T0305251

Lured by the
American Dream

THE ASIAN AMERICAN EXPERIENCE

Series Editors
Eiichiro Azuma
Jigna Desai
Martin F. Manalansan IV
Lisa Sun-Hee Park
David K. Yoo

Roger Daniels, *Founding Series Editor*

*A list of books in the series appears
at the end of this book.*

Lured by the American Dream

Filipino Servants in the
U.S. Navy and Coast Guard,
1952–1970

P. JAMES PALIGUTAN

**UNIVERSITY OF
ILLINOIS PRESS**
Urbana, Chicago, and Springfield

© 2022 by the Board of Trustees
of the University of Illinois
All rights reserved
1 2 3 4 5 C P 5 4 3 2 1
♾ This book is printed on acid-free paper.

Cataloging data available from the Library of Congress
ISBN 9780252044595 (hardcover)
ISBN 9780252086670 (paperback)
ISBN 9780252053603 (ebook)

This work is dedicated to my father,
Proceso A. Paligutan, 1930–2017.

Dad, I hope this book makes you proud.

Contents

Acknowledgments ix

Introduction. A "Metaphysics of Absence":
    Filipino Americans in the Margins of U.S. History 1

Chapter 1. Colonial Past, Neocolonial Present 23

Chapter 2. The Navy's Search for Postcolonial Servants 46

Chapter 3. Adrift from the American Dream. 67

Chapter 4. Tales of Resistance 94

Chapter 5. The Navy's "Filipino Servant Problem" 115

Chapter 6. Achieving the American Dream 139

Epilogue 149

Notes 151

Bibliography 169

Index 175

Illustrations follow page 66

Acknowledgments

The years spent researching and writing this book pendulated between misplaced meandering and intellectual reward, darkness and illumination, uncertainty and surety. As this book reached its final stages, the cumulative energies expended are in hindsight a homage to family and a proverbial labor of love as much as an arduous effort at scholarship. That this work on a personal level transcends its narrow historical and topical purview, directly relating to my own family's place in America, can only be explained as a blessing. This fact unsettles the notion of academic research and writing as "work," while redefining it—in this case, at least—as an impulse governed by a quest for self-knowledge.

The debts incurred along this quest are numerous. It is not an overstatement to say that this book would likely never come to fruition had it not been for the guidance of Yong Chen, my graduate adviser and dissertation chairperson. He held an unwavering confidence in me as a graduate student even during times of my grave doubt, and his guidance and reassurances were very crucial to the completion of this project. Professor Chen's scholarly expertise, experience, and wisdom regarding things of true importance in life will never be forgotten, and an *"utang na loob"* (Tagalog for "internal debt"—a Filipino outlook implicating lifelong gratitude and payback) was established since the day I asked him to be my graduate adviser. I cannot speak highly enough of my friend Yong Chen, and I hope I can adequately repay him through the years.

A great intellectual debt is owed to Yen Le Espiritu, whose incisive comments and critical eye has made this work undoubtedly much stronger than originally conceived. Her erudition left no topic unturned and exposed holes in my thinking imperceptible by me before our discussions. There is a reason why she is one of the most popular professors at the University of California San Diego, and her kindness and generosity are well known to all her students. The field of Asian American Studies has greatly benefitted from the pioneering work of Le Espiritu.

Mike Davis, maverick scholar and gifted wordsmith, has been a tremendous guide throughout my intellectual *Bildung* as a would-be historian and academic. Each of our conversations, sometimes veering into late hours over glasses of beer and wine, was always memorable, touching upon subjects as variegated as family, race relations in Los Angeles, Samoan street gangs, Manny Pacquiao and the history of boxing, General Harrison Gray Otis and the Philippine-American War, the big island of Hawai'i, and of course, Filipino navy stewards. Mike's genuine warmth, capacious memory, and spellbinding erudition never failed to astound me; needless to say, his trenchant comments were indispensable in the successful completion of this work.

I especially thank Emily Rosenberg for generously offering her insights regarding this work. A giant in the field of modern U.S. history, she in her scholarly work has enriched the intellectual landscape of the discipline, and no serious scholar interested in such diverse topics as U.S. foreign policy, history and memory, economic history, and American modernity can ignore her work. Her generous critiques were important in making sections of this work more lucid and historically accurate and thus a stronger work overall.

Special mention goes to Dorothy Fujita-Rony, who introduced me when I was a first-year graduate student to the intellectual landscape of Asian American Studies, an academic terrain that I will never cease exploring. I am also indebted to the professors, teachers, and mentors I have had throughout my educational development, including Dickson Bruce, Alice Fahs, Ken Pomeranz, Mark Poster, Heidi Tinsman, Anne Walthall, Jon Wiener, and R. Bin Wong at the University of California Irvine. Thanks also to my teachers at San Diego State University's philosophy department, especially Steven Barbone, Deborah Chaffin, J. Angelo Corlett, Andrew Feenberg, Robert Francescotti, Tom Weston, and Mark Wheeler, who were all critical in my intellectual development. I also thank Regina Akers and the helpful staff at the Naval Historical Center in Washington, DC, and Nathaniel Patch at the National Archives II in College Park, Maryland. Also, a shout-out to my colleagues throughout the years, especially Brittany Adams, Brooke Bui, John Crocitti, Christina Ghanbarpour, Catherine Christensen Gwin, Bill Jahnel, Gloria Kim, Kristin Marjanovich, Jonathan McCleod, and Eric Reyes. Thank you so much for your advice, guidance, and support.

I was excited to receive an e-mail from Dawn Durante, senior acquisitions editor at University of Illinois Press. Dawn was nothing less than superb in her efforts to make this project come to fruition, whether offering generous writing and structural suggestions, composing and sending letters of support for research grants, or accommodating special requests. Upon her move to the University of Texas Press, I had the pleasure of working with acquisition editors Alison Syring and Dominique Moore. They have continued UIP's tradition of geniality and comradery, and I am very grateful to both of them. I also thank all those involved at the press, especially the anonymous reviewers and the Asian American Experience series editors, whose generous contributions have led to an improved work. Also, this endeavor in expressing gratitude would not be complete without acknowledging Mary Lou Kowaleski, whose keen copyediting skill contributed to a more polished version of this book while teaching me how to be a better writer.

And, of course, I cannot overstate my profound appreciation toward all those who agreed to be interviewed for this project and sincerely hope that this written work sufficiently honors the sacrifices they have made in order to achieve the American Dream for themselves and their families in the United States.

Lastly, I owe debts that can never be repaid to my family: my father Proceso "Paulie" A. Paligutan; my mother, Cecilia; my brother, Earl; my sisters, Eleanor and Janice; my brother-in-law, Lou "Happy" Pontanares; my sister-in-law, Geraldine Bautista Paligutan; my nephews and nieces, Andrew, Chelsea, Emily, Jillian, Sam, Pearl, Perri, Cedric, and Christopher; and all members of my extended family in the United States and the Philippines. Also, much love to all my friends, especially to all my fellow musicians, whom I have collaborated with and learned from throughout the years. You have all affected me in immeasurable ways, and I am truly blessed to have you all in my life.

Lured by the
American Dream

A "Metaphysics of Absence"

Filipino Americans in the
Margins of U.S. History

The very first Asians to settle in the United States were Filipino seafarers. Referred to as "Manilamen" while laboring in the Manila-Acapulco Galleon Trade, these Filipinos would disembark from their vessels upon American shores as early as 1765, settling in parts of coastal Louisiana.[1] Subsequent Filipino immigration to the United States would not occur in significant numbers until the American occupation of the Philippines following the brutal Philippine-American War. What began as a meager stream of Filipino migrants in the earliest years of imperial rule would develop into a significant migratory flow; eventually, by 2020, Filipinos would constitute the third largest Asian American population in the country.[2]

By the mid–twentieth century, another group of Filipino seafarers would follow the pelagic pathways forged by the pioneering Manilamen: Filipino nationals enlisted in the U.S. Navy and Coast Guard during the post–World War II era. The origins of Filipino recruits into the U.S. military can be traced as far back as 1901, amid the effort to "pacify" the islands before occupational rule. Although this practice endured through the proceeding decades, the recruitment numbers of Filipinos in the U.S. Navy and Coast Guard would reach significant levels by the 1950s and 1960s, the immediate decades following the granting of Philippine independence in 1946. This particular surge in Filipino recruitment after independence is explained by a labor problem faced by the U.S. Navy at the time, as mounting resistance increasingly displayed by African American sailors imperiled the navy's labor supply of "stewards." A "rating" (i.e., naval occupational category for enlisted men) considered the most menial of navy jobs and overwhelmingly comprising persons of color, stewards were essentially domestic workers laboring for the comfort and well-being of naval officers. In practice, however, stewardship unofficially entailed duties considerably beyond those of domestic service, which redefined the steward rating as akin to that of a personal servant. With the rising crescendo of black protest against their subsidiary positions during the civil rights era, the U.S. Navy looked to its erstwhile colony to replenish its supply of nonwhite stewards.

The experiences of Filipino sailors serving in the U.S. Navy and Coast Guard between 1952 (the year that navy recruitment of Filipinos was initiated after Philippine independence) and 1970 (the beginning of the dismantling of the navy's racial restrictions) would in many ways mirror that of earlier African American stewards in their encounters with institutional discrimination, exploitation, and lack of rating promotion. A taken-for-granted assumption held by naval recruiters was the notion of Filipino passivity: the belief that Filipino stewards would remain a docile and tractable labor force, unlike African Americans at the time. Due to the Filipino stewards' increased economic power coupled with cultural stereotypes largely attributable to the ideology of Orientalism,[3] it was hardly expected that Filipinos in the navy and coast guard would follow the examples of resistance displayed by those they were meant to replace.

Yet, as will be discussed, Filipino stewards in the navy and coast guard did, in fact, engage in a variety of resistance strategies in the face of their systemic exploitation, ones that included nonconfrontational resistance, direct complaints to flag officers and naval chaplains, flooding naval bureaucracy with rating transfer requests (despite its futility due to naval policy), disobedience, and even labor stoppage. In spite of their near invisibility within the navy and coast guard, Filipino resistance percolated upward to the highest echelon of naval officialdom, eventually serving as a decisive factor in the navy's move to finally eradicate the antiquated steward rating. As argued in this oral history, Filipino stewards were crucial historical agents of institutional change within the navy and coast guard in the elimination of exploitative racialized servant labor. Through the exercise of their agency, Filipino stewards—the supposedly "weakest" element in the hierarchical navy—played a *direct* role in the reversal of race-based policies practiced by the world's most powerful military force, a fact yet to be academically explored in depth until this work.

As servants consigned to sequestered spaces within a neocolonial milieu of the navy warship, the stewards' experiences mirror the plight of previous Filipino immigrants while presaging the predicament of future generations of Filipino Americans within U.S. society. Indeed, despite their preponderance as an immigrant population, Filipino Americans past and present have occupied the margins of the American cultural, political, and social landscape.

Scholars of Filipino American studies, particularly, lament the invisibility of Filipinos within American historical memory, despite an interlocking relation borne out of U.S. imperialism—that of colonizer and colonized. Given the enduring historical amnesia of America's imperial past, it is little wonder that both the Philippine-American War and the subsequent U.S. colonization of the Philippines often remains forgotten, ignored, or dismissed as a minor footnote in U.S. history. Such denial of empire, it can be argued, is likely correlated to the peripheral status of Filipino Americans in the United States throughout its immigration history.

Further underlining Filipino Americans' absence are the prevailing stereotypes of persons of Asian descent in America, both negative and positive. The caricature of Asians as "perpetual foreigners"—inscrutable, unassimilable, and uncivilized—is not yet entirely expunged from American cultural, historical, and racial imaginaries, despite the presence of Asian Americans of extended generations. Even positive depictions, such as Asian American exceptionalism expressed in the category of "model minorities," serve to decrease the visibility of many Asian Americans who do not conform to such stereotypes. Large segments of Asians in America, in fact, are not members of the educated and professional classes. Indeed, with capitalism's implacable search for cheap labor overseas, many Asian immigrants were pulled abroad as low-wage, low-skilled labor: plantation workers, agriculturalists, cannery workers, industrial laborers, domestic workers, and service-industry workers. While praise of Asian American success emanating from mainstream accounts may be encouraging, it amounts to a sin of omission in the failure to extol the labor of those Asian immigrants standing in the outer edges of society.

The lives of Filipino sailors enlisted in the navy and coast guard during the postwar years serve as a prism refracting such aforementioned historical relations. Their experiences not only encompass important categories of race, colonialism, immigration, and labor in the migratory flow of Filipino Americans but their positionalities as postcolonial servants in the U.S. military also stand as an illustrative case of imposed exclusion—a condition experienced by many Filipino immigrants relegated to the periphery of American society, polity, and history.

This state of affairs likely finds its origins with the earliest attempts of American lawmakers, intellectuals, and nationalistic writers to uncover the meaning of the American nation. In their efforts to define and/or posit the immutable and universal features of America, a taken-for-granted correspondence between "nation" and "whiteness" played a role in eliding the historical presence of nonwhites—especially Asians, who were cast as aliens waylaid outside of nation. Although national histories and commentaries of the past often strived to locate and define the *essential* aspects of the American nation, I refer to the deliberate erasure of the racial Other as a racial "metaphysics of absence."[4] Of course, such a metaphysical (and thus ahistorical) viewpoint—that is, affixing a natural correspondence with "American nation" and "white skin"—is one that represses a particular historical dissonance: the presence of racial Others since the inception of the United States. The roots of this racial metaphysics are likely traced to the U.S. self-designation as a member of Western civilization. Yet, the obvious difference compared to the civilizations of Europe is America's foundational history—that is, its origins as European-settler colonial society in the New World, replete with indigenous populations and racialized slavery. It has only been recently, in relative terms, that Asians in America have been confronting this crisis of underrepresentation in a more frontal manner (especially with the formation of Asian American Studies as an academic discipline), while pressing their claim as essential members of America's racial landscape. Indeed, ethnic histories such as this work serve to eviscerate such metaphysical assumptions about the "racial being" of America.

The tropes of racialization, exclusion, labor exploitation, resistance, and agency, all ubiquitous themes in Asian American Studies, are hardly missing in the account of the migratory experiences of these Filipino navy men. Yet. while their lives may indeed be viewed as a fractal of the whole, it is equally true that these Filipino sailors and their families constitute a unique diasporic population in Asian American history and thus should not be denied a sui generis historical analysis. What follows is an oral history of post–World War II Filipino sailors in their encounter with the nation and its institutions— a study whose angle of vision is based upon the immigrant Other as they turned toward America. It is hoped that this work will adequately serve as a project of reclamation, even as their marginal statuses as postcolonial subjects, perpetual foreigners, and inferiorized servants threaten to vanquish their historical place to the dustbin of U.S. history.[5]

The Colonial Connection: Colonized and Racialized Labor

Numerous tomes of scholarly work are devoted to the study of the construction of race in the crucible of modern Western colonialism, an event of seismic consequence in world history. One inexorable aspect of Western imperial expansion is the migration of racialized colonial subjects from their own colonized territory ("periphery") to the colonizer's country ("metropole"). Yet, these events—colonialism and immigration—should not be conceived in a simplistic cause-and-effect fashion. Rather, both movements must be understood as mutually constitutive—that is, both migratory flows (colonizer to periphery and colonized to metropole) historically constitute a single migration process rather than separate linear migration movements. This double-aspect view of immigration is perfectly rendered in the scholar Yen Le Espiritu's representation of colonialism and immigration as two sides of the same historical coin. Thus where applicable, contemporary scholarly analysis of persons of darker skin migrating to places such as the United States, Great Britain, France, and other former colonial empires must account for the centrality of overseas colonialism, expansionism, and/or interventionism in the precipitation of immigration originating from the developing world. As Espiritu reminds us, it is a somewhat overlooked fact that most of modern immigration to the United States comprises ethnic groups whose country of origin has sustained a form of political, economic, and social relation with the United States.[6]

The process of colonial expansionism necessarily linked to immigration from the colonized Global South inheres in another crucial theme: labor. In the case of the United States, the history of overseas expansion into the Pacific region cannot be decoupled from economic goals.[7] Granted, monocausal explanations of key historical events should strain credulity, yet in the case of twentieth-century presence in the Pacific, the United States' overall desire for economic access to Asian markets looms as an inescapable causal factor (although certainly not the sole factor). This economic dimension, furthermore, involves not only the Pacific region as a market for American goods but also as a source of cheap labor for American industries at home. Indeed, even before turn-of-the-twentieth-century expansion, U.S. industry recognized the profit-enhancing benefits of hiring Chinese labor in the Western industries of mining, agribusiness, and railroad construction. Being paid half the wages of a typical American worker, Chinese laborers were historical precursors to the exploitative usage of Asian labor, as witnessed in the following century by the examples of Japanese, Korean, and Filipino agriculturalists, Filipina nurses, and Filipino servants in the U.S. Navy.

Much of current academic work on immigration from the colonized Global South to the United States has reconsidered immigration outside the standard approaches, often framing political and economic domination as tantamount to neocolonial hegemony. To provide just a few examples, it is found in contemporary scholarship surrounding the largest immigrant group to the United States—Mexican immigration. The scholar Gilbert G. Gonzales, in his book *Guest Workers or Colonized Labor*, argues that the Bracero Program should be reconsidered not simply as an agreement between two sovereign nations but, rather, as an expression of U.S. economic domination over "neocolonial Mexico."[8] Within the neocolonial context, Mexican labor is hardly nonexploitative but reconceived by Gonzalez as "indentured labor." Similarly, Pierrette Hondagneu-Sotelo argues that an analysis of Mexican immigration cannot be dissociated from the colonialism of the past as well as its current manifestation in the form of globalization.[9] This explanatory paradigm readily applies to many immigrant groups of color: Vietnamese, Salvadorans, Puerto Ricans, Cubans, Pacific Islanders, Koreans, and others.

Recent scholarship in Filipino American historical studies similarly transcends the traditional push-pull model, enhancing it with an interpretive framework that accords primacy upon American colonialism as a structural condition shaping Filipino immigration. In the succinct words of Espiritu, "Filipinos went to the United States because Americans went first to the Philippines."[10] In fact, arguably no other case of Filipino American migration centralizes the role of colonialism and neocolonialism more so than Filipino sailors during the post–World War II era. Arriving to enlist at U.S. Navy bases in the Philippines—veritable symbols of a colonial past and a neocolonial present—these new recruits, driven by the American Dream, embarked upon warships serving to protect American vital interests across the globe. A remnant of a colonial practice—that of the colonized servant in servitude of the colonizer—was extant within the colonial "contact zones" of U.S. Navy and Coast Guard vessels, where such colonial domestic workers would labor to ensure the comfort of naval officers.

Yet, it is not just the correlative migration patterns of Filipino migrants to the United States that would interweave with U.S. formal colonization of the archipelago. As will be extensively discussed, the architectonic of U.S. colonialism would assume form and substance through a miscellany of measures reputedly imposed for the sake of Filipino racial elevation. An ideological by-product of this imperial project would be a worldview evangelized by American occupiers in the supposed inherent superiority of Western civilization and, by extension, the white race. This belief system would be important not only in justifying American occupation of a vital geostrategic region in the Pacific but also in dampening native feelings of revolt against their colonial masters. Even the granting of formal independence in 1946 would be construed as still another act of benevolence, a gesture symbolizing their students' mastery of the art of democracy. Of course, with neocolonial structures ensuring continued economic and military control, the United States no longer needed to don the habiliments of a colonial master in the Philippines.

These years of postindependence are the specific historical context for the Filipino subjects of this study, as the recruitment of thousands of Filipino male citizens would be enabled by neocolonial structures enduring past Philippine independence. In her study of Filipina nurses, *Empire of Care: Nursing and Migration in Filipino American History*, Catherine Ceniza Choy pinpoints the colonial hospital-training system combined with the postindependence Exchange Visitors Program as instrumental institutions facilitating this ubiquitous labor flow by the 1960s and 1970s.[11] Similarly, in the case of Filipino navy men, the Military Bases Agreement of 1947, a paramount expression of neocolonial domination, not only guaranteed American military presence in the newly sovereign nation through the century but also permitted the continued recruitment of Filipino citizens into the U.S. military based upon need. Still, why would Filipino young men at the time, proud of their country's newly gained sovereignty and national identity, remain disinclined to join the military ranks of their newly independent country, only to prefer enlistment with a foreign one instead? The answers lie with the protean effects of colonial and neocolonial domination in both economic and ideological aspects. During the mid–twentieth century, Filipino recruits were lured by the American Dream as well as an expected fraternity with white America, beliefs gained through American-styled colonial education and culture. At the same time, these persons were pushed from their country by the dim prospects for employment as the Philippine economy languished in the thrall of neocolonial dependency. Enlistment in the U.S. Navy was viewed as an ideal remedy for their economic hardships while providing an avenue for their adventurism. As one can see, both agency-oriented and structural factors encouraging voluntary recruitment were shaped in large measure by the residual effects of formal colonization.

The immigrant lives of Filipino navy men during this time would be marked by distinct migratory patterns when compared with both earlier agriculturalists and, later, nurses, domestic workers, and professionals. Dorothy Fujita-Rony's work on Filipino agribusiness workers, *American Workers, Colonial Power: Philippine Seattle and the Transpacific West, 1919–1941*, for example, discusses how such laborers, navigating the transpacific trade networks and traveling from one agricultural site to another, viewed Seattle as a "colonial metropole" in the West.[12] Other scholarly works in Filipino American Studies, such as Dawn Mabalon's *Little Manila Is in the Heart*, Rick Bonus's *Locating Filipino Americans: Ethnicity and the Cultural Politics of Space*, and Espiritu's *Home Bound: Filipino American Lives across Cultures, Communities, and Countries* are similarly anchored to a specific geographical region.[13] The life of a young sailor, in comparison, precluded the possibility of long-standing community formation and strong social ties fixed upon geographic region—there was no fixed "colonial metropole" for such workers. Rather, they found themselves aboard U.S. naval ships roaming the seas, engaged in a mission to protect the Free World during the Cold War. Yet, at the same time, such navy ships were akin to miniature colonial societies, comprising darker-skinned subjects providing servant labor for the superiors. Filipinos and other racial minorities were relegated to the peripheral areas of the ship, just as in any colonial city, laboring in the most menial of tasks and occupying the lowest stations of the navy's hierarchical labor system. Aboard such warships, Filipino servants were at once former colonials and foreign workers after independence—they were the colonized immigrant Others whose main duty was to serve. With respect to status, their unique position shares uniqueness with the subjects of JoAnna Poblete's book *Islanders in the Empire: Filipino and Puerto Rican Laborers in Hawai'i*, a discussion of "U.S. colonials" migrating from one colony to another (to be specific, the labor diasporas of both Puerto Rican and Filipino workers to the plantation fields of Hawai'i) rather than from "periphery to metropole." In the cases of both Poblete's subjects and those of this work, a profound sense of liminality surrounds their journeys, whose trajectories have been determined by U.S. colonialism.[14]

Transnationalism Meets Colonialism in Filipino American History

The transnational turn in immigration scholarship is apparent in the profusion of recent immigration studies. This innovative approach questions the founding assumptions of the traditional Chicago School of immigration studies, namely, the central importance of borders separating nation-states, as well as the presupposition of unilinear stages (arrival, settlement, assimilation) undertaken by immigrants from one nation to another. In contrast, transnational analysis eschews a prior commitment to the artificial geographical boundaries of sovereign nations, focusing not upon full assimilation but upon hybridized identities; not upon full settlement but upon dual incorporation amid the constant cycle of immigration/reemigration. In doing so, the transnational approach exposes the lens of the traditional framework as shortsighted, often beclouded by American exceptionalism in the assumption of full assimilation leading to an overstated "melting pot" to describe American identity.

As initially conceived, the conceptual model of transnationalism befits contemporary immigration in the context of globalization; that is, the movement of "transmigrants" amid an era of novel technological advancements, thus more enabled to forge transnational social fields interconnecting their countries of origin and of settlement. Yet, some aspects of transnational linkages—reemigration, remittances, exchange of information, immigrant involvement in homeland politics, to name a few—have precedents in earlier immigration histories. Are the claims of transnational theory, such as the claim of novelty in current immigration patterns, somewhat overstated? Do transmigrants truly resist assimilation to a much greater degree than their migratory predecessors?

Overall, the study of Filipino immigration to the United States offers interesting answers to such questions while also expanding its historical purview. Scholars of Filipino American Studies remind us that Filipino transnational immigration can rarely escape the long shadow of American colonialism, which, as discussed, is inextricably bound with the corollary migration of (post)colonial subjects from periphery to metropole. Similar to Choy's transnational study of Filipina nurses, *Empire of Care*, which locates its historical context of transnational analysis with the incipient period of American colonialism,[15] so, too, will this work constantly hearken back to America's program of "benevolent assimilation" and its institutions,[16] ones that would eventually intersect with Cold War militarism and civil rights reform.

Filipino sailors in this study were certainly postcolonial, but were they transnational? A central innovation found with transnational immigration studies lies with the migrants' fluid relation to their geographical place of settlement, whereby the notion of "home" incorporates both places of origin and settlement, forging social spaces as sites of "reterritorialization."[17] Yet, how is one to conceptualize the experiential trajectory of migrants that do not permanently settle in any particular geographical region within their host country while also left unanchored to their sending country (in profound ways to be discussed) as a condition to their recruitment? In the case of Filipino postcolonial stewards, notions of "home" and "national belonging" are noticeably unmoored from any specific geographical locus, because these young, unmarried recruits considered the naval ship as their actual home. A typical enlisted sailor transferred stations every few years, reporting to a different naval ship stationed in a different region of America. The regional location of the home port, however, was not truly the young sailor's "home" when serving in the U.S. Navy; rather, home was the actual ship, where many single sailors worked, ate, and slept even while docked onshore. And, of course, navy ships would be deployed offshore for many months at a time. In this context the oceans of the world, rather than national spaces, are diasporic spaces for these Filipino navy men. Yet, even within the ship, Filipino sailors were relegated to demarcated spaces—racially and occupationally. Thus, the Filipino stewards' immigrant experience was distinguished by the radically migratory and marginal nature of their labor. In constant movement aboard ships provocatively viewed by the cultural theorist Paul Gilroy as "chronotopes" operating beyond national boundaries,[18] these sailors embodied the condition of "free-floating signifiers" occasioned by their unique sense of indeterminacy. Furthermore, such Filipino recruits would also find themselves nearly cut adrift from both nations while navigating the interstices between both. Filipino stewards at the time, for example, were foreign Others in America, yet they would also be denied the opportunity to marry and the right to vote in the Philippines upon choosing to enlist in a foreign military. Taken together, the unique positionalities of Filipino stewards give new meaning to contemporary notions of "deterritorialization."[19]

To be sure, they do share broad similarities with other migratory waves of Filipino laborers. Filipino migrants that preceded navy stewards, as former colonial subjects, were not immigrants in the traditional sense. In official terms they were neither foreigners nor citizens but colonial wards arriving in America, though similarly confined within a racialized zone of in-betweenness, as poignantly narrated in Carlos Bulosan's novel *America Is in the Heart: A Personal History*. Stated in more academic fashion, Filipino migrants were thrust within a "limbo of alterity and transitionality," according to scholar E. San Juan Jr.[20] Furthermore, scholars such as Dorothy Fujita-Rony, in her book *American Workers, Colonial Power*, note the transitory character of earlier Filipino agriculturalists in the West (known as "*Manongs*"), whose everyday lives were marked by constant movement and impermanence due to the seasonal nature of their jobs.[21]

For the Filipinos of this study, however, the conditions of impermanence and constant mobility are made more striking given the fact that most of them were stationed aboard navy vessels, symbols, and purveyors of U.S. military power. In this way these Filipinos in a literal sense did not escape the hegemonic structures of neocolonial "place" and "space." Filipino sailors onboard navy vessels in the high seas gave new embodiment to Asian American indeterminacy and liminality. As stated, for these young migrants, the roving ship was literally their "place of settlement"—a transnational space without geographical fixity but, rather, in constant movement throughout the globe. A comment by Proceso "Paulie" Ada Paligutan, a retired former steward in the U.S. Coast Guard, underscores the radically transitory character for these Filipino migrants: "If you're single and you don't have any relatives . . . the ship is your home."[22]

In terms of contemporary Filipino immigration, a close parallel to Filipino stewards is found with a contemporary labor force also constituted by male seafarers—Filipinos laboring aboard cargo ships for the international shipping industry, as studied in Kale Fajardo's ethnographic study *Filipino Crosscurrents: Oceanographies of Seafaring, Masculinities, and Globalization.* Fajardo analyzes how the Philippine state, as intermediary and booster of Filipino seamen labor, constructed Filipino masculinities (that is, as masculine *bayanis*, or "heroes") due to their valuable contribution to the Philippine economy.[23] Also viewing oceans as diasporic spaces, Farjardo's ethnographic studies of these Filipino laborers reveals how the ship—again, a transnational social space in itself—also serves as sites of gender performativity, wherein masculinities are sometimes constructed in nonnormative ways. As will be discussed, the radical nature of the Filipino steward's liminality would similarly result in the constant flux of identity when "border crossing": from the lowest station of the navy's pyramid due to the servile nature of stewardship, to the upper echelon of male power upon his periodic visits home due to his "social remittances"—economic power, social capital, and the like. What truly distinguishes Filipino sailors compared to contemporary Filipino shipworkers, however, is the ambiguous national status of the former.

The contemporary labor flow of Filipino seamen working for the global shipping industry takes us from early U.S. colonization in the Pacific to the neoliberal policies of the current economic age. In the works by scholars of Filipino American Studies studying more recent transnational labor diasporas, we see how the Philippine state, under the clutches of neoliberal policies, has shared places with neocolonial institutions in precipitating the labor migration flow of today. Robyn Magalit Rodriguez's work, *Migrants for Export: How the Philippine State Brokers Labor to the World*, reveals how the Philippine government became the world's largest "labor brokerage state," partly accomplished through state-managed redefinitions and reinscriptions of citizenship and nationalism. Today's overseas foreign workers (OFWs) are celebrated as heroes, both nationally and locally, due to their indispensable economic role in the Philippine economy.[24] Yet, the ramifications of this economic state of affairs exacts a heavy toll among those Filipino families with breadwinning members cast to far-flung areas of the world, as discussed in Rhacel Salazar Parreñas's *Servants of Globalization: Women, Migration, and Domestic Work* and Valerie Francisco-Menchavez's *Labor of Care: Filipina Migrants and Transnational Families in the Digital Age.* With parents separated from spouses and children, the "pain of transnational parenting" (to use Parreñas's phrase) bespeaks the sacrifice of long-term separation and profound emotional suffering experienced by the transnational family. Yet, at the same time, the vicissitudes of the state-sponsored family separation has led to innovative ways by which Filipino transnational families manage to maintain and care for each other.[25] In contrast to the plight of contemporary transnational families, Filipino enlistees of this study were initially prohibited from marriage as a condition for recruitment so long as they remained naval stewards. Nonetheless, it is apparent that the category of family formation intersected with economic gain and state-sponsored recruitment even in the case of Filipino sailors.

In summary, the historical reality of the Philippines' colonial past is an inescapable factor in comparison with other transnational migrant populations in modern history, complicating the transnational framework. Compared with current Asian American immigrants, for example, the transnational consciousness of Filipinos remains interpellated by U.S. colonial technologies of power, such as an American-influenced educational system, an American-styled political system, popular culture, and language.[26] As will be revealed, the implications of the Philippine colonial past figure prominently in the formation of these men's multiple subjectivities, shaping their outlook toward adjustment to life in America. What distinguishes the migratory experience of Filipino stewards from other Filipino diasporas is their very incorporation within the U.S. military apparatus. The U.S. Navy served both as a neocolonial institution and an employer of Filipino domestic labor. They were literally unanchored to a geographically determinate place of settlement during their enlistment periods; indeed, their "host location" aboard naval ships, in constant movement within denationalized spaces while global in reach, was an ultimate expression of indeterminacy. When Filipino stewards were finally able to overcome rating restrictions and raise families in America, they would eventually settle mostly in coastal cities, such as San Diego and Long Beach, California, and Virginia Beach, Virginia, places with large navy installations. In many ways, this migratory group of U.S. navy men was among the progenitors of contemporary Filipino overseas contract workers pulled to destinations all over the globe.

Racialized Domestic Laborers in the U.S. Military

As mentioned, the occupational rating of stewardship was essentially a form of domestic servant labor provided for naval officers. The tradition of stewardship within the modern U.S. Navy and Coast Guard was indissociably linked to race, because stewards were overwhelmingly persons of color. African Americans mostly dominated the rating of stewardship as the Old Navy transitioned to a modern navy at the turn of the twentieth century (though smaller fractions of Caucasians, Chinese, Japanese, and other foreigners were recruited as stewards, messmen, and cooks). A policy shift toward the heavy recruitment of Filipino stewards took place after World War II, when African American sailors pressed their claims for equal work conditions. Naval recruiters particularly favored Filipino recruitment due to their efficiency and alleged docility. In short, the steward rating was overwhelmingly a nonwhite rating dominated at certain points by either Filipinos or African Americans, depending upon fluctuating naval policies. Even as piecemeal victories were gained in the future against the discriminatory practices of the U.S. military, racial discrimination would not be officially expunged from naval occupational policy until the mid-1970s.

The place of Filipino stewards in the study of immigrant domestic work is not only articulated to the category of race but also gender. There is a rich field of scholarly work studying the plight of immigrant women domestics serving the middle- and upper-class families of more affluent countries. The predominance of women domestics is not surprising given the function of gender ideology in the relegation of women to the private sphere, in the naturalization of their roles as caregivers of family and caretakers of the home. As women began to branch out in the world of work, most were consigned to labor believed to correspond to their "essential capabilities." Thus women were to overwhelmingly constitute the ranks of domestic workers.

Recent studies of women domestic workers foreground the role of structural and institutional factors—colonialism, globalization, nation-state, and family are a few examples—as shaping this gendered migration. Parreñas, in *Servants of Globalization,* recontextualizes the subjective experiences of Filipina domestics not only in the macroprocesses of colonialism and globalization but also within institutional factors, such as households and social networks, thus providing a multi-theoretical account of this diasporic phenomenon.[27] Scholars examining other ethnic groups have similarly insisted upon transcending the push-pull explanatory framework. In an important work exposing the plight of Latina domestic workers, Hondagneu-Sotelo, in her book *Doméstica: Immigrant Women Cleaning and Caring in the Shadows of Affluence*, does not neglect the significance of globalization not only in the precipitation of Latinx immigration to the United States but also in the creation of domestic work realized with the migration of families constituting the professional-managerial class to the "global city" of Los Angeles.[28]

Analyzed in comparative terms, the case of Filipinos stewards conspicuously stands as a unique diasporic population of domestic workers: male sailors recruited by the military of their erstwhile colonizer to perform domestic work, in addition to other jobs of servitude, such as fetching coffee, shining shoes, serving the officer's family members, and running errands, within the homosocial space of the U.S. Navy warship. A comparative glance into the lives of Filipino stewards with those of women domestics brings their experiences into broad relief. In her book *Issei, Nisei, War Bride: Three Generations of Japanese American Women in Domestic Service*, Evelyn Nakano Glenn reveals the problem of injured self-esteem endured by Japanese women domestics in their encounters with dominant society.[29] In the case of Filipino stewards, such injury to their self-esteem was added to the insult threatening their masculinity. Doubtless, many of these Filipino men were quite masculine in their outlook and demeanor; what was denigrated as "women's work" was an inescapable aspect of everyday toil. How did such men handle such insult and injury? Did these men hide the servile, "feminized" nature of their jobs from friends and family in their native country?

This particular study of a "bachelor society" of domestic workers is part of the developing academic work focusing upon gendered domestic labor.[30] Prior to enlisting, their Otherness was evident in their subject positions as racialized perpetual foreigners and neocolonial subjects. As articulated to their status as inferiorized servants, these Filipino sailors, not unlike working-class immigrant women of color, arguably endured a form of triple oppression" in their encounter with dominant society. While the difference of gender obviously individuates their experiences, similarities and parallel experiences abound upon comparison. Whether cleaning the chambers of their superiors or serving the meals to them, these stewards not only found ways to redefine their masculine identities as proud workers but also forged cultures of resistance in reaction to their exploitation.

Moreover, this work shows how the case of Filipino stewards in the navy and coast guard is constitutive of a long history of mistreatment and labor exploitation regularly practiced within the U.S. military, both of minorities and women. Indeed, this feature of systemic discrimination and differential treatment has hardly dissipated, given the recurrence of scandals involving women enlistees and ethnic minorities. Past practices of racial discrimination within the U.S. Navy and Coast Guard are thinly veiled in the relegation of minorities to the bottommost ranks of its occupational rating system. African American sailors were visibly exploited as messmen, stewards, and cooks, details of which are vividly described in Richard Miller's *Messman Chronicles*.[31] Filipino stewards, sharing a common experience of labor exploitation with African Americans, must be recognized as integral to the story of the U.S. military's insensitivity toward exploitative racialized labor in practice. It is hoped that this study of a racialized and colonized labor force will do justice in this very aim.

Methodology, Arguments, and Chapter Overview

This history is in large part a work of oral history. The epistemic concerns surrounding oral history are widely recognized: the unreliability of memory, the truth-value of subjective experience, the validity of anecdotal evidence. Despite such issues, oral historians consider the spoken experiences of marginalized persons as legitimate repositories of repressed history, usually elided from the meta-narrative of mainstream national history. At its epistemological core, I feel that the production of history—in the last instance—is an interpretive enterprise, notwithstanding the necessary presence of an objective layer in all legitimate histories. Inductive generalizations can be forcefully asserted in light of uniformity of experiences and acknowledged consensus revealed among interview subjects. In the end, oral testimonies are recoveries of hidden histories that would otherwise be ephemeralized, destined to history's dustbin; the task of the historian in this case is to ensure their consignment to posterity.

Beside these methodological concerns, I faced other challenges that may be unique compared to other academic oral histories: the direct connection of family (since my father and several uncles were subjects for this study). While seemingly advantageous due to direct access, on the other hand, the act of maintaining critical distance proved to be a genuine concern. The ideal bifurcation between insider/outsider was admittedly tenuous during some of these interviews, a separation necessary if one strives toward a disinterested interpretation (in the sense of being "outside" the personal emotions of subjects).[32] I grew up hearing many of these stories, and they have become sedimented layers of my family's immigrant history that cannot be entirely divested of personal emotion.

Another area of potential concern relating to interpretation is more intellectual rather than personal and emotional. That is, the intellectual stance I assume in this work is from the critical perspective. This work *critically* examines a racialized domestic-servant tradition, not to mention other historical categories, such as American exceptionalism, imperialism and colonialism, and the U.S. history of race relations. Such a stance lies in contrast to more value-free approaches, let alone celebratory and triumphalist renditions of historical interpretations. The various interviewees, it can by stated with certainty, were or are all proud retirees and loyal Americans. The navy or coast guard was formative in their lives and remains the centerpiece of their individual identities. While their statements occasionally evoke resentment over their past mistreatment, it is also plausible that some interviewees may be leery of a wholly critical stance regarding their beloved navy or coast guard.[33]

Despite such concerns, I have deliberately maintained this intellectual approach since the archival evidence irrefutably lends support to Filipino claims of exploitation—stated otherwise, Filipino retirees are merely retelling and expanding upon the reality of race-based differential treatment acknowledged within official naval documents written decades ago, filed away quietly in the National Archives and Records Administration (NARA) and discoloring with age. As will be shown, not only did some navy officials and flag officers support keeping the steward branch as a non-Caucasian one but some also expressed contempt toward proposals to terminate the tradition. In the end, the details of a racialized labor force disclosed in this work are accurate, regardless of whether one is critical, sympathetic, or indifferent of this practice. Any evaluative concerns formed by the reader regarding the specific details disclosed in this work can remain personal opinion.

Methodologically, I chose to conduct interviews of retired U.S. Navy and Coast Guard veterans currently mostly in southern California, especially in San Diego. At first glance this choice may appear restrictive in terms of region, but San Diego remains a major U.S. Navy town, wherein resides a significant population of naval retirees compared with other regions containing large Filipino populations. Indeed, it was not at all difficult finding willing subjects in San Diego for the interviews collected—word of mouth as well as newspaper announcements within the local Filipino press were sufficient enough in the search for prospective subjects. Annual gatherings—both formal and informal—of Filipino navy retirees are regularly held in San Diego, with other retirees from different areas often traveling to San Diego for these reunions, which, unfortunately, are becoming smaller with each passing year. Sadly, since the completion of this work, many of the subjects, including my own father, have passed on; consolation at least can be found in the knowledge that a chronicle of their early experiences in America is found in this work.

As a work of oral history, this book is an earnest effort to ensure that the voices of these Filipino sailors will be heard, rather than being restricted outside the margins of our national history. I interviewed nineteen retired ex-stewards recruited by the U.S. Navy or Coast Guard between the mid-1940s through the early 1970s. Each subject was queried about his personal background, premigration experiences, the circumstances leading to recruitment, the signing of steward contracts, early experiences in America, the nature of labor as a steward, and personal opinions concerning the restrictions and regulations exclusive to Filipino servicemen, as well as the ways, if any, he protested the restrictive conditions in which he remained for years, if not decades for some. The duration of each recorded interview varied considerably, with some lasting less than one hour to several others necessitating several sessions. This variation largely depended upon the subject—some interviewees were laconic in their speech; others were quite dramatic storytellers, their spoken memories at times perambulating to distant tangents. Despite a high degree of uniformity regarding their early lives as officers' stewards, a variety of opinions were expressed regarding their overall views of the navy and coast guard as "oppressive" institutions. For most, there still remains discernable resentment over their mistreatment and devaluation as persons; for others, their "revenge" was silently projected into the future in the form of their children's success in America; for a few, despite their acknowledgment of racial discrimination, no resentment was expressed at all. Across the board, however, all Filipinos acknowledged the tradeoff related to permanent stewardship, and almost all involved in this subject had no regrets about their lives in the navy or coast guard.

An inescapable task of the historian is to explore the archives in search of new information and evidence. In conjunction with the spoken voices of Filipino sailors, the uncovering of written documents relating to their plight provided details without which such oral testimonies might be questioned as lacking in official evidence. The Naval Historical Center Library in Washington, DC; the National Archives at College Park, Maryland; and the University of California Libraries at the Irvine and San Diego campuses were essential in the uncovering of evidence and/or providing expansive historical information, thus providing ballast to the oral testimonies within this work. The archival material includes official training manuals; official statements regarding recruiting criteria of Filipinos; letters sent by Filipinos—often desperate in tone—to U.S. naval recruiting stations; newspaper articles; and naval psychiatric studies of Filipino stewards, as well as official naval correspondences and memorandums circulated by the Bureau of Naval Personnel (BuPers). Such documents, I will show, demonstrate how the recruitment of Filipino stewards would eventually materialize as the navy's "Filipino servant problem," an issue whose clear resolution (that is, termination of race-based domestic work) was met by considerable protest among some high-ranking officers even during the age of civil rights.

In sum, the approach of this work is to provide an expansive historical context explaining the utilization of Filipino servant labor in the U.S. Navy, to present and interpret the subjects' experiences gained through oral testimonies, to connect these memories to official archival sources found in both the National Archives II and the Naval Historical Center, and to hopefully contribute an important chapter to Filipino American history with the argument that through their resistance strategies, Filipino stewards played a determinative role in the navy's decision to finally terminate its hidebound practice of racialized domestic labor.

The chapters that follow at once assume a chronological shape while emphasizing topical themes. Chapter 1 serves as a historical and, at times, theoretical disquisition on the centrality of American colonialism in the origination of Filipino immigration to the United States. Scholars in the field of Filipino American Studies have argued that due to American colonialism the "racial formation" of Filipino Americans begins before actual emigration.[34] It is therefore instructive to discuss the historical, ideological, and economic dimensions behind America's colonial foray in the Philippines. Filipino American marginality today can be plausibly linked to their status as former colonial and present neocolonial subjects; their near invisibility in U.S. society is historically connected to the erasure of U.S. war and imperialism in the Philippines within the historical consciousness of most Americans. While the historical and conceptual terrain of this chapter is quite expansive and at times abstract, it is instructive to gain an in-depth understanding of how U.S. imperial presence in the Pacific—and in the Philippines, in particular—is directly connected to Filipino American presence in the United States.[35] The formation of Filipino navy men in the U.S. Navy was indeed an effect whose cause is traceable to U.S. colonialism, which in this case intersected with American exceptionalism, capitalist expansion, and cultural hegemony. The various causal links of this historical chain will be explored in this chapter. While some older works are cited alongside recent scholarship in the chapter's historiography, I believe that the reader stands to profit in the engagement with different approaches to Philippine colonization, thus examining the colonial dimension of U.S.-Philippine relations from different angles of vision, whether economic, political, ideological, or cultural.

The subsequent chapters follow a uniform structure in the discussion of Filipino experience within the U.S. Navy and Coast Guard. As an introduction to each chapter's general topic(s), the particular experiences of my father, Proceso "Paulie" Ada Paligutan, are first highlighted in the form of a storytelling vignette. Paulie's detailed narratives capture some of the shared experiences among Filipino sailors while also revealing the unique details particular to his own early life as a Filipino steward; of course, such particularities vary with each individual interviewee. The rest of the chapter interweaves the broader historical context with the specificities of steward experiences, all the while informed by the voices of other Filipino subjects.

Chapters 2 and 3 relate to the Filipinos recruit's early experiences within a foreign military and country. Again, neocolonial presence looms large in these episodes, as Filipino recruitment was greatly facilitated by preexisting colonial institutions, materially in the form of U.S. military bases in Philippine soil and ideologically by way of the American Dream inculcated since childhood through the practice of U.S. "benevolent assimilation." Here the neocolonial dependency between the former colonizer and ex-colony is exposed as a prior structural condition for the former's use of native labor to solve the navy's labor problems. This fact serves to denaturalize recruitment itself: it is not simply a matter of Filipino young men seeking an escape from economic immiseration toward a "land of plenty," as presupposed in many push-pull analyses of immigration. As the initial elation commonly experienced among them began to fade, the realization of their marginal consignments within these military institutions led to disenchantment and discontent. For most, this meant that their initial plans to pursue the American Dream had to be deferred.

A common observation among non-Filipinos at the time was the perceived passivity and docility of the Filipino sailor. Often, such mythic renditions were formed due to certain ideological misconceptions of Asians as found in Orientalism—a Western ideology born out of European imperialism. Orientalism presupposes fundamental and essential differences between the East (Orient) and West (Occident), engendering the dubious conclusion that "Orientals" cannot fully assimilate to Western culture. Oriental men, according to this view, are viewed as essentially weak, effeminate, and passive. Visual attestation may have been formed via the outward image of Filipino stewards as passive, hardworking, loyal, and enthusiastic. Yet, these superficial observations masked the reality of Filipino protest, manifested in passive and active forms. Chapter 4 penetrates the surface of often-feigned Filipino alacrity. Contrary to outward appearances of Filipino passivity, these stewards were able to forge a culture of resistance in the face of their enforced marginality within an environment where not only was open contempt against superiors harshly reprimanded but also the consequences of chronic disobedience and labor stoppage surely meant incarceration and deportation. Indeed, for some, such punitive repercussions did little to quell the impulse toward revolt against their secondary positions, a decision that would irreversibly negate their chances of life improvement in a country much more affluent than home. The culture of protest and resistance discussed in chapter 4 should be viewed as continuous with other examples of Filipino laborers protesting unfair labor conditions, such as the Filipino Federation of Labor established in the sugar plantations of Hawai'i, and the pioneering efforts of Larry Itliong, Philip Vera Cruz, and the Filipino agricultural protesters in the United Farm Workers.[36]

Chapter 5 is primarily the result of archival findings regarding the navy and coast guard's "steward problem," which by the 1960s extended beyond the black/white dichotomy to encompass primarily Filipino stewards. By then, Filipinos were the preferred race by the navy's top brass to fulfill the roles as servants, owing to their supposed docility, clean appearance, efficiency, and—curiously—their smaller stature. To quote an African American sailor: "The officers preferred the Filipinos. They complained [that we African Americans] were country boys who didn't know how to wait tables, that we were too tall, and that we were not clean as compared to the Filipinos."[37] Attributions of docility were greatly misplaced, however, and as will be shown, the nature of Filipino mistreatment, exploitation, and oppression would not escape the attention of naval administrators, due to Filipino protest.[38] What was earlier kept hidden, suppressed, or ignored (especially since some admirals and captains grew attached to their Filipino stewards and could not imagine not having servants) was now openly acknowledged among naval policymakers, and this work argues that the reality of Filipino oppression would not be known by the navy's top command if it was not for a culture of resistance percolating upward and finding its mark. Stated otherwise, the imminent change in the navy's practice of colonial servitude was in large part the result of Filipino protest and not merely symptomatic of a wider national trend in the liberalization of racial attitudes during the civil rights era.

The final chapter largely centers on a historically important chief of naval operations, Adm. Elmo "Bud" Zumwalt, who instituted reforms more than twenty years after President Harry S. Truman desegregated the U.S. military. Zumwalt's formative experiences leading to the crystallization of his reformist zeal directly involved his own Filipino stewards, who pleaded for his assistance in their attempt to migrate beyond the steward rating. Due to inertia within the navy's occupational rating system specifically imposed upon Filipino sailors, Zumwalt's attempts to help his stewards with advancement was met with so much unexpected friction that the young officer was suddenly forced to reconsider his earlier views regarding the navy's race relations as naïve. Indeed, Zumwalt would eventually change the complexion of the U.S. Navy—from a monochromatic portrait surrounded with dark borders toward a mosaic of different colors—in the navy's heralded era of reform during the 1970s, spurred by African American and Filipino complaint and protest. Such changes finally led to the end of the deferment of the American Dream for many of these Filipino sailors.

Thus the American Dream was not exactly a colonial lie; yet at the same time, the entire truth was not revealed to Filipino recruits regarding the disproportionate amount of sacrifice, patience, and even acts of protest necessary to clamber up its promised heights. Even their colonial textbooks, which taught Filipino students that the exploration of a "frontier" combined with hard work and dedication led to material success, were hardly forthcoming about the institutional barriers experienced by persons of color striving to reach this universal American ideal. This reality underscores the necessity of understanding not only the ideological component but also the economic, political, and racial dimensions behind colonialism in the Philippines. The following chapter aims to dissect the manifold ways in which American colonialism serves as the fulcrum of Filipino American history; thus, it is necessary to start from the beginning of imperial rule in the Philippines.

CHAPTER ONE

Colonial Past, Neocolonial Present

Proceso Ada Paligutan, called "Paulie" by his friends, was a proud retiree of the U.S. Coast Guard. This is readily apparent by the ubiquitous presence of coast guard memorabilia throughout his home: the plaques and awards prominently displayed on the walls of his study, the numerous pictures of longtime coast guard and navy friends, the highly conspicuous coast guard decal emblazoned on the bumper of his car. Yet, even after nearly thirty years of retirement, there remained a discernible tinge of resentment when asked about his early years in the service. Although retiring as a respected senior chief (a very high rank for enlistees), his early years in the U.S. Coast Guard can be aptly described as a prolonged experience of servitude and subservience while denied occupational mobility. Recruited as a Filipino national into the military of his country's former colonizer, Paulie was consigned to the most menial occupational rating in the navy and coast guard: that of an officer's "steward," whose duties were basically equivalent to that of a domestic servant. Due to his status as a foreign national, he and other Filipino recruits in the navy and coast guard were prohibited from entering other occupational ratings. For a significant number of years, Paulie wallowed inside the ranks of a postcolonial labor force within the U.S. military, whose duties were not unlike those historically associated with colonial labor throughout the history of Western imperialism: native servant labor performed for their white colonial masters.

Despite this prolonged period of servile duty, the opportunity to enlist in the U.S. Navy was an enormously life-changing event for the typical Filipino young recruit during the post–World War II era. Especially for him and others mired in economic destitution, this sudden reversal of fortune greatly transformed his life, as his earnings would place him well above the average income earner in a poor country. Given the tremendous odds due to the sheer number of applicants vying for the job, this dramatic economic transformation was nearly miraculous, likely conceived by such beneficiaries as an act of benevolence extended from their former colonial master. Indeed, many Filipinos at the time considered the half-century of American colonial occupation itself as a fortuitous chapter in Philippine history, insofar as Filipinos benefitted from the gifts of public education, democratic government, and modern reforms. Even after independence in 1946, Filipinos proudly imagined a natural affinity and fraternity with America as "little brown brothers and sisters" of the most powerful and influential nation in the world.[1]

Such a belief was a vestige of the colonial aims proclaimed by American occupiers after the islands were annexed as a U.S. territory in 1898. From the outset, Americans justified the colonization of the Philippines as driven by a moral imperative—the racial uplift of Filipino natives through the spread of American civilization within their fledgling colony. The American colonial project was to be the transformation of Filipinos in mind and body, from "primitive" savages to enlightened subjects. This moral justification for American colonization of the Philippines is a key starting point in understanding not only the Philippine nation as it developed through the twentieth century but also the history of Filipino immigration to the United States during the twentieth century. As will be shown, it particularly applies to the immigration of Filipino recruits into the U.S. Navy and Coast Guard. In order to understand this connection, it is necessary to discuss how "race"—as a both a historical and theoretical category—had figured significantly in the U.S. justification for expansionism, as well as how exceptionalism shaped the nature of American colonial institutions in the Philippines, ultimately connecting this interrelation to the various factors that would precipitate Filipino immigration to America. This chapter discusses how exceptionalism was centrally important not only as an ideology justifying continental expansion but also in the U.S. colonial management of the Philippines. It critically examines various U.S. colonial practices in the Philippines while recasting benevolent assimilation as a colonial technology of control and power. By the end of this chapter, it is revealed how U.S. colonialism and neocolonialism factored immensely in the creation of a labor pool of migrant workers, even after the granting of Philippine independence. Indeed, the voluntary enlistment of Filipino recruits is but one example of a labor force shaped by prior colonial domination, while migrating under the aegis of American neocolonial institutions within the former colony.

Race, American Exceptionalism, and U.S. Expansionism

The colonial occupation of the Philippines following the Spanish American War stands as a singular event in the history of U.S. expansion.[2] By the 1890s, with land now extending from sea to shining sea, the United States did not mask its ambitions of expansionism and colonial nation building beyond its newly established continental boundaries. American civilization now followed upon the heels of the powerful empires of Europe in their effort to carve up the world.

Yet despite outward similarities, the architects of U.S. empire declaimed pronouncements of exceptionalism justifying its extension toward new frontiers, ones that parted company with the naked aggression characterizing European imperialism in Asia and Africa at the time. American imperialists appealed to a moral obligation justifying the occupation of the Philippines, a duty to guide a "backwards Filipino race" from darkness to light. While vigilantly maintaining distance from the native population predicated upon racial and cultural superiority, American colonizers, nonetheless, expounded an imperial project that President William McKinley called "benevolent assimilation," which entailed the racial uplift of a benighted race through the largesse of representative democracy, Western culture, and the practices of modernity. Indeed, this "civilizing mission" to spread enlightenment among native Filipinos is at once an instance of American exceptionalism par excellence while also serving as an ideological veneer concealing the economic and geopolitical desideratum of Pacific domination.

America's self-referential designation as a benevolent empire is continuous within a wider narrative of U.S. exceptionalism throughout its history, an article of faith that remains deeply woven in the fabric of American beliefs. The long history of American expansionism was typically justified by exceptionalist claims to the supposed vacant lands in the American West. Just as with Philippine colonization, prior territorial aggrandizement upon the North American continent was explained by the moral righteousness of the act itself. All the while, notions of American exceptionalism wielded a talismanic ability to shroud America's imperial conquests—continental and overseas—in a fog of historical amnesia. Just what is revealed about U.S. expansionism once this fog is lifted?

To begin, the very foundation story of America itself is bound to notions of exceptionalism and civilizational superiority, as seen with the image of the New World as a New Jerusalem, settled by exceptionally stalwart, pious, and enterprising English Puritans establishing a "shining city on a hill." Occupying land imagined as vacant, these Puritan settlers avowedly held belief in the divine right to build a model community comprising God's chosen people, a Puritan trope that would be reinscribed in future claims of American exceptionalism centuries after Puritan settlement. Yet, this moral plot would not be without immoral consequences, as it would play an ideological role in the genocidal displacement of Native Americans due to their putative state of "savagery" and "primitivism." Thus a direct line can be traced from early forms of moral exceptionalism justifying English settlement to the eventual forced removal of racial Others to clear the way for white expansion, leading to the rare historical case in modern history of racial replacement within a given continent.

The American Revolution itself was justified as a necessary consequence following a "long train of abuses" against colonial liberty perpetrated by the British monarch and Parliament, a crucible that the revolutionary Thomas Paine framed, in exceptionalist language, as a world historical event inaugurated by a chosen people of history—that is, the English colonials soon to become Americans. Upon rupturing the umbilical relation between the colonies and its mother country of England, the extrusion of American settler movement would proceed unremittingly, forging the settlement of frontier described by Thomas Jefferson as an "empire of liberty." Jefferson's vision illustrates how even the Founders—standard bearers of liberty in the modern world—failed to discern the fundamental incongruity between empire and freedom. Indeed, American leaders and settlers self-assuredly preached that the geographical spread of American civilization was coextensive with the spread of the American creed—that the constitution followed the flag. This unique character of American egalitarianism would not escape the notice of the famous scholar Alexis de Tocqueville, who by the 1830s announced that the United States stood as an exceptional nation in all of Western civilization insofar as it had established a stable and vital functioning democracy bereft of feudal constraints.

By the mid–nineteenth century, the American expansion across continental territory would be described in exceptionalist terms bespeaking a teleology ordained by God—a "manifest destiny to overspread the continent allotted by Providence for the free development of [America's] yearly multiplying millions."[3] With the close of the Western frontier officially announced by the government in 1890, the historian Frederick Jackson Turner in 1893 celebrated white pioneers as driving American history, which he defined as a line of civilization inexorably moving westward toward the shores of the Pacific Ocean as America conquered savagery. Turner's thesis is cited as a pronouncement of American exceptionalism, as it attributes America's unique engagement with the frontier as the very source of America's essential values and ideals, such as ingenuity, innovation, resourcefulness, and of course, the spread of democracy.

As viewed today, Turner's celebratory frontier thesis is roundly criticized due to a pair of exclusions: first, in his definition of American civilization in exclusionary terms—that is, defined by what it is *not* (the savage racial Other), thus reminding us of how expansion hinged upon race; second, in his privileging of "civilization" as the primary engine of American territorial expansionism while downplaying capitalist expansion as a primary factor. In Turner's mind, "free land" in the West (to use his own phrase) may have referred to a political state of affairs, yet this entailed a land free of a race that remained savage. Indians were part of the landscape that needed to be tamed. Turner's recurrent idealism justifying westward movement also conceals the linkage between continental expansion and commercial growth. Modern historians have since revisited geographical expansionism during the nineteenth century as inextricably bound with capitalist expansion.[4] Just as the spread of markets reached its continental ending point, the United States during the 1890s, already immersed in an unprecedented period of intensive industrialization amid social and political upheaval, now faced a new economic exigency—the need for overseas markets due to economic overproduction.[5]

Yet, just as Turner's thesis mistakenly elided the reality of the market as an engine of history in continental expansion, so, too, is there a danger in ascribing casual priority upon the economic dimensions behind the search for colonies abroad. A more nuanced interpretation of U.S. overseas expansionism necessarily involves consideration of a variety of causal factors prompting the emergence of the United States as a competitive empire by the 1890s. Recent scholars have rejected overly economistic interpretations in their work, instead viewing economics as one strand in a causal web that includes social and cultural factors.

Historians peering through the interpretive lens of culture, for instance, connect expansionism to the categories of race, gender, and class to provide novel factors that plausibly connect to overseas imperialism. The historian Gail Bederman's work *Manliness and Civilization* argues that middle-class manhood during the last decades of the 1800s, due to underlying social strife and economic crises at the time, sought its redefinition with the rougher lower-class immigrant masculinities while abandoning the Victorian ideals of high-minded self-restraint and gentility.[6] The recasting of middle-class gender customs to include masculine aggression and physical strength would occur not only with the entrepreneurial middle class but among the genteel upper class, as famously embodied by the aristocrat Theodore Roosevelt's masculinist exploits, writings, martial ethos, and gendered philosophy (the "strenuous life"). Crucial to Bederman's thesis is how this redefinition of manhood was tied to white supremacy: that is, the new masculinist ethos at the time was constructed through racial domination of nonwhites.[7] From here, it is apparent how gender and race connect to the spread of white "civilization," which again is a central aspect of "benevolent assimilation."

The scholar Kristin Hoganson, for example, argues that the jingoistic exhortations of American imperialists during the outbreak of the Spanish-American War in 1898 particularly resonated with men seeking an outlet for the expression of martial spirit and at the same time provided an opportunity to fulfill the role of earner and family provider in the aftermath of the Depression of 1893, obligations that were attached to middle-class male gender roles yet unfulfilled due to the economic crisis.[8] The taming of new frontiers now found in the Caribbean and Pacific—a new "errand into the wilderness," to borrow historian Perry Miller's well-known phrase—was thus a means by which men could regenerate and reclaim masculinity and male supremacy. Of course, the affinity of male power and whiteness was evident in the prior inferiorization of Native American and African American men, whose political and social disfranchisement was, in large part, justified by their supposed unmanliness and lack of civilization. Moreover, men of darker races, according to nineteenth-century evolutionary-based pseudoscience, were simply not advanced enough intellectually and morally to practice the Western political arts of democracy and self-government. Such essentialized gendered beliefs directed at nonwhite men were components of nineteenth-century racial ideology that effectively marginalized them from the political sphere. This articulation of manliness, racial dominance, and civilization would be grafted upon the "muscular" foreign policy dictating American overseas expansion by the end of the nineteenth century, eventually being transposed to a new frontier across the Pacific Ocean.

A New Frontier in the Pacific

With the prosecution of war against Spain in 1898, U.S. Navy Commodore George Dewey's fleet easily destroyed the Spanish navy protecting its largest Pacific colony. A sovereign Philippine republic was established that same year after more than three centuries of Spanish colonial rule. At the outset, American officials reassured the Philippine nationalist leader Emilio Aguinaldo that the new republic's sovereignty was a foregone conclusion.

Yet, the uneasy coexistence of two victorious forces occupying the same ground began to crumble, creating a new tension-filled frontier of would-be combatants separated by race. As with their earliest encounters with Native Americans along the "gender frontier" in colonial Anglo-Indian interaction,[9] the inevitable confrontation of Anglo-Saxon men and Filipinos was impinged by prevailing gender stereotypes. Filipino men were essentialized as effeminate, soft, weak, and unmanly (despite the tenacity and bravery eventually displayed against American soldiers in combat). As discussed in Kristin Hoganson's book, the expansionist George Becker believed that the perceived reversal of gender customs in Philippine culture, whereby women were producers while men seemingly chose not to work, was evident not only in the inherent indolence of Filipino men but also their lack of capacity for self-government.[10] Filipinos were further Orientalized as savage, uncivilized, and lacking in honor; they were infantilized as "grown-up children" in need of supervision from civilized races.[11] This racial imaginary of Filipinos was a necessary prelude to the benevolent assimilation program justifying colonization of the Philippines.

Importantly, a sizable number of influential American politicians, activists, writers, and intellectuals—collectively known as the Anti-imperialist League—was staunchly opposed to American occupation. Is not the expropriation of overseas territory, they argued, against the grain of the American ideals of freedom and democracy? Yet, this forceful argument would be countered by pro-imperialists through turning the anti-imperialist argument on its head: the formal colonization of the Philippines is exactly justified in the name of democracy, an ideal demanding its export abroad, they argued, suturing their argument to the lofty duty of racial uplift. Filipinos must be rescued from the dark cave of savagery, and America, by virtue of its racial superiority, is charged with this moral obligation by God and history. The prominent U.S. senator Albert J. Beveridge expressed this sentiment in unequivocally racial terms:

[The Philippine] question is deeper than any question of party politics. . . . It is elemental. It is racial. God has not been preparing the English-speaking and Teutonic peoples for a thousand years for nothing but vain and idle self-contemplation and self-admiration. No! He has made us the master organizers of the world to establish system where chaos reigns. . . . He has made us adept in government that we may administer government among savage and senile peoples. Were it not for such a force as this the world would relapse into barbarism and night. And of all our race He has marked the American people as His chosen nation to finally lead in the regeneration of the world.[12]

Even the famous literary figure Englishman Rudyard Kipling, in his poem "The White Man's Burden," reminded Americans of their solemn duty to bear the burden and bring civilization to a backward Filipino people—"half-devil, half-child."[13] Unlike the forcible expropriation of land and displacement of Native Americans practiced under manifest destiny, the benevolent assimilation of the Filipino native would be compelled by moral compassion toward a lesser race—what the scholar Vicente L. Rafael calls "white love."

Eventually, the ideology of benevolent empire loudly trumpeted by American imperialists contributed decisively to the political defeat of the anti-imperialist factions within the U.S. Congress.[14] Holding in abeyance the contradiction of empire and democracy, definite talk of Philippine annexation was now on the lips of influential leaders (some of whom did not forget to remind others of the added geostrategic value of the archipelago as a gateway to the lucrative markets of Asia).[15] Even before the altruistic largesse of benevolent assimilation was extended, the American military forces, once greeted as allies and liberators, were now sized up by resentful natives as an occupying army. The conditions of possibility for a democratic experiment in the Philippines, imperialists realized, must entail a sort of "creative destruction" for democracy—the use of bullets and bayonets was the prerequisite for instituting the ballot.

Hostilities between the two opposing armies quickly flared into the open, developing into full-scale warfare. The Philippine-American War, beginning in 1899 and officially ended by the United States three years later (despite unabated hostilities in the countryside and southern regions for over a decade thereafter), significantly exceeded the previous Spanish-American War in intensity, duration, expenditure, and military and civilian casualties. Superior arms and tactics deployed by the American military forced the Filipino army to adopt guerilla warfare initially considered dishonorable and "unmanly" by their adversaries. The bravery and near fanaticism displayed by Filipino soldiers and insurrectos in the battlefield would eventually inspire the awe, fear, and even admiration of their American enemies. The tenacious resistance of Filipino guerillas, some armed with only *bolos* (native machetes), prompted the U.S. Army to adopt tactics of torture, civilian mass relocation and mass murder (referred to as "depopulation campaigns"), shooting Filipinos "for sport," scorched-earth policies, and "reconcentration" camps occupied by hundreds of thousands of villagers and peasants sympathetic to the cause of Philippine independence.[16] Despite heavy censorship of the press, word spread among the American public that their soldiers, ostensibly fighting with benevolent intentions, were ordered by U.S. Army officers to conduct war in an "uncivilized" manner: to raze entire villages; kill women and children indiscriminately; engage in torture techniques, such as the infamous "water cure" (today known as waterboarding); and to take no prisoners among surrendering Filipino troops.[17]

The justifications for committing such atrocities largely pivoted upon prevailing assumptions undergirding racial and gender ideologies and while wedded to the discourse of civilization—that American troops must meet the dishonorable, unmanly tactics of guerilla warfare conducted by native savages with more atrocious means; that the practices of massacre, torture, and civilian internment were a justifiable recourse when fighting an inferior race undeserving of civilized combat. The code of civilized warfare simply did not apply to an uncivilized race. Moreover, scholars have noted that many seasoned American officers and soldiers fresh from the killing fields of the American West during the Indian Wars exported with them an intense hatred for the racial Other, as well as prevailing stereotypes of racial images pertaining to Native Americans and African Americans, ones that were readily applied to Filipinos. The racial epithets of "Indians," "savages," "niggers," and "goo-goos" (a derogatory designation invented for Filipinos) directed toward natives were employed interchangeably as distinctions without a difference. After the official end of the war, although the Filipino's racial status would be elevated from the category of savagery, the unpacified remnants of insurgent resistance in the "boondocks" (an American slang word invented during the war derived from the Tagalog word "*bundok*," meaning "mountain") would retain their racialized status as "niggers" and "Indians."

The defeat of the Philippine revolutionary army and insurrectos at the hands of the occupying army meant that the memories of atrocities visited upon Filipino soldiers and civilians would be momentarily effaced. Indeed, in the textbooks of U.S. history, the entire episode of the Philippine-American War would be continually reinterpreted as a minor "insurrection" compared to the U.S. war against Spain, despite the higher costs in American lives and military expenditure, not to mention the Philippine-American War's significance as the first American war fought in Asia (to be followed by military conflicts with China, Japan, Korea, Vietnam, Cambodia, and Laos resulting from American expansionism in the Pacific theater). The combined military and civilian death toll of Filipinos (extending past the war's official end) can only make the mind reel: the Filipina historian Luzviminda Francisco projects that cumulative casualties, taking into account deaths resulting from epidemic diseases and starvation exacerbated by the war, amount to the staggering figure of over one million Filipino deaths. More conservative figures estimate up to twenty thousand Filipino military deaths and three hundred thousand civilian deaths.[18] One can imagine, however, that some American policymakers saw the brutality of the war a necessary means to the goal of civilizing Filipinos.

Benevolent assimilation was thus inaugurated by a race war necessitating wholesale devastation and psychological trauma wrought by America's wartime policies and practices while costing the lives of an untold number of Filipinos cast as uncivilized half-devil, half-child and racialized as savages, niggers, and goo-goos. With the end of hostilities in sight, it was reasoned that the white man's burden to administer democratic government and to teach Filipino "children" the responsibilities of civic virtues could begin in earnest. Yet, such an undertaking, in principle, could not occur according to the wartime metaphysics of race, whereby the Filipino was defined in essentialist terms by savagery. Before and during the war, Filipino natives were designated to the lowest rungs of the uncivilized world—inferior to even "the most ignorant Negro," according to the administrator (and eventual U.S. president) William Howard Taft.[19] Thus discernible at the wake of pacification was a marked shift in the imperialist racial metaphysics: no longer enemies, Filipinos were reconstructed in the more familial and paternalistic terms as "little brown brothers." This reinscription of race was deemed a necessary condition for the creation of a racial colonial state inclusive of Filipino participants in the governance of the fledgling colony.[20]

Such fluid racial constructions would continually persist within the colonial state through the ensuing decades, thus marking the incipient stages of Filipino *American* history even before migration toward the metropole. Lisa Lowe and Yen Le Espiritu remind us that the racial formation of Filipino Americans did not begin upon settlement in the United States; rather, its origins are found within the colonial racial state, whereby racial construction by the colonial state and its contestation by racialized groups were already underway. Hence, the racial formation of Filipinos as "little brown brothers" serves as an early formation that preceded future legal constructions, such as "wards" and "nationals." Indeed, the construction of the "docile Filipino native"—a stereotype attributed to Filipino stewards in the U.S. Navy—is all the more conceivable once constructed by a paternalistic and putatively benign colonialism.

Although Filipinos acquiescing to American rule may have ascended a degree in colonial American race making, they were, nonetheless, preordained by virtue of their "Asiatic" physical features to remain outside the imagined community of the American nation.[21] The "Philippine Question" revolved around the issue of citizenship: with U.S. acquisition of overseas territory, should the Philippines' millions of inhabitants be recognized as citizens endowed with rights guaranteed under the U.S. Constitution? With the North American continental expansion, the Constitution followed the flag—would this also occur in the Pacific frontier?

This novel situation regarding the status of native colonials provoked the xenophobic anxiety of American policymakers unable to imagine "little brown brothers and sisters" incorporated into white America. In the interest of preserving white nationhood, American legislators enforced the "differential inclusion" of Filipino subjects.[22] Geographically, such a designation would be expressed with the official classification of Philippine territory as "unincorporated territory." Unlike earlier continental territory, whereby the condition of racial replacement allowed for state formation and admission, the newly acquired Philippines was inhabited by seven million dark-skinned natives at the time. As seen with the U.S. Supreme Court decision over the 1901 Insular Cases, the official classification as unincorporated territory hinged upon race; to quote the historian Daniel Immerwahr: "The main majority [Supreme Court] decision contained warnings about including 'savages' and 'alien races' within the constitutional fold."[23] With the Insular Cases, American officials declared that native inhabitants of unincorporated territory would be legally prohibited from gaining U.S. citizenship. In order to preserve the naturalized affinity of American citizenship with whiteness, the U.S. government essentially deemed the Philippine colony as belonging to, yet not a part of, the United States.[24]

Thus, in the case of the Philippines, the sacrosanct American belief that the Constitution follows the flag was suspended. The overriding concern of Congress to preserve a white nation, legally formalized since the 1790 Nationalization Act, underwrote the indeterminate status of Filipinos under U.S. colonial rule; the various designations of "brothers," "wards," and "nationals"—but not citizens—of the United States adumbrated their interstitial positionalities as immigrants within the imperial metropole itself. The future migratory waves of agricultural and cannery workers, soldiers and sailors, and nurses and doctors would occupy an ambiguous space wherein Filipinos, mostly seen as reliable and cheap laborers by Americans at home, were ironically viewed as needed yet unwanted. As argued by the theorist Lisa Lowe, the legal exclusion of Filipinos and other Asian subjects from citizenship during pre–World War II America served as a legal discourse sublating the contradiction between the needs of the industrializing economy (i.e., cheap labor) and those of the state (i.e., racial homogeneity).[25]

Benevolent Imperialism or Colonial Technologies of Power?

While the invasion of the Philippines in 1898 was occasioned by destructive force of the U.S. military, subsequent colonial policy for civilian governance of the islands was imbued with the missionary spirit of progressivism. Indeed, the next wave of colonizers to arrive—administrators, government officials, and educators—were disciples of progressive reformism sweeping throughout the United States in the wake of the new century. As civilian purveyors of benevolent assimilation, administrators aimed to govern not by military force but, rather, by moral fiat; they sought to persuade Filipinos of U.S. sincerity in carrying out policies that promised to rescue native society from its supposed backwardness.

With the Organic Act of 1902 granting authority to implement a colonial state within the newly conquered territory, progressivism's transformative vision—the moral, political, and social elevation of the fledgling colony by way of American tutelage—was now underway. Progressive imperialism extended to almost every aspect of everyday life: language, education, political governance, health and sanitation, and medicine, among others. The progressivist faith in expertise was transplanted across the Pacific Ocean as one more constituent of Western knowledge systems inflicting violence upon the native mentalité. Moreover, American administrators sought to finalize the conquest of the islands (as well as U.S. Caribbean possessions) through mastery of the geography, indigenous life, and native habits of the mind, as witnessed by the profusion of scientific and ethnographic knowledge production during occupation. As one can see, such "knowledge/power" regimes (as advanced by the philosopher Michel Foucault) were at once instilled and invented by a "second wave of American occupiers" to reach the Philippines.[26] These regimes reveal the interdigitated relation of knowledge and power in the colonial setting—how power determines regimes of knowledge while knowledge produces regimes of power.

The interpenetration of knowledge and power and their connection to benevolent imperialism in the colonial Philippines offer a fascinating dimension of analysis in the endeavor to demythologize American benevolent imperialism. Scholarly works by Vicente L. Rafael and Warwick Anderson, among others, expose the implementation of ostensibly reform-minded programs and policies as colonial technologies of power wielding and subtle forms of domination, ultimately facilitating the discipline and control of native bodies. Such scholars transpose Foucauldian notions of "knowledge/power," "biopower," and "governmentality" from its original European historical setting onto the colonial milieu. According to this approach, colonial administrative policies and reforms implemented in the name of progress are recast as disciplinary techniques, at once shaping the colonial subjectivities while managing the colonial population en masse. In Foucault's schema, the exercise of power is not a top-down process as conceived in more totalizing explanatory frameworks, such as Marxism and most schools of traditional political philosophy. Rather, Foucault reconceptualized power as operating at the capillary level, as a process of diffusion emanating from no individual or group in particular. Interestingly, such postmodern formulations of power—being everywhere but from nowhere in particular—offer compelling interpretative frameworks in both the shaping of colonial subjectivity and subjugation, although it remains contentious whether its application onto colonial power structures retains the original meaning conceptualized by Foucault.[27]

Arguably, the most effective colonial technology of power under American colonialism was found in the program of universal education for all Filipinos, a knowledge/power discursive formation par excellence. Previously, under Spanish rule, the withholding of secular education from most Filipinos was an important instrument of control, insofar as the revolutionary potentialities of an uneducated native population tended to remain dormant. Indeed, the Spanish parish friars who oversaw the education of the few privileged natives were determined not to loosen their monopolistic hold upon secular knowledge, being tolerant of only religious topics as legitimate teachings.[28] Notwithstanding a "dark age" with the denial of education among the Filipino lower and peasant classes, the "enlightened" class of educated Filipino elite (appropriately named the *Ilustrados*, or "the learned"), some of whom ventured from periphery to metropole in pursuit of higher learning, gained a political education imbued with the liberal ideals of the Enlightenment, and subsequently demanded local reforms of education, humane treatment by friars, and the building of public infrastructure in their homeland.[29] One preeminent member of the Ilustrado class, Jose Rizal—a physician who would become the national hero of the Philippines—produced remarkable literary works that satirized the colonial and religious orders while crystallizing a Filipino identity in embryo. Rizal's fiery pen would help spark the movement from elite reformism to populist revolution, led by Rizal-inspired "organic intellectuals," such as Andres Bonifacio and Emilio Jacinto. The denial by Spanish colonizers of universal education among the broad masses was proven ineffective in staving off native revolt.

American colonizers, aware or not of the unintended consequences resulting from Spanish educational policy, pursued the opposite path in the name of racial uplift and democratic progress. For a backwards race to advance toward democratic self-government, it was crucial that Filipinos become students of the "superior" ways of American civilization—the historical exponent of democracy and liberty among modern nations. As education was foundational to a democratic society in America, it was reasoned that the same educational opportunities should be readily available within the new colony aspiring toward political, economic, and moral elevation. The gift of education would be presented by a new group of civilian "pioneers" possessed with progressivist missionary zeal—American teachers. As early as 1901, the USS *Thomas* transported 509 American educators voyaging to a new frontier where a race war was still being fought, dedicated in their mission to spread Western knowledge and achieve mass literacy in English among the native population.[30] The arrival of the "Thomasites," many of whom were women, served to alter the complexion of the masculine tableau established by earlier American military aggressors. An explicit message was sent with the arrival of educators and administrators, that the American imperialists were not exactly disingenuous in their stated ambition of benevolent assimilation. Indeed, the succeeding waves of civilian educators and civil government workers were not greeted with the distrust and derision reserved for the imperial army; rather, the program of universal education, as with democratic elections, was embraced not only by the native elite but also by the urban and rural lower classes that, not unlike the freedmen and freedwomen after the U.S. Emancipation, stood to benefit the most with the provision of free education, a right denied to them for centuries owing to fear of popular uprising.

In the interest of national advancement of the Filipino people, was the program of free universal education truly a gift? Prima facie, it seems that colonials would have nothing to lose but their ignorance; yet a more critical analysis reveals the educational program to be crucially instrumental in forging the chains of colonial dependency. Again invoking Foucault's notion of knowledge indissociably linked to power, scholars have transvaluated colonial education from a gift promoting racial uplift to a technology wielding disciplinary effects. The effectivity of education as a disciplinary technique is particularly evinced in the exposure of white supremacy in all its variants to the broad mass of the native population.[31] Aiming to expunge traditional knowledge—dismissed as supernatural and irrational—from indigenous consciousness, compulsory education served to create a tabula rasa of the native mind to be newly inscribed with Western narratives, histories, and epistemologies presented by educators as universal truths. As passive recipients of colonial education, Filipino students were inculcated with a hierarchical worldview that located their intermediary positions between civilization and savagery. Such a worldview naturalized and essentialized the putative superiority of Western knowledge, American culture, and white bodies. The subtle form of power diffused from this disciplinary technique was demonstrated in the apparent interpellation of native consciousness readily accepting hierarchical ideas of white superiority and native inferiority, with the upshot being the internalization of subordination while quelling revolutionary impulses latent within the restructured native mind. To teach Filipinos of their inherent inferiority as implied in colonial education was to inculcate the expected responses of docility and loyalty toward their benefactors.

The Filipino nationalist historian Renato Constantino, in his essay *The Miseducation of the Filipino*, understood the disciplinary effects of colonial education well before the publication of Foucault's works on knowledge/ power.[32] Writing during a period of antiestablishment protest in the mid-1960s, Constantino's provocative thesis not only explained the apparent aim of colonial education in producing docile and compliant colonial subjects but also admonished the Filipinos' tendency to apotheosize American culture and society over their own, a practice arguably extant to this very day. Recognizing the role of colonial education in the American early efforts of pacification, Constantino notes the historical timing of the implementation of public education in the face of intransigent military resistance directed toward the new occupational army. He delineates these themes in the following passage:

> From its inception, the educational system of the Philippines was a means of pacifying a people who were defending their newly-won freedom from an invader who had posed as an ally. The education of the Filipino under American sovereignty was an instrument of colonial policy. The Filipino had to be educated as a good colonial. Young minds had to be shaped to conform to American ideas. Indigenous Filipino ideals were slowly eroded in order to remove the last vestiges of resistance. Education served to attract the people to the new masters and at the same time dilute their nationalism which had just succeeded in overthrowing a foreign power.[33]

It was previously mentioned that mainstream historical narratives as taught in American schools and universities have consistently relegated the Philippine-American War—America's "first Vietnam," as one critical journalist called it—as a minor footnote in U.S. military history, thus contributing to the historical amnesia persisting not only over this deadly conflict but also the event of Philippine colonization itself. The remarkable success of education in effecting this erasure of historical memory is made more striking when considering its efficacy within the colonial setting itself. Millions of Filipino schoolchildren, sharing the same textbooks as students in mainland

America, were taught of the civilizing mission of the American colonizer impelled by "white love," in consequence denying them the truth of a ruthless race war, as well as nationalist teachings espoused by Filipino leaders resisting American rule. The stature of Filipino revolutionary heroes was made diminutive next to towering American leaders, such as George Washington and Abraham Lincoln. Many Filipinos, as students of U.S. history, practitioners of American-styled democratic government, and consumers of American culture, might have believed in an "imagined fraternity" with Americans (to borrow Carlos Bulosan's phrase) or may have accepted their secondary status vis-à-vis whites; yet one seemingly universal recognition among Filipino colonials was the inconceivability of Filipino superiority over their white colonizers. Such was the consequence of the Filipinos' colonial "miseducation." The following observation by Constantino, poignant while indignant, deserves attention:

> With American textbooks, Filipinos started learning not only a new language but also a new way of life, alien to their traditions and yet a caricature of their model. This was the beginning of their miseducation, for they learned no longer as Filipinos but as colonials. They had to be disoriented from their nationalist goals because they had to become good colonials. The ideal colonial was the carbon copy of his conqueror, the conformist follower of the new dispensation. He had to forget his past and unlearn the nationalist virtues in order to live peacefully, if not comfortably, under the colonial order. The new Filipino generation learned the lives of American heroes, sang American songs, and dreamt of snow and Santa Claus.[34]

Initially imagined as "savage" and "barbaric," Filipinos were coerced not only to reform their minds and reconstitute their identities but also to "refashion their bodies." Just as the lack of widespread literacy and education among the colonials was indicative of native backwardness, so, too, did colonialists correlate the apparent lack of healthy bodies and sanitary conditions (defined, of course, by American standards) as outward evidence of their inherent primitiveness. As with educational reform, progressive colonialists imagined the institutionalization of hygiene practices and sanitation regimes not only as a progressive step toward modernity but also as an act of altruism for the sake of moral uplift; they considered disease control and medicine as integral components of race improvement. Native bodies (as well as those of white soldiers separated from their "natural" environment) were the subjects of the "colonial laboratory," to use Anderson's phrase, where the latest theories and practices of medicine and disease prevention could be tested and implemented upon a colonial population.

The role of medicine, sanitation, and hygiene as disciplinary techniques should be readily apparent, for such discursive regimes penetrate to the most private aspects of one's life. Viewed through the optics of race and gender, such technologies of power not only contributed to the gendered discourse of Filipino male bodies—continually stricken by "colonial pathologies" in an environment inhospitable to Westerners—as "weak" and "fragile" compared to strong and healthy white bodies but they also served to naturalize a constructed biological and physiological distinction between the races. Anderson explicates this particular point in his uncovering of hygiene reform as an instrument of discipline and surveillance deployed in the colonial setting. After their initial encounter of a new tropical terrain and climate, American doctors and medical experts underwent a fundamental shift in their theories concerning the etiological role of tropical pathogens upon the Western body. This epistemological shift allocated the causal role in disease from the tropical environment itself to that of native bodies. American bodies inflicted with dysentery, diarrhea, malaria, parasites, and so forth were contaminated less by their surroundings but primarily through racial contact. According to Anderson, the subsequent American fear of contact with native bodies and contagion was the major impetus behind hygiene and sanitation reform.[35] Such reforms were constitutive of the prevailing racial discourse justifying benevolent imperialism insofar as it essentialized fundamental differences between the white and "tropical" races, designating the native as a sort of biological Other in conformity with the hierarchical view of race prevalent at the turn of the century.

Perhaps no other technology of power better accents the Otherness of Filipino colonials than that of administrative and ethnographic studies conducted by the initial wave of scholars and government experts arriving to the islands. This is so insofar as they attempted to delimit specific definitional boundaries between colonialists and colonials to be constituted as official state knowledge. These demarcations, of course, were determined largely by race. American experts conducting the research remained constrained within an epistemological straitjacket—evidenced in the taken-for-granted dualisms of West/non-West, observer/observed, and civilization/savagery—that rendered their findings to be contaminated by preconceived racial prejudices. The "objective gaze" of the ethnographer, for instance, could not retreat from a subjective stance taking for granted a cavernous gap between Western and native societies, thought worlds, and cultural expressions, a bias whose foundation was structured upon essentialized and hierarchical views of race.[36]

The scholar Rafael, for instance, exposes the 1903 Census, completed to mark the supposed end of the war and the outset of civilian rule, as a discursive regime yielding disciplinary effects beyond its pretext of making intelligible the peoples of the newly acquired colony. The overall effect of surveillance (in Foucault's sense) of the population was achieved in reducing Filipinos subjects as objects of study conforming to preconceived statistical categories. Says Rafael: "Through continuous and discrete observations, the targets of benevolent assimilation could be identified, apprehended, and delivered for disciplinary subjugation."[37] Upon becoming subjects of surveillance following classification, Rafael argues that native bodies became better disposed toward the goal of assimilation under the auspices of benevolent imperialism. An arduous task undertaken by colonial experts in collaboration with the native elite class, the completion of the census signified several important resonant themes throughout early Philippine colonialism: the formation of a colonial technology of power (as with the census' intermediary function between benevolence and discipline); the "objective" survey of a new colonial landscape; the categorization of racialized colonials according to Western classification systems; the demarcation of racial space and place; and the advent of American/ native-elite collaboration as a critical component of benevolent imperialism.

Genealogy of a Neocolonial State

By 1901 Washington ordered the transfer of power from military to civilian rule despite wartime conditions, signaling its solid commitment toward colonial state building. Replacing U.S. Army General Arthur MacArthur was the civilian governor Taft, who set in motion a "policy of attraction" meant to add solidity and stability to an uneasy alliance formed between colonized elites and their imperial masters. Such an alliance was a critical component of America's imperialism whose precepts and protocols were interwoven with the ideals of democracy. According to this imperial vision, America's gift of democracy would be exemplified through the participation of members of the educated and elite classes (so long as their nationalist tendencies have been expurgated) in the political arena, an approach in contradistinction to the colonial practices of European imperial aggressors. Through the appointment of native elite to political offices and bureaucratic positions, the United States sought to demonstrate its own brand of overseas colonialism, one driven not by gold and glory but by historical duty.

Just how democratic was the practice of benevolent assimilation if political power was to remain in the hands of the undemocratic elite? Indeed, it is exactly the alliance of imperial officials and native elite that would define democracy in colonial Philippines, an illicit marriage that would evolve as a patron-client relation persistent throughout colonial and neocolonial relations. With the recognition of the sybaritic land-owning class as corulers (preceded by a loyalty oath), colonial governance resulted, more or less, in the re-creation of preexisting social hierarchy rather than the democratic redistribution of political power, although now allowing a degree of social and political elevation for qualified and educated middle-class bureaucrats.

Remember, however, that in the beginning of American colonial rule, such conciliatory gestures of power sharing with the elite class were for the most part chimerical. While providing native officeholders with a *feeling* of democratic participation, the situation assured that American control was never in jeopardy.[38] Moreover, the policy of Filipinization, not unlike colonial education, worked effectively to prevent the recrudescence of Philippine nationalism among the elite and middle classes. Thus, it has been cogently argued, the initial effort to win the "hearts and minds" of Filipinos through the sharing of power was less a concern for moral and political advancement than a strategy aimed toward subjugation and control, to ultimately render native bodies more docile for the exigencies of American imperialism. Nonetheless, American colonizers grasped the critical importance of Taft's "attraction policy" as a supposed concession granted for the consolidation of a social base for U.S. rule.[39]

Economic concessions, furthermore, would be granted to the native elite in return for their allegiance. As the scholars of Philippine colonization Daniel B. Schirmer and Stephen Rosskamm Shalom point out:

> Political office was not the only reward the Philippine elite got in exchange for acquiescence in the loss of Philippine sovereignty. In 1909 the passage of the Payne-Aldrich tariff law opened the markets of the U.S. to wealthy Philippine landowners so that henceforth they prospered from the sale of the raw products of their plantations (sugar, hemp, tobacco, coconut oil) in tariff-free U.S. markets, . . . Those in the United States who sponsored and organized the colonization of the Philippines realized two achievements with far-reaching impact: they helped form a Filipino elite that was for years to come a reliable social and political base for the exercise of U.S. influence, and they helped to create a neocolonial psychology that affected both the Filipino elite and the mass of the Filipino people, bringing with it enduring attitudes of subservience to the United States.[40]

Schirmer and Shalom thus trace the forging of neocolonial bonds to the colonizer's overtures of power sharing and profit making made toward the colonial elite, engendering the formation of a nascent comprador class reliably loyal and beholden to American authority. Even as American administrators gradually loosened their grip in governance, as with the grant of wider political latitude for Filipino leaders during the Commonwealth era (which promised independence within a ten-year span), the cumulative effect in creating a neocolonial psychology to promote the subjugation of the colonized was for the most part obtained.[41]

Indeed, complicity and control fostered through benevolent assimilation were the means to achieve the less-spoken ends of economic penetration and geostrategic occupation. American imperialists loudly advocated the occupation and annexation of the Philippines ostensibly to refashion a nation in America's own image, yet would never consider the possibility of mass settlement, never mind its incorporation as a possible state (as with Hawai'i). As "unincorporated territory," American imperialism in the Philippines was a departure from the settler movement of the North American continent, whereby settled territory would be fully integrated into the existing U.S. federal system upon expropriation of land and segregation of the native inhabitants.[42] Furthermore, as earlier stated (and perhaps more important in the minds of Americans), it was fallacious to argue that "Asiatics," through the blessings of democratic tutelage, could hence be endowed with the qualifications to integrate with American nationhood. Noninclusion was a foregone conclusion determined by skin color. Thus what distinguishes the colonization of the Philippines was the practice of direct and formal colonialism—distinct from American "informal" colonialism practiced in certain Latin American states—yet without the mass settlement of Americans upon expropriated territory as witnessed with the close of the Western frontier.[43] Regardless of the rhetoric of benevolent assimilation, formal colonialism in the Philippines would become purely administrative, arguably in service of the realpolitik goals of an open market for American commerce as with the establishment of American military presence in the Pacific region in order to safeguard its vital interests.

Although the furtherance of elite accumulation of wealth was a sine qua non in securing their allegiance, elites were careful to mask such complicity within their quasi-nationalist political rhetoric espousing national self-determination. Both American and Philippine scholars examining the patron/client relation of Philippine colonialism trace a reliable continuum of elite behavior dictated by an overriding concern in maintaining their economic power. Such was true during Spanish colonial rule and would continue to persist throughout the progressive stages of American colonial rulership—from American military rule through Filipinization and the Commonwealth era. Indeed, Philippine elite-class interests were to be glaringly exposed during Japanese occupation in World War II, whereupon the majority of elite allegiance shifted from the vanquished American colonial power to a succeeding Asian imperial power in return for their own economic and political preservation, not to mention the augmentation of wealth through war profiteering. Yet with the imminence of Japanese defeat, the very same elites suddenly abjured their affiliation with imperial Japan, explaining their collaboration as driven by duress. Notwithstanding the plausibility of this claim, it did not hide the fact that not a few Filipino elite businessmen profited from wartime-related industry, such as the provision of food and supplies to both Japanese and German armies.[44] Astonishingly enough, in place of summary punishment for treason (as witnessed in postwar France's purge of Vichy collaborators, for example), the most prominent of Filipino wartime collaborators were not only pardoned but were eventually restored to their prewar political positions. Nothing underscores the symbiotic relation of American colonial administration and the Philippine elite better than U.S. Army General Douglas MacArthur's pardoning of prominent Filipino elite whose unhidden collaboration with the Japanese was widely known. Many of these individuals were to occupy the highest political offices upon the granting of independence in 1946, including the well-known collaborator Manuel Roxas, the first president of the sovereign Republic of the Philippines.

A Cheap and Exploitable Labor Force

After 1946 the Philippines' status as an independent nation was more nominal than real, due to the residual economic subjugation and political domination wielded by its former colonizer. Neocolonial dependency exposes the decolonized sovereign nation as a category mistake: independence stands more as an abstract relation than an existing state of affairs. For such Third World countries, decolonization has meant that while their erstwhile colonizers have packed their bags and lowered their flags, imperial presence remains calcified due to the colonizer's remaining geostrategic and economic interests in the region. This is structurally reinforced in the various demands put forth before colonies as necessary conditions for independence. For instance, Philippine law enacted after independence granted investment privileges to U.S. capital in Philippine markets.[45] The Bell Trade Act of 1946 ensured that U.S. investments remained protected in the fledgling nation. The law required the establishment of a "system of preferential tariffs between the two countries, it placed various restrictions on Philippine government control of its own economy and required the Filipinos to amend their constitution to give a special position to U.S. capital."[46] Moreover, American geopolitical concerns justifying imperial presence were not suspended. The Military Bases Agreement of 1947 granted the United States jurisdiction of Philippine territory whereupon the establishment of U.S. military bases could be undertaken without interference from the Philippine government. Strictly prohibited was the military presence of other countries in the same country. Furthermore, the Military Bases Agreement granted the allowance of further recruitment of Filipino nationals into its armed services.

The unholy alliance of Philippine and U.S. business and political elite, exacerbated by their rampant corruption, has resulted in the tremendous disparity between rich and poor magnifying in the decades following independence. While there was considerable economic growth in the Philippines in the twenty-five years after World War II, economists noted that the increases in real per capita gross domestic product did not result in a "visible impact on the poorer half of the population."[47] The economic prospects of the vast majority of Filipinos after 1946 grew dimmer, while the ruling elite profited handsomely from their patron/client relation with their former colonizer. Shalom, in his book *The United States and the Philippines: A Study of Neocolonialism*, explodes the myth of progress under neocolonialism based upon empirical evidence pertaining to the living standards of the poor after independence. Based on studies conducted by the Philippine Bureau of Census and Statistics, income distribution between 1956 and 1965 become more skewed between the richest and the poorest of the Philippine class system. During this time, the share of income for the lowest three-fifths of the population declined while that of upper-income groups increased—the top 5 percent of income groups reported more income than the bottom 60 percent.[48] This empirical reality of economic inequity was manifest in the growing slum populations of the major cities of the Philippines, the world-high infant-mortality rate and malnutrition among children, the alarming increase in the school dropout rate, the drastic increase of provincial migration to metropolitan areas due to agricultural depression, the increasing number of women working in prostitution, and so forth. The growing economic disparity between rich and poor was a grim portent of a developing "anti-development state" whose roots could be genealogically traced to the establishment of American colonial and Philippine elite collaboration.[49]

Such structural conditions are causally related in the creation of an "international labor pool." According to Antonio Pido, these networks of inequality retard the development of decolonized nations into economically and politically viable nation-states. In effect, they create and perpetuate the structural factors that precipitate emigration. To quote Pido: "Structurally they lead to the creation of an international pool of labor, ready and willing to go wherever and whenever they are needed."[50] One can see how Filipino

laborers recruited by the U.S. Navy between 1952 and 1970 form a constituent migratory group of a larger international labor pool. Viewed by U.S.
employers as cheap labor, these overseas workers were, in a sense, following
the migratory footsteps of earlier Filipino agricultural laborers in the west.
Of course, this time the employer was not American agribusiness but the
U.S. military. Both the U.S. military and corporate capitalism arguably share
parallel interests in their involvement within the transpacific economy.[51] Not
surprising, some Filipino nationalists contend that the chief function of the
U.S. bases was less to protect the Philippines from communism abroad and
more so to ensure the safety of American investments within its former
colonial possession.[52]

Navy Stewards: Precursors of Today's Filipino Overseas Workers

This chapter frames the historical context for the eventual recruitment of
erstwhile colonial subjects into the U.S Navy and Coast Guard. As scholars
of Filipino American Studies emphatically affirm in their work, the embers
of this historical moment would travel far into the future, impacting Filipinos at home and abroad in profound ways—culturally, economically, and
politically. While the legacy of benevolent assimilation has been argued as
having some positive benefits, the fetters of colonial subjugation would not
be cast off so immediately, making independence a more nominal gesture.
In the case of Filipino immigration, American colonialism would leave its
impact upon the structural factors engendering migration. As discussed
in the following chapter, Filipino men enlisting in the navy—constituents
of an international pool of labor—would not be driven solely by economic
interests but also by a host of factors largely determined by the legacy of U.S.
colonialism.

CHAPTER TWO

The Navy's Search for Postcolonial Servants

The story behind Proceso "Paulie" Paligutan's recruitment into the U.S. Coast Guard in 1955 reveals how specific enabling conditions related to American colonialism and neocolonialism interwove with contingency and good fortune. During the early 1950s, Paulie was a college student in the Philippines, away from his small hometown barrio, when he received news that his family's land, the yardstick of one's economic well-being in the provincial areas of a poor county, had been ravaged by an extraordinarily powerful typhoon, leaving only detritus where once stood a small coconut plantation. The plantation was his family's source of meager profit that not only silenced their hunger pangs during the war but also through careful planning and sacrifice managed to send him to the University of San Carlos in the city of Cebu several islands away. Paulie was the first in his family to leave the barrio in pursuit of a college degree; now he learned that the typhoon cruelly took away his chance to elevate himself above the conditions of life he had known since a child. Yet, his brief experience of a better life in Cebu only deepened his longing for something novel and adventurous, for nothing but joblessness and idle moments awaited him at his home barrio. Perhaps it was in the big city of Manila, he thought, where his fortunes lay.

Thankfully, Paulie's father, Marcelo, greeted his son's decision with support, although only able to provide him with a meager sum of pesos for his pocket. In 1952 Paulie headed north, joined by two buddies seeking similar prospects. Manila is the biggest city in the Philippines, a mecca for those provincials bold enough to pursue a life richer in money and excitement. For most, the pilgrimage was not a sunny tale of upward mobility, for it was not uncommon that hapless rural migrants would remain trapped in the chaotic maelstrom of city life while mired in urban poverty. Yet, Paulie and his friends, he proudly recalled, were adventurists. They welcomed the hustle and bustle, the huge anonymous crowds, the endless line of vehicles in the city streets and the blaring of car horns heard above the familiar din of the rooster's crow.

No amount of grit, however, could stave off the reality of poverty. What he called home in Manila was a dilapidated structure of four walls surrounding a dirt floor, covered by a roof of corrugated sheets of metal. What little food they were able to get was shared among themselves. They even shared their clothes. In order to satisfy his nicotine habit, Paulie stood outside the bars of Manila, standing nonchalantly as he looked for half-smoked cigarettes thrown out the window. This was his life for several years—a hardscrabble existence typical of poor, unemployed men in Manila. Paulie's ordeal with urban poverty is a reminder of the aforementioned effects wrought by neo-colonial mechanisms upon the Philippine economy, ones that relegated it to a state of dependency and underdevelopment following its independence. Such conditions would trickle down to particularly affect the urban poor, who would face widespread unemployment and lack of mobility.

Eventually, Paulie and his friends found themselves living in the nearby city of Cavite, home of the U.S. Navy installation called Sangley Point. This navy installation was one of many that dotted the coast line of the newly in-dependent Philippines, yet it was particularly important for would-be Filipino sailors as the site of the navy's recruitment center. The Philippines was home to the largest military installations outside the United States at that time, ow-ing to negotiations between the United States and the Philippines before the latter's independence. Another concession was the continued recruitment of Filipino men, now sovereign citizens rather than colonial subjects, into the U.S. military. This condition was a central neocolonial arrangement leading to the enlistment of Filipino servants.

It was in the city of Cavite that Paulie's life would irretrievably change. Here he managed to befriend a neighbor, an older man named Manding, who lived in one of the nicer houses of the street. One night over beers, Manding revealed that he worked a clerical job at the recruitment center in Sangley Point. Almost sheepishly, Paulie asked him about the possibilities of employment within the navy base. Manding's response revealed a much more ambitious plan: "How would you like to enlist in the U.S. Navy?"

It was widely believed in the Philippines that Filipinos recruited into the U.S. Navy were a lucky group, judging by the line of young men stretching for blocks beyond the recruiting station, a common sight in Cavite. Whenever these chosen-few sailors returned home, they proudly strutted around in their

U.S. Navy uniforms—signifiers of their elite status. It was as if their identities were reconstituted overnight: a nondescript commoner transformed into a rich and adventurous pioneer of America. To the envy or adulation of onlookers, these new recruits spent lavishly, won the attention of the prettiest women, and sent home remittances that in many cases drastically reversed their family's financial misfortunes. Their flashy clothes, their confident swagger, their tall tales of a country whose wealth was boundless: such images coalesced to form the impression that Filipino sailors in the U.S. Navy held the most promising and adventurous job a young man could hope for. Yet, it also seemed impossibly out of reach—just how did these recruits manage to be selected over the tens of thousands desperate for the chance?

Manding revealed a possible solution to this puzzle upon intimating the connections he had developed with the recruiting office. "Just fill out the application, and I will place it on top of my supervisor's stack." Although wearied by lean years of poverty, Paulie was now overcome with excitement upon realizing that his dreams of America were no longer out of reach. He received his "calling card" (interview appointment) in the mail a week later. Aware of the rigorous examination process that selectively weeded out most prospective candidates, he anxiously wondered if he possessed the mental and physical attributes that would separate him from the others. Paulie recalls glancing at his rather gaunt frame, wondering if he was healthy enough to pass the physical examination. Immediately, he sought advice from Manding, who unfortunately had no reassurances to dispense—only this: "I hear that many sailors eat a lot of bananas before their physical exam to quickly gain weight."

On that most important day of his life during the summer of 1955, Paulie entered through the gates of the navy base with a distended belly from eating too many bananas. It seemed as if he had entered America itself. The interior of the base was unlike the crowded and polluted streets outside the gates; to him it was uncommonly clean and orderly. Never in his life did he see so many white people at one place; they looked as if they were giants. Suddenly, an awareness of his skin color, something he had never experienced, overwhelmed his consciousness. It was a strange experience: the mere exchange of glances with these white men, he remembers, triggered in him an awareness of racial difference—and of inferiority.

Summoned into a different room, Paulie proceeded to take the mental examination. As he read the questions and attempted his answers, he remembered the stories his father, Marcelo, used to tell him about his experiences as a houseboy for an American official. Having gained a glimpse of the American's life of ease, Marcelo dreamed that his children would be given a chance at a similar fortune. He imparted onto them a fascination with American culture. Paulie regularly followed a piece of advice his father told him: "Son, whenever you can, read the English newspaper so you can be more familiar with America." As he took the mental exam, Paulie realized that his father's beliefs contributed to the confidence he felt as he answered exam questions pertaining to American civics, history, language, and other information he learned from school. His confidence was soon shaken during the physical examination process. As various men measured his height and weight, examined his body as if he was a specimen, and asked questions about diseases and parasites he had known since childhood, he felt his chances dim while under the medical gaze of these inspectors. At the end of his physicals, Paulie was directed to a waiting room where the other eager yet anxious Filipinos waited for their next instructions.

After a long wait, an American recruiter finally entered the room and instructed the men to fall in line. One by one, the recruiter approached each man, reviewed his application, and then instructed him to either stay in line or step aside. The American finally approached Paulie, their eyes meeting while he told Paulie to stay put. At the end of the process, the recruiter directed the men who stepped aside to head back toward the gates. Turning to Paulie's small group, the recruiter, with a smile, uttered the words Paulie longed to hear: "You guys are lucky—you made it."

After the recruiter's words prompted a few hollers and congratulations among themselves, the would-be enlistees were given further instructions. Only four weeks were granted to notify their families and take care of personal matters. Then the recruits were to report punctually at "0500" back to the base, bringing no personal possessions—only one change of clothes and a few dollars. Before embarking to the United States, they were to sign their contracts that would officially enlist them into the U.S. Navy. As he walked the noisy streets back home, Paulie knew that his life was about to change even beyond his wildest dreams. Indeed, it was the American Dream itself that awaited him on the other side of the Pacific Ocean.

Paulie's narration of his recruitment experiences provides a glimpse of the typical circumstances and historical backdrop that fundamentally addresses the question, "Why were there so many Filipinos in the U.S. Navy?" The recruitment of Filipino nationals into service of a foreign military was greatly facilitated by the abiding presence of U.S military installations in the former colony. Colonial subjectivity also serves as an important factor in their recruitment. According to the colonial metaphysics of race, the subordinate position of racial subjects to their imperial masters is naturalized, a relation sustained even beyond national independence. The role of culture in this regard cannot be overstated. The discussion of colonial education highlighted its critical role in inculcating white superiority and native inferiority, spreading American values, and justifying colonial rule. The same consequence would be realized with American popular culture: movies, music, literature, modern advertising, mass media, and information. The cumulative effect of a half century of American colonial rule (not to mention more than three hundred years of prior Spanish rule) is the formation of a totalizing ideological barrier repressing the will to establish a Filipino identity hermetically sealed from external influence.

From the U.S. Navy's perspective, Paulie's recruitment was in actuality not an act of benevolence but, rather, a pragmatic move related to a personnel issue—Filipino recruitment was a solution to a labor problem the navy faced. The navy's sudden need for racialized domestic labor after World War II found its replenishment in the ready supply of young men facing the possibility of poverty, former colonial subjects who were also fervent believers in the American Dream. This chapter focuses upon the premigration backgrounds of the various subjects involved in this study, as well as the historical and contingent factors that intersected in their recruitment histories, and discusses how American imperial designs upon the Pacific region evolved with the inauguration of the American century. In widening our lenses from the specific colonial context in the Philippines, the various reasons are explored as to why the United States looked to the Pacific—not the Atlantic—as its chosen sphere of influence for the twentieth century.

This discussion is crucial in understanding how the neocolonial presence of the U.S. military served as a structural precondition facilitating the recruitment of Filipino citizens, a fact that denaturalizes the recruitment process beyond reductive analyses foregrounding individual economic calculus in the escape from poverty.

The Navy's Search for Domestic Servants

The recruitment of Filipino young men into the U.S. military was initiated during the earliest years of colonization, when President William McKinley authorized the recruitment of five hundred Filipino enlistees in 1901.[1] Through the ensuing decades, Filipino sailors had a small but steady presence in the modern navy, although enlistment numbers of Filipinos would ebb and flow according to changes in recruitment policy. Through these years, Filipinos would labor alongside African American sailors and a few other racial minorities within the steward and messman ratings. Upon the granting of Philippine independence in 1946, this recruitment policy was momentarily closed as Filipinos transitioned from colonial wards to Philippine citizens.

The eventual resumption of the practice of Filipino recruitment after the Military Bases Agreement of 1947 was continuous with the American view of Filipinos as an exploitable labor force. Filipino farm laborers in the past, for example, represented a logical solution to the agricultural labor problems of Hawai'i and California and were effectively used in breaking strikes in the plantations of Hawai'i during the 1920s and 1930s.[2] After the war, similar use-value of Filipino labor power was applied in the Cold War decades, when African Americans in the U.S. Navy, previously restricted to the lowest occupational ratings, protested their lowly working conditions. Once again, the United States would look to the Philippines for a solution to labor problems.

The use of minority sailors as stewards and messman—the most menial jobs within the modern naval rating system—has an interesting past that is indissociably bound to race. African Americans recruited into the modernizing U.S. Navy (as it transitioned from the wooden ships powered by wind to the modern steel vessels powered by steam) found themselves trapped within de facto segregated spaces of navy ships, unable to gain promotion in occupations beyond such jobs. As previously stated, the colonization of the Philippines at the beginning of the twentieth century witnessed the beginning of Filipino recruitment. With the rising tide of Jim Crow segregation, the U.S. Navy began to openly discourage black enlistment while relying more upon Filipino recruits and, to a lesser degree, other racial minorities. This led to a momentary drop in African American recruitment numbers. Thus before the 1930s, the ethnic composition of mess attendants in the U.S. Navy shifted toward being dominated by Filipinos; at the same time, there was a shrinking number of African Americans, as well as even smaller numbers of Chinese, Japanese, Samoans, Puerto Ricans, or Chamorro/Guamanian stewards.

However, a shift back to the increase in African American steward recruitment was initiated by concerns over the allegiance of noncitizens within the naval ranks in the event of war; furthermore, in the specific case of Filipino mess attendants, it was anticipated that the recruitment of Filipinos would no longer be sanctioned with the granting of Philippine independence with the Tydings-McDuffie Act (1934) promising independence in ten years, an event that seemed imminent at the time.[3] According to the historian Richard Miller, the reinstatement of African American recruitment before World War II was a pragmatic solution to such concerns, although many navy officials were tentative in their endorsement of the policy change due to egregious racist beliefs about blacks.[4] Another change in the naval steward demographic therefore occurred, whereby African Americans regained the majority over the dwindling numbers of Filipino recruits.

During World War II, the exploitation of African Americans in the U.S. Navy was not relegated to the mess hall; black recruits were also assigned to dangerous, high-risk tasks. Such was the case that led to the infamous Port Chicago mutiny, whereby black navy men, tasked to load explosives onto navy ships, refused to resume their duties after an enormous explosion at the site cost the lives of hundreds of African American enlistees.[5] This highly publicized mutiny during wartime foreshadowed an uneasy relation between African American navy men and naval officialdom after the war's end, whereby increasing demands for racial desegregation and equal working rights were put forth by African American sailors as well as civil rights groups.[6] The conservative navy brass was forced to acknowledge the demands of black navy men and allow them promotion in rate, but the officers preferred not to readily give up the antiquated tradition of servitude for naval officers without first seeking a remedy to this labor problem.

The perceived solution lay in a provision of the Military Bases Agreement of 1947 between the United States and the Philippines: the right of the United States to recruit Filipino citizens into U.S. Armed Forces. As indicated in naval records, the official reinstatement of Filipino recruitment after the Military Bases Agreement of 1947 did not begin in earnest until further negotiations were finalized by 1952. Even before then, it was known that negotiations were underway between the United States and the Republic of the Philippines regarding specific details of Filipino recruitment, as shown in an inquiring letter from Antonio N. Artuz to the Department of Naval Personnel, dated March 23, 1950: "I wish to seek official confirmation from your office relative to the veracity of rumors going on around here to the effect that in the forthcoming, immediate future there will be opened recruiting offices here in the Philippines, to take in for enlistment persons who want to join the U.S. Navy."[7] Inquiries such as these flooded the U.S. Navy's Recruitment Division at this time and were answered with the standardized response denying Filipino recruitment "rumors": "Current enlistment regulations require that applicants ... *must be American citizens*, native born or fully naturalized, between the ages of 17 and 31 years. ... At this time there is no plan to establish a U.S. Navy Recruiting Station within the Philippine Islands."[8]

An agreement to the negotiations was finally reached by the beginning of 1952, authorizing the recruitment of a thousand Filipino citizens per calendar year, effectively reversing the requirement of American citizenship; two years later, an amendment increased the number to two thousand per calendar year.[9] This annual recruitment ceiling was in place through the 1950s and

1960s. Once again, the ever-vacillating policy surrounding the preferred racial group for naval stewardship would shift from African American to Filipinos during the post–World War II decades, this time due to social and political pressures wrought by the civil rights movement.

With the renewed increase of Filipino stewards by 1952, the specific requirements behind the reinstatement of Filipino recruitment were delineated: applicants must be citizens of the Republic of the Philippines and must have attained their eighteenth but not their thirty-first birthday; applicants must be "physically examined in accordance with the provisions of the Manual of the Medical Department of the U.S. Navy. . . . Particular attention shall be given to diseases of the lungs"; applicants must obtain a "minimum score of 42 (NSS [Navy Standard Score]) on AQT [Applicant Qualification Test] #6."[10] Continuous with earlier "bachelor societies" common to past Asian American immigration since the 1840s, the U.S. Navy required that only single men enlist: "Applicants must be single and have no one solely or partially dependent upon them for support. Each applicant will be cautioned that should he have a wife or any other dependents, including parents, and withhold such information, his enlistment will be considered by the Department of the Navy as perpetration of a fraud against the United States Government and he will be subject to discharge without trial, under other than honorable conditions."[11]

Sangley Point in the city of Cavite was established as a central recruiting station for hopeful Filipinos, and a common sight during this time was a line that stretched around the gates, comprising young men hoping that enlistment in U.S. Navy might solve their economic problems while providing them with an avenue for adventure in America. As Paulie Paligutan's earlier narrative of his recruitment reveals, enlistment in the U.S. Navy was, first and foremost, a remedy to financial hardship. Interviews conducted of retired Filipino stewards reveal that economic necessity was indeed the primary factor in their decision to join the U.S. Navy. Correspondence sent by Filipino young men inquiring about job opportunities was often redolent of desperation and frustration. A letter from Felix P. Mamaril to the chief of naval personnel, for instance, narrates a desperate struggle to unsuccessfully enter the Sangley Point recruiting station after previous letters sent were not met with a reply, leading to still another letter tinged with frustration to the secretary of the navy: "Another reason is that I am getting fed-up for not having a steady employment. In fact ever since, I quit studying due to financial deficiencies, I have been without a job and right now the unemployment problem here in the Philippines is very very bad and in fact much worse."[12] A letter from Abelardo Angeles reveals a similar predicament: "I am nineteen years of age ... registered with the Roosevelt Memorial High School. ... I am too interested in the U.S. Navy beside it's my ambition, I cannot continue my collegiate studies due to our poverty and I shall be jobless."[13]

However, not all Filipino applicants lacked employment and higher education. In actuality, many stewards enlisted after 1953 were either college educated or attending college, holding or pursuing degrees, such as engineering, business, and commerce. Some were studying for medical degrees, hoping to eventually become physicians in the U.S. Navy. Moreover, a considerable number were employed, although they typically held low-paying jobs that offered no financial promise during a period of economic infirmity (for the lower classes) at the time. Before his recruitment in July 1955, Tony Javier worked as a butcher at the U.S. naval base at Sangley Point while also attending college at Far Eastern University. Although pursuing a degree in business, he was acutely aware of the grim economic prospects awaiting the typical college graduate. Tony remembers how good fortune played a role in his recruitment: "I was working in the Navy commissary store. ... I was lucky that I knew somebody and they recommended me. ... It was hard to get in, with all this unemployment in the Philippines. And a lot of these young men, even if they finish college, they don't have any jobs at all. ... There's a lot of them with college degrees in the Coast Guard at that time."[14]

Sergio Norombaba faced similar circumstances before his recruitment. Although nearly finished with his studies in commerce, he was lured into joining the U.S. Navy when the opportunity presented itself. Recruited in May 1960, Sergio judged that a stint in the navy offered more economic promise than a business career in the Philippines. As he recalls: "Everybody wants to get in. ... That was your chance to be able to upgrade your life. ... I was almost graduating from college in the Philippines, and I know there were so many college grads at that time, and yet so many of them don't have jobs."[15]

A third-year student at the University of the Philippines, Diliman (the most prestigious university of the Philippines), Jesus "Jesse" Reyes was one year away from a degree in foreign service when he decided to join the U.S. Navy in January 1966. Watching his father, a government worker, struggle to pay for the college tuition of Jesse's two sisters and himself compelled Jesse to make an abrupt turn in his life course. Of course, this decision was not solely influenced by familial obligations—as Jesse recalls, an older first cousin (who was later killed in Vietnam) had already been working in the navy for five years, and their homecoming conversations were replete with tales about an incomparable place called America. As Jesse remembers: "When going home on vacation, he was regaling me with all the stories about how nice it is [in America,] ... all the women they see in the liberty port. ... [At first,] it wasn't my idea [to join], but I kinda looked at my dad, he was really working hard, he couldn't make ends meet with three of us in college."[16] Upon spotting an advertisement placed by the U.S. Navy in the newspaper the *Manila Chronicle*, Jesse decided that joining the navy would not only alleviate the financial burden his father shouldered but also provide Jesse with similar adventures experienced by his cousin.

The impression of America as the "land of opportunity" held almost equal sway in the decision to enlist in the U.S. military. Indeed, many young Filipinos cited their own adventurism, a willingness to explore the uncharted frontier of the United States and stake their claim as a factor overlapping with economic need in their desire to join the U.S. Navy. A letter by Rudolfo M. San Juan to Lt. Commander C. J. Barry reflects both such push-and-pull factors in his desire to enlist: "It's [*sic*] approval would mean a lot to me. It would emancipate me from my job-seeking worries. I would be in a better position to save more money. . . . Furthermore, I think I might take American citizenship, too. Somethingmore [*sic*], it would provide [me] with adventures galore."[17] Similar sentiments are expressed by Federico Bona, who was recruited into the U.S. Coast Guard in 1964: "There were many reasons [why I joined], number one is financial, because I'd be able to help my mom in raising my brothers and sisters; number two is adventure—I wanted to see the States."[18] Sailing east toward America was imagined as a path toward a fabled land of overabundant wealth and new experiences for these young men. A life of adventure in America coupled with economic promise was exactly the definition of the American Dream for these young men.

As mentioned, it was foremost the regnant power of the American dollar that convinced these hopeful applicants to leave behind the familiar spaces of home, family, and nation. As Paulino Maestre, working as a busboy before his recruitment in 1959, recalls when questioned by his American naval interviewer: "'Why do you want to join the U.S. Navy? You are Filipino, you should join the Philippine Navy.' [I answered,] Because the salary is 'dollar.' And they were thrilled: 'This guy's honest.' So I think that made me qualified."[19] Two commonly held beliefs by Filipinos at the time were that all Americans were rich and that the misfortune of poverty all too familiar among most Filipinos somehow passed over the United States. This was especially impressed upon some Filipinos premigration who were interacting with Americans in the Philippines. Vicente Bianes, originally from Eastern Samar, was a college ROTC student while working for a Philippine shoe manufacturer before his recruitment. After his ROTC squad leader urged him to submit an application at Sangley Point alongside his, Vicente was surprised to receive a calling card a week later, especially since his earlier applications to the Philippine

Navy and Army were rejected. He vividly recalls his excitement when being accepted into the U.S. Navy, for it meant that the riches of America might be awaiting him as well: "I was very happy about [my recruitment] . . . because before I joined the Navy, the American people there in Samar—in Guiuan, in Leyte, they were very rich people."[20] Norberto "Bert" Amano was another interviewee who held such a view. A self-described adventurist, Bert worked as a golf caddy for U.S. naval officers before his recruitment at age twenty-two. He tersely sums up the commonly held belief about Americans: "Everybody who lived there in America was rich."[21] Reynaldo "Rey" Pellos, a second-year college student before his recruitment in 1962, began his American Dream early in life: "Everything [in America] is green, everything is good, everything that I see and heard about America is beautiful. Ever since my first year in high school, I'm already dreaming, already thinking about going to America."[22] Tony Javier held this belief of America and Americans when he was growing up in Cavite City near the U.S. naval base: "It's the land of opportunity, and God blessed the American people because they had almost everything at this time."[23]

The Filipinos' idealization of America is not surprising, given the global economic dominance of the United States during the postwar decades, not to mention the vestiges left by America's "benevolent assimilation" inculcating such beliefs through colonial education and American culture. Yet for many Filipinos, the stark reality of structural conditions occluding upward mobility in the United States was most likely obscured by the ideological meta-narratives of equality, freedom, and individualism also propagated by the American belief system. American colonial teachers regaled their Filipino students with stories of the American Dream—ordinary individuals achieving upward economic and social mobility by simple virtue of hard work within a country proudly announcing its equality of opportunity. As earlier discussed, critical scholars and writers have cited American culture itself, manifested in education, government, language, and popular culture, as a colonial technology of power employed in the project of native subjugation while stultifying the native will toward resistance against colonial rule. American-style education was particularly effective in this regard. In contradistinction to Spanish colonial practice, the U.S. government developed a program of free and universal education conducted in the English language; while a generous gift, on the one hand, it also served a purpose in quelling resistance to colonial rule and winning influence with the mass of Filipino people, on the other. American educators constituted a "second army of occupation"—to again invoke Filipino historian Renato Constantino's phrase—following military conquest. Whether the internalization of native subjugation was a primary, incidental, or unintended effect of Philippine modernization remains a subject of debate; regardless, the result of this policy was noticeably effective in bolstering "the hold of the U.S. government on the popular mind in the Philippines, to undermine the influence of Philippine nationalism, and to inculcate ideas of white superiority."[24]

The effectivity of this practice of "epistemic violence," to borrow a term from Gayatri Spivak, is reflected in Paulie's recollection of how his premigration belief of America was formed: "I had seen a lot of American movies. Plus, I learned it in history classes, because we studied U.S. history."[25] His remembrance of colonial space further served to accent the white colonizer's putative superiority: "I was in Olongapo, a navy town. The town of Olongapo, you can see the difference when you go inside the base. It's well stream-lined—it's clean, you know? When you go outside the gate to the town, it's back to 'Filipino style.'(laughs) There's no order! Even the smell inside the base. . . . It's different."[26] This statement invokes Frantz Fanon's observation of colonial space: "The colonial world is divided into compartments," wherein the Manichean demarcation of space separating the colonizer and colonized is essential in reinforcing imperial rule.[27] This geography situates the clean, well-organized, well-developed space of the colonizer alongside the dirty, unorganized, unkept quarters of the colonized. Such a dichotomy serves as a justificatory framework in the subjugation of the putatively "inferior" native; of course, the colonizer fails to recognize the fallacy in confusing cause for effect. Paulie's contrast of the ordered space within the U.S. military base with that of the chaotic space of the Filipino town of Olongapo is a further reminder of American neocolonial presence in the Philippines.

Although the U.S. Navy and Coast Guard actively sought young Filipino men to serve as stewards, enlistment into the U.S. military was not easy, since it was extremely competitive due to the annual quota effective by 1954 of only two thousand recruits. Those lucky applicants chosen to undergo preliminary evaluations and interviews within the naval base received a calling card in the mail specifying the date of their mental and physical examinations. Federico Bona was enrolled in the University of the Philippines, Los Banos, when he decided to return to his hometown of Baguio to help his family with their financial struggle. Upon hearing of the opportunity to join the U.S. Navy, he decided to submit an application, and a week later he was fortunate to receive a calling card for the exam process. He passed the physical and mental exams easily and soon thereafter discovered how lucky he was to be chosen: "I was lucky because in my group . . . we started with two thousand [applicants], and out of that group, only thirteen were recruited, and I was number thirteen." For the unlucky applicants failing to pass the exams, the news was usually devastating, since pursuing the American Dream surely would have been the solution for the economic hardships experienced by most of the applicants and their families. Bona explains, "Lots of [candidates] . . . especially from other islands, they come from a farm and their parents are farmers, they even sell their *carabao* [water buffalo] just for them to go to Manila, just to take the examination. There are lots of those who didn't pass . . . and they were crying. 'What will I do now, my father sold his *carabao*.' . . . What can they do?"[28]

Enlisting in the last months of colonial rule, Lucio Pontanares's amusing story reveals how he "recruited himself" into the navy in 1946, the same year as Philippine independence. Prior to his enlistment and by the end of World War II, Lucio was hired as an office clerk for an American doctor in Sangley Point. This doctor had the responsibility of medically examining young Filipino candidates hoping to list. Evidently, exploitative work practices began even before Lucio enlisted in the navy—the American doctor instructed his new office clerk how to perform the unpleasant job of bodily examinations. "After a couple or three times, I was assisting him. One day, he let me do it alone, observing me, and I thought he know that I could handle it. And then he told me, 'Okay, Pontanares, you take care of the whole thing. . . . I'm a busy man.'" Ironically, Lucio's exploitation eased his recruitment into the U.S. Navy. In the interim between Philippine independence and the Military Base Agreement, the U.S. Navy would have to suspend its recruitment of Filipino stewards. Lucio remembers the historical background: "The Filipino president didn't want Filipino boys to join the U.S. military forces anymore, because he wanted to start building his navy, his air force, his marines, his coast guard. . . . So the American authorities cannot say anything. So there was no more recruiting. . . . My office will be demolished! And I [will be] a civilian! Oh shit, I'll have no more job! What kind of life will I have?"[29] When Lucio was instructed to recruit his last group of Filipino sailors, he included himself and his nephew on this final list. He remembers that while the American doctor eventually realized what Lucio had done, the doctor did not say a word, pretending not to notice.

Prior to the 1950s, although enlistment was still competitive, the U.S. Navy was less stringent regarding the educational background of Filipino applicants. As discussed, African Americans began to fill the rating of stewardship in the navy in the early 1930s; at this time, the navy and coast guard viewed Filipinos as merely supplementary to black stewards, and one's educational level or natural intelligence was then not yet considered preferential. Lucio, a steward "old-timer," commented: "In my level, there were a lot of Filipino boys who did not write at all. They were just physically fit and know how to wash dishes, know how shine shoes of the officers, make the bed, walk the dog, wash the socks and garments of the family of the officer."[30] The fact that educated Filipino stewards recruited since 1952 performed exceptionally well on the job compared to earlier old-timers prompted the U.S. Navy to implement more-stringent mental examinations by the 1950s while showing preference toward applicants with at least some college education.

The completion of both the physical and mental and written exams was an anxious moment for these stewards. A sizable number of Filipino men must have known beforehand that they failed to meet certain physical requirements. The weight requirement, for example, was 115 pounds, and the height requirement five feet, three inches, yet a number of these Filipinos were rather diminutive young men. Teodulo "Doloy" James Coquilla, jobless and homeless as a young man for five years following the completion of high school, was recruited into the navy in September 1964; he recalled his amusing yet poignant story of the desperate circumstances surrounding his recruitment in Sangley Point:

> My God, I don't even know how to speak English, . . . [so] my friend said, "I will write the application in my words." . . . He advised me to send the application three times a week: one in Monday, one in Wednesday, one in Friday. So in September 1964, I received a calling card from the naval recruiting office in Sangley Point. . . . But there was problem because I was 108 pounds, but the cut off was 115 pounds, so I need 7 more pounds to be able to come up with the desired weight. Then the recruiting officer sent me home to Manila and [told me to] start eating bananas. That's what I did. . . . After one month I went back to Sangley Point, [they] put me on the scale, and I only gained five pounds. . . . But what I did, when the lieutenant said, "'I'm sorry, you lack two pounds. I cannot accept you,'" I grabbed his waist and started crying and said, "If you don't accept me, I will kill myself!" . . . You know what happened? . . . He waived the two pounds, and that was the start of my navy career.[31]

Julian Ortiz was an unemployed nineteen-year-old in 1959. Desperately seeking employment, he wrote the following letter to the recruiting office in Sangley Point, believing it would be a long shot:

Dear Sir:
I would like to join the US Navy.
Thank you, Sir.

He was surprised and ecstatic upon receiving his calling card several weeks later. Julian has vivid memories of his anxiety once he was called to take his physical exam. As he humorously recalls:

You know how Filipinos are so small? And I was skinny at the time. My sister-in-law said, "Julian, before you take your physical exam, you gotta start eating bananas." I was riding on the bus back to the recruiting office. Man, my stomach was hurting [from eating bananas]. . . . When they were measuring my weight . . . I couldn't stand up steadily—I was pushing some weight [on the scale]. . . . When they were measuring my height, man, I was trying to stretch! (laughs) I was trying to pass![32]

The Western medical gaze thoroughly inspected the native body—ears, eyes, throat, X-rays, dental exams, blood tests, body cavities—the search for symptoms of "exotic" disease.[33] A century after Asians were detained on Angel Island for weeks (unlike their European counterparts on Ellis Island) due to the fear of "yellow peril," one cannot help but notice the striking parallels.

According to the men interviewed for this work, the mental exam consisted of three areas: the general-knowledge test, written test, and interview. The general-knowledge test consisted of basic arithmetic, basic science, and "common sense" questions in English. The written exams tested the candidate's English reading comprehension skills. Bona remembered, "I would say it's high school level. You had to compute fractions, then they let you read a story [for the written test] . . . and they will ask you a questions about that story."[34] The interview phase was perhaps the most challenging and anxiety-provoking. Candidates were asked to engage in English conversation with their American interviewers or take dictation in order to test their English writing skills and spelling. Gerardo "Jerry" Silva recalled an interesting tactic used by naval examiners to test the applicant's English comprehension during the interview: "They ask you, 'What's the color of the ceiling?' If you don't look up [to the ceiling], you fail. 'How many buttons do you have in your shirt?' If you can't count it, you fail, because there's a lot of people applying for it."[35] Interestingly, some of the questions within the general exam favored the poorer applicants over the wealthy ones—Ernie Cabanes's following claim suggests that some questions were pictorial, name matching, or identifications in English: "It's a common-sense exam, but a lot of [rich] college graduates failed it, because they don't know what pliers look like, because they're rich! They don't even know the use of pliers or a screwdriver!"[36]

As one can see, U.S. Navy recruiters chose to recruit those natives whom they believed dutifully internalized their colonial lessons. The colonial mechanisms in place served not only to quell resistance to imperial rule but also to influence Filipino natives to pursue the American Dream across the Pacific Ocean, fulfilling the labor needs of the colonizer's economy and military in the same process. Yet, American designs in the Pacific did not end with the half century of Philippine colonization. The following section discusses why the Pacific region was the chosen American sphere of influence during the twentieth century. The historical backdrop provided explains why U.S. military bases in the Philippines, as well as neocolonial control of the former colony, in general, was deemed vital to the aims of U.S. foreign policy elites during the height of the Cold War.

Imperial Garrisons in the Pacific

The famous photograph of General Douglas MacArthur wading toward the shores of Leyte Gulf, thereby fulfilling his promise to return to the Philippines, is a synecdochic image of American imperial benevolence in the mainstream history of U.S.-Philippine relations. With his return to colonial territory, MacArthur and the U.S. military forces fulfilled the moral ideal of benevolent imperialism in upholding its paternal responsibility toward its colonial subjects. This celebrated historical event momentarily erased the controversial abandonment of the colony by the imperial general years earlier, an act now seen as forgivable in light of Japan's imminent defeat.[37] The return of the imperial military to the Philippines foretold a state of affairs that would remain intact for an extended time during its postcolonial history: the prolonged presence of the U.S. military upon independent Philippine soil.

Interestingly, America's desired condition of enduring military presence in the colony stood precariously in the balance before World War II. The Tydings-McDuffie Act of 1934, promoted as a supreme gesture of imperial benevolence to its colony, promised independence to the Philippines after a ten-year transitional period.[38] Notably, the act reversed previous negotiations for the continued presence of U.S. military forces upon Philippine sovereign territory, a concession considered a victory for more nationalist Filipino politicians. Yet after MacArthur's army and the United States reclaimed the war-torn colony from Japan a decade later, Philippine leaders found that independence had to be renegotiated with the United States, including the issue of imperial military presence within the newly decolonized republic.

The renegotiation over the conditions for independence was influenced by novel specificities faced by U.S. foreign policy in the wake of the postwar era. With the Japanese empire finally driven to its knees after Hiroshima and Nagasaki, the United States assumed the mantle of the preeminent economic and sole atomic military power in the world. Despite these facts, the U.S. demilitarization efforts through the ensuing years were hardly on the scale witnessed at the end of the previous global war.[39] The standard interpretation of U.S. postwar militarism after World War II is typically explained by the heightening ideological tension and brewing military conflict between the United States and the Union of Soviet Socialist Republics (U.S.S.R.). To be sure, mutual distrust had characterized their relationship since the 1917 Russian Revolution (as seen with American expeditionary forces in military conflict with the Bolsheviks in Siberia, followed by the post–World War I domestic Red Scare). The unfolding of World War II saw the United States and Great Britain cautiously conceding to an alliance with Joseph Stalin after Adolf Hitler's violation of the Non-aggression Pact. As early as the Bretton Woods Conference in 1944, a meeting of Allied countries to plan the postwar economic world, the agreed participation by the U.S.S.R. seemed to augur well for the Allied participants. The escalation of U.S.-U.S.S.R. rivalry due to their divergent ideologies and political economies led Stalin to veto participation in the negotiations, a portent of Cold War conflict.[40] As postwar animus between the two countries seemed headed beyond the rattling of sabers, American political leaders reasoned that the global presence of its armed forces was a necessary bulwark against the Soviet menace. Thus, according to the conventional script, U.S. postwar militarism was undertaken as a defensive posture in order to check the imperial ambitions of Stalin's U.S.S.R., whose militaristic tendencies were perceived as bound to a desideratum of worldwide influence.

As a traditional interpretation of the outbreak of the Cold War, this prevailing interpretation appears uncontroversial. Yet, a more critical view of the outbreak of Cold War tensions reveals that the conventional reasons for heightened American postwar militarism obscure the context of America's realpolitik ambition in the global economic system. As the U.S. economy reached its apogee of power and influence after the war, American political and economic elites deemed it necessary to establish a new economic and political global order, one advantageous to the longevity of open markets and Western capitalism. With the global reach of the Great Depression a not-so-distant memory, American leaders reasoned that global policies of reversing protectionism and imposing open markets were necessary to avert the possibility of another global depression in the postwar world. Indeed, the Bretton Woods Conference itself, a seminal event that, for one, overturned prewar protectionist policies occluding the movement of American capitalism to new markets, was indicative of the U.S. intention of postwar global economic influence; it is understandable why Stalin decided to part from this agreement. Furthermore, American leaders felt that the political and economic transformation of the world into its own image—as nation-states adopting liberal democracy and open-door capitalism—would make obsolete the empire-based alliance system, thus preventing the possibility of still another global conflagration. Indeed, the Great Depression itself was a breeding ground for the rise of populist fascism, whose popularity was fueled by economic misery afflicting Germany, Italy, Hungary, and other European countries. The obvious obstacle to this postwar vision was the U.S.S.R.'s implacable efforts to internationalize their own political economy and ideology. For the sake of global political and economic stability, full measures needed to be undertaken to prevent this, including the expansion of U.S. military presence to enforce this vision.

America's economic and military predominance coincided with the movement of global decolonization during the postwar era. European colonial powers were now greatly weakened owing to two cataclysmic world wars occasioned by European interimperial rivalry, and some strained in their efforts to cling to their colonial possessions. As the end of the war sounded the death knell of European imperialism, its former colonies—comprising darker-skinned races—would be subject to a new global hierarchical system designating them as the Third World. The United States, in relative terms, stood relatively unscathed by the war. Thus, with the collapse of the remaining European empires as with the economic and political weaknesses of Europe itself, the presence of a vacuum in the postwar topography of power balance invited the global reach of American military might, an unprecedented event in the history of imperial projection. An inescapable concomitance of this reality was the proliferation of U.S. Armed Forces throughout the globe. As the world's sole economic hegemon, the United States assumed the duty of safeguarding the international free-enterprise system, potentially global in scope.

Such an analysis, one that departs in significant ways from traditional interpretations of the Cold War, is not recent post facto revisionism. The economist Harry Magdoff, at odds with orthodox understandings of U.S. postwar militarism at the time, argued the above point in an article written during the Cold War:

> [A] substantial portion of the huge [American] military machine . . . is the price being paid to maintain the imperialist network of trade and investment in the absence of colonialism. The achievement of political independence by former colonies has stimulated internal class struggles in the new states for economic as well as political independence. Continuing the economic dependence of these nations on the metropolitan centers within the framework of political independence calls for . . . worldwide dispersion of U.S. military forces and the direct military support of the local ruling classes. . . . The main substance of U.S. overseas power . . . is spread out over 429 major and 2,972 minor military bases. These bases cover 4,000 square miles in 30 foreign countries, as well as Hawai'i and Alaska.[41]

Magdoff astutely dovetails postcolonial class struggles within decolonized nations with those pertaining to U.S. control of global capitalism. A trend in U.S. postwar foreign policy—the threat (and in many cases, the use) of U.S. military power to prevent socialist and national liberation movements from gaining political power for the purpose of breaking free from U.S. capital dependency—was established as standard operating procedure. In the particular example of postwar Philippines, this practice would be exemplified in the collaboration among U.S. military advisers, Philippine government officials, and Philippine counterrevolutionary armed forces in their military campaigns against the communist peasant armies, the "Huks" and the New People's Army (NPA).

The linkage among U.S. militarism, empire, and overseas capital expansion, as advanced by analysis based upon world-systems theory, unsettles the logic explaining American postwar foreign policy as largely defensive in posture (a view in accordance with the official policy of containment), as reflexive reaction to the inherent tendency of communism toward global expansionism.[42] It serves to puncture the prevalent Western belief that only socialism inheres in militarist expansionism, in contrast to the "democratic peace" that results from a capitalist world system, while questioning the Manicheanism of U.S. foreign policy (reflected in Paul Nitze's call for militarization in a National Security Council paper, NSC 68). In fact, viewed from explanatory frameworks positing the existence of dual imperial formations, it is Washington that became embroiled in militaristic "hot wars" outside its spheres of influence more so than the Kremlin.

What is more, such an interpretation exposes continuity rather than rupture between a supposed pre-1941 American isolationism and Cold War interventionism. Granted, while the United States did indeed face novel conditions emerging from the ashes of World War II, it is arguably a mistake to claim that its global dominance resulted in U.S. foreign policies largely discontinuous with those of a bygone era of a supposed isolationism. As argued in the previous chapter, one can trace a line of seeming inevitability from nineteenth-century continental wars against Native Americans and Mexicans to the U.S. military's hegemonic presence in the Pacific region in the following century. Such expansionist movement inextricably linking U.S. commerce and militarism abroad has been described by various scholars as "open-door imperialism"—not a few contemporary scholars have linked American military adventurism of the twenty-first century with that of the preceding one as constituting a narrative arc of U.S. empire.[43]

Thus, due to the overriding necessity of consolidating military strength, the proliferation of U.S. military bases marked the outset of the postwar era.

As priority was placed upon the task of establishing a Grand Area open to U.S. trade and investment,[44] U.S. leaders demanded the preservation of military bases upon Philippine territory as an absolute condition. The Military Bases Agreement of 1947 stipulated a miscellany of conditions, including the following: the rent-free occupation of U.S. military bases on Philippine soil for a ninety-nine-year period; the condition of extraterritoriality for U.S. citizens, both military and civilian, affiliated with the bases; the exclusion of armed forces from other nations upon Philippine territory; and the legal right to recruit Filipino nationals into the U.S. Armed Forces.[45] Philippine leaders were given little choice in negotiating the status of U.S. military bases, with full knowledge that American officials would withhold economic aid from the country should political resistance be visited upon such terms and conditions.[46] Since 1947, despite presumptions of a preestablished harmony between colonizer and colonized arising from American benevolent rule, the presence of U.S. troops upon Philippine sovereign territory has not been immune from controversy. American officials claim that not only does the American military protect the Philippines from enemies both external and internal but also that the bases are vital to a healthy Philippine economy. Yet, nationalists not only protest the rent-free occupation violating Philippine sovereignty but also the attendant social problems exacerbated by the omnipresence of a foreign army, most notably the problem of prostitution.[47]

In summary, the historical logic driving westward continental expansion during the nineteenth century found its conclusion with the establishment of U.S. military bases in the Pacific, the largest of these installations found within the former colony of the Philippines. Arguably, the geostrategic purpose of U.S. military presence in the Pacific during the Cold War corresponded not simply to the supposedly defensive stance postulated by containment strategy but also served a function in aggressively safeguarding the flow of U.S capital throughout the postwar open-market system. Particularly, it would be the naval installations in the Philippines that would serve as neocolonial institutions allowing for the recruitment of Filipino nationals in the U.S. Navy and Coast Guard even after independence was granted in 1946.

Lured by the American Dream

In spite of President McKinley's stated goal to uplift the new colonial subjects, the United States had more often viewed Filipinos as a solution to U.S. domestic-labor problems, whether serving as replacement workers in the plantation fields of Hawai'i, fulfilling labor shortages in Western agribusiness, or recruiting Filipino young men to serve as domestic servants during the civil rights era. This latter source was largely facilitated by existing neocolonial structures in the Philippines—at the time the largest military installations outside the continental United States—as well as legal conditions that allowed for the recruitment of Filipino citizens into the armed forces of their former colonial masters. Also crucial were the legacies of benevolent assimilation—primarily, public American-styled education taught in English, American popular culture, and the ideological meta-narratives of freedom and upward mobility, which inclined Filipinos to enlist in the call for service while transforming them into pioneers exploring the frontier of America. However, the American Dream that awaited them on the other side of the Pacific Ocean, they would soon discover, had to be momentarily deferred upon realizing their marginalized roles within the navy, thus eviscerating their imagined fraternity with America, a belief earlier formed as colonial subjects.

U.S. Coast Guard bootcamp graduation photograph of Proceso "Paulie" Paligutan (first row, middle), father of the author.

U.S. Navy bootcamp graduation photograph of Ireneo "Rene" Amano (second row, second from the right). As described in this work, Amano would eventually be incarcerated and discharged from the U.S. Navy for inciting Filipino disobedience.

Personal cleanliness and good health are required of all food service personnel.

A petty officer or other person senior to you will inspect you daily for cleanliness and neatness.

The Navy requires that all food service personnel be inspected each week by a medical officer.

Get ready for medical inspection by washing your hair, shaving, bathing, cleaning your fingernails and teeth, and putting on a clean working uniform.

For your own welfare and to avoid spreading germs, report to sickbay when you have an infection, a cold, or otherwise don't feel good.

Report to sickbay if you have reason to believe you have been exposed to venereal disease. Early treatment means early cure.

Above and opposite: Photographs from the Stewardsman Training Manual of Filipino steward recruits being trained by an African American head steward. Upon the reinstatement of Filipino stewards by the early 1950s, African American stewards were typically charged with the training of Filipino TAs (i.e., steward apprentice). Eventually by the 1960s, Filipino stewards would significantly outnumber African Americans, especially due to lower voluntary enlistment and re-enlistment of black sailors during the civil rights era.

Pers-B6211-ebg

2 June 1953

P14-4

From: Assistant Director, Recruiting Division (Pers-B6a)
To: Director, Recruiting Division (Pers-B6)

Subj: Information concerning the enlistment of individuals in the
       Steward Group

1. Any man, regardless of race, color, or creed is eligible for enlistment in the United States Navy provided he is a citizen or national of the
United States, meets the established mental, moral, and physical requirements, has not more than one dependent and has attained his 17th but not
his 31st birthday. Written consent of parents or guardian is required for
men under 18 years of age.

2. Enlistment in the Navy as Steward Recruit is strictly voluntary and has
no bearing on race, color, or creed. Each applicant applying for enlistment
in the Regular Navy is required to complete the following statement on his
application for enlistment in the Regular Navy in his own handwriting:

>   "I hereby apply for enlistment in the Regular Navy for a term of
>   _____ years. If accepted, I understand my enlistment will
>   (SPELL OUT)
>   be effected in the rate of _____ which is agreed between the
>   (SPELL OUT)
>   Recruiting Officer representing the United States and myself."

3. Quotas for Steward Recruit - Steward Apprentice - Stewardsman - Steward
are included in all mental groups.

4. Upon entering the Navy all personnel are sent to a Recruit Training
Center for fourteen weeks indoctrination and basic training, guidance, and
classification. Upon completion of this period, training for the rating of
Steward may be obtained by study at a service school or through the accumulation of experience on the job and the study of manuals provided for this
purpose.

5. It is believed that the reenlistment of Steward Group ratings under continuous service is above those of other rating groups. Reenlistment in the
Navy as a whole is approximately 52%.

6. The opportunities for advancement in the Steward Group are good.

                                    Very respectfully,

                                    K. B. SMITH

By the 1960s, naval officials grappled with a public image problem of steward labor connected to servant labor. Yet as reflected in this official document dealing with this controversy, most naval officials refused to acknowledge steward labor as the exploitation of *racial* minorities; nowhere in this correspondence is the issue of race even mentioned. This serves as a reminder of the navy's worldview naturalizing the correspondence between dark skin and servitude.

STEWARD RATING NAME SURVEY QUESTIONNAIRE

The Navy's enlisted Rating Review Board is currently considering various changes in the Steward rating. One of these changes is the desirability of a name change for the Steward rating.

To assist in evaluating this proposal this questionnaire is designed to give you an opportunity to express your recommendations toward changing the name of the Steward rating.

You have been chosen as a representative of the other Stewards throughout the Navy in this survey. It is important that you answer the questions accurately and sincerely. It is not necessary to indicate your name or other identification on this sheet. When you have completed the questionnaire fold the page in thirds, seal with tape, and mail.

1. DO YOU FEEL THE NAME OF THE STEWARD RATING SHOULD BE CHANGED?
   Please check (x) appropriate box.

   NO ☐
   YES ☒
   UNDECIDED ☐

2. REGARDLESS OF YOUR ANSWER IN QUESTION #1 ABOVE, PLEASE INDICATE YOUR CHOICES FOR A NEW NAME IF A CHANGE IN RATING NAME FOR STEWARDS IS APPROVED:

   1st CHOICE   Go-foR.

   2nd CHOICE   PAGE.

   3rd CHOICE   Peon.

3. WHAT IS YOUR PRESENT PAYGRADE IN THE SD RATING?
   Please check (x) appropriate box.

   E-9 SDCM ☐   E-6 SD1 ☐   E-3 SN ☒
   E-8 SDCS ☐   E-5 SD2 ☐   E-2 SA ☐
   E-7 SDC ☐   E-4 SD3 ☐   E-1 SR ☐

AFTER COMPLETION FOLD IN THIRDS, SEAL WITH TAPE, AND MAIL.

By the early 1970s, naval officials considered a host of strategies in the attempt to rectify its public relations problem connected to the steward's job, including a superficial proposal to change the name of the rating. Questionnaires were distributed among stewards to gain their initial reaction to this preferred proposal. As reflected in these surveys, stewards were forthright in the understanding of their subservient roles; such notions ran counter to officialdom's view that servant labor did not exist in the navy.

STEWARD RATING NAME SURVEY QUESTIONNAIRE

The Navy's enlisted Rating Review Board is currently considering various changes in the Steward rating. One of these changes is the desirability of a name change for the Steward rating.

To assist in evaluating this proposal this questionnaire is designed to give you an opportunity to express your recommendations toward changing the name of the Steward rating.

You have been chosen as a representative of the other Stewards throughout the Navy in this survey. It is important that you answer the questions accurately and sincerely. It is not necessary to indicate your name or other identification on this sheet. When you have completed the questionnaire fold the page in thirds, seal with tape, and mail.

1. DO YOU FEEL THE NAME OF THE STEWARD RATING SHOULD BE CHANGED?
   Please check (x) appropriate box.

   NO   ☐
   YES   ☒
   UNDECIDED ☐

2. REGARDLESS OF YOUR ANSWER IN QUESTION #1 ABOVE, PLEASE INDICATE YOUR CHOICES FOR A NEW NAME IF A CHANGE IN RATING NAME FOR STEWARDS IS APPROVED:

   1st CHOICE ___Slave___.

   2nd CHOICE ___Officers mama___.

   3rd CHOICE ___Galley Rats___.

3. WHAT IS YOUR PRESENT PAYGRADE IN THE SD RATING?
   Please check (x) appropriate box.

   E-9 SDCM ☐   E-6 SD1 ☐   E-3 SN ☒
   E-8 SDCS ☐   E-5 SD2 ☐   E-2 SA ☐
   E-7 SDC ☐   E-4 SD3 ☐   E-1 SR ☐

AFTER COMPLETION FOLD IN THIRDS, SEAL WITH TAPE, AND MAIL.

E3-1 is not SN its TN, TA and etc. I love my rating, please indicate it right.

STEWARD RATING NAME SURVEY QUESTIONNAIRE

The Navy's enlisted Rating Review Board is currently considering various changes in the Steward rating. One of these changes is the desirability of a name change for the Steward rating.

To assist in evaluating this proposal this questionnaire is designed to give you an opportunity to express your recommendations toward changing the name of the Steward rating.

You have been chosen as a representative of the other Stewards throughout the Navy in this survey. It is important that you answer the questions accurately and sincerely. It is not necessary to indicate your name or other identification on this sheet. When you have completed the questionnaire fold the page in thirds, seal with tape, and mail.

1. DO YOU FEEL THE NAME OF THE STEWARD RATING SHOULD BE CHANGED? Please check (x) appropriate box.

    NO ☐
    YES ☒
    UNDECIDED ☐

2. REGARDLESS OF YOUR ANSWER IN QUESTION #1 ABOVE, PLEASE INDICATE YOUR CHOICES FOR A NEW NAME IF A CHANGE IN RATING NAME FOR STEWARDS IS APPROVED:

    1st CHOICE _SLAVE_.

    2nd CHOICE _SERVANT_.

    3rd CHOICE _HOUSE BOY_.

3. WHAT IS YOUR PRESENT PAYGRADE IN THE SD RATING? Please check (x) appropriate box.

E-9 SDCM ☐	E-6 SD1 ☐	E-3 SN ☒
E-8 SDCS ☐	E-5 SD2 ☐	E-2 SA ☐
E-7 SDC ☐	E-4 SD3 ☐	E-1 SR ☐

AFTER COMPLETION FOLD IN THIRDS, SEAL WITH TAPE, AND MAIL.

STEWARD RATING NAME SURVEY QUESTIONNAIRE

The Navy's enlisted Rating Review Board is currently considering various changes in the Steward rating. One of these changes is the desirability of a name change for the Steward rating.

To assist in evaluating this proposal this questionnaire is designed to give you an opportunity to express your recommendations toward changing the name of the Steward rating.

You have been chosen as a representative of the other Stewards throughout the Navy in this survey. It is important that you answer the questions accurately and sincerely. It is not necessary to indicate your name or other identification on this sheet. When you have completed the questionnaire fold the page in thirds, seal with tape, and mail.

1. DO YOU FEEL THE NAME OF THE STEWARD RATING SHOULD BE CHANGED? Please check (x) appropriate box.

   NO ☐
   YES ☑
   UNDECIDED ☐

2. REGARDLESS OF YOUR ANSWER IN QUESTION #1 ABOVE, PLEASE INDICATE YOUR CHOICES FOR A NEW NAME IF A CHANGE IN RATING NAME FOR STEWARDS IS APPROVED:

   1st CHOICE *SERVANTS*.

   2nd CHOICE *MAIDS*.

   3rd CHOICE *SLAVE*.

3. WHAT IS YOUR PRESENT PAYGRADE IN THE SD RATING? Please check (x) appropriate box.

E-9 SDCM ☐	E-6 SD1 ☐	E-3 SN ☑
E-8 SDCS ☐	E-5 SD2 ☐	E-2 SA ☐
E-7 SDC ☐	E-4 SD3 ☐	E-1 SR ☐

AFTER COMPLETION FOLD IN THIRDS, SEAL WITH TAPE, AND MAIL.

STEWARD RATING NAME SURVEY QUESTIONNAIRE

The Navy's enlisted Rating Review Board is currently considering various changes in the Steward rating. One of these changes is the desirability of a name change for the Steward rating.

To assist in evaluating this proposal this questionnaire is designed to give you an opportunity to express your recommendations toward changing the name of the Steward rating.

You have been chosen as a representative of the other Stewards throughout the Navy in this survey. It is important that you answer the questions accurately and sincerely. It is not necessary to indicate your name or other identification on this sheet. When you have completed the questionnaire fold the page in thirds, seal with tape, and mail.

1. DO YOU FEEL THE NAME OF THE STEWARD RATING SHOULD BE CHANGED?
   Please check (x) appropriate box.

   NO ☐
   YES ☑
   UNDECIDED ☐

2. REGARDLESS OF YOUR ANSWER IN QUESTION #1 ABOVE, PLEASE INDICATE YOUR CHOICES FOR A NEW NAME IF A CHANGE IN RATING NAME FOR STEWARDS IS APPROVED:

   1st CHOICE   SLAVE .

   2nd CHOICE   SERVANT .

   3rd CHOICE   MAID .

3. WHAT IS YOUR PRESENT PAYGRADE IN THE SD RATING?
   Please check (x) appropriate box.

   E-9 SDCM ☐   E-6 SD1 ☐   E-3 SN ☑
   E-8 SDCS ☐   E-5 SD2 ☐   E-2 SA ☐
   E-7 SDC ☐   E-4 SD3 ☐   E-1 SR ☐

AFTER COMPLETION FOLD IN THIRDS, SEAL WITH TAPE, AND MAIL.

CHAPTER THREE

Adrift from the American Dream

In the fall of 1955, Paulie Paligutan left the Philippines to pursue the American dream. His brother, Adriano, and his neighbor Manding, the very person responsible for Paulie's new foray in life, came by the navy base to bid him farewell. As they parted ways, there were no tears, no emotional good-byes. Paulie wanted nothing more than to rush past the gates of the navy base. He remembers quite vividly the sight of Manding's wide smile, his dark sunglasses failing to conceal a face beaming with pride. Paulie then turned to Adriano and tossed him a brown package—it was a bundle of Paulie's civilian clothes he no longer needed. Waving one last time, he hurriedly entered the gates of the navy base, fearing that they might close before he got inside.

He and other recruits were directed to the "transient barracks," where roughly one hundred nervous yet excited Filipino enlistees waited for their next instructions. The very first order issued to them as new recruits came as they fell in line for immunization. Afterwards they were instructed to sign their contracts that officially enlisted them in the military. During this procedure, he was told of his assignment to the messman branch to work as a "steward apprentice." It was not explained to him the exact nature of the steward's job, although he readily admits he was never interested to hear further clarification of what the job entailed. He was given two options of service periods, four years or six years. Roughly one-third of the group was randomly designated as enlistees for the U.S. Coast Guard. For Paulie, it did not matter whether he joined the navy or coast guard, and he signed the coast guard contract without hesitation, choosing the six-year option. As he was issued his new navy attire, along with socks, underwear, caps, shoes, and jackets, he recalls the pride he felt as he discarded forever the ragged civilian clothes that he was wearing. His next experience was with the breakfast "chow" in the mess hall. Paulie and the other Filipinos were overwhelmed by the abundance and variety of food, some of which seemed strange to them. Amusedly, he remembers being disappointed that there was no rice served and that his first encounter with "American food" was not particularly enjoyable.

The journey east to America took eighteen days, making stops in Guam and Honolulu before arriving at San Francisco, where they were to undergo basic training and steward school. On the trip to America, Paulie was assigned duty at the sick bay, where he and another Filipino were responsible for keeping the area clean, buffing the floor, and other related jobs. The work was so easy, especially in contrast to the laborious work in the fields of his family's plantation—if this was the extent of hardship working for the navy, he thought, his stint was going to be a breeze. As with the other Filipinos, he was determined to work hard and demonstrate before his superiors his worthiness as a sailor of the U.S. Coast Guard. Along the trip, he made friends with other Filipino recruits. They shared stories of unemployment, lack of opportunity, and of the responsibility to provide for their families. For Filipinos, "family" denotes not only one's immediate members but also one's nephews and nieces, uncles and aunts, and even "fictive family" members emerged through compadrazgo relations. Most Filipinos still felt intimidated in the presence of white sailors, and Paulie recalls that they did not really speak openly with them on the journey to the United States.

After a journey of nearly three weeks, the ship arrived at San Francisco in late September 1955. Excitement was palpable on each Filipino countenance as he gained his first glimpse of the American mainland. The Golden Gate Bridge, a landmark symbolizing a new beginning, loomed just ahead of them, shrouded in fog. As Paulie finally disembarked, he observed his new surroundings that somehow felt familiar to him, although he was now thousands of miles away from home. This was the America he had seen in the movies and read about in books and magazines, a place teeming with energy as everyone around him seemed in a needless rush, and the many cars looked new and drove fast. This exciting first encounter was quickly disrupted by the navy chief loudly barking orders to the men to fall in line. The thirty sailors joining the coast guard, they were notified, were to be bused to nearby Alameda for basic training, while the navy recruits would travel south to San Diego for boot camp.

Although he had heard about the grueling experiences of boot camp, for Paulie it was hardly strenuous at all—in fact, it was a much better experience than his life as an unemployed young man in Manila. Basic training had its challenging moments, but at least he had three big meals a day, plus clothing and shelter. Keeping his amusement inside, he was surprised how many of the other trainees struggled in training camp. Some of them hardly knew how to swim and were surprisingly weak, all the while loudly complaining about the so-called rigors of training. For Paulie, boot camp in Alameda was fun—an adventure he always dreamed about. Even the "indoctrination" classes, which taught trainees about life in the coast guard, were not a problem for him, despite anxiety about his language abilities.

After twelve weeks of training camp and indoctrination, the recruits received additional training in their assigned occupational rating. Paulie was going to attend steward school at nearby Government Island (today called Coast Guard Island), yet everyone he asked was destined to another training center. At the steward school he expected to see at least a few new friends from his mostly white boot-camp cohort, but immediately apparent upon arrival at Government Island was that all the recruits were either Filipino or black. Whispers of this glaring racial divide were exchanged among the Filipinos, quietly wondering why their group was segregated from the rest.

The answers to such questions would be known after four weeks of steward training. Upon receiving strict instructions on how to fix beds, set tables, serve food, and clean living quarters, the stewards realized that their occupational rating was akin to that of a personal servant for naval officers. Was it the color of their skin, they began to wonder, that determined their occupational status within the U.S. Coast Guard? At this point, even this race-based policy did little to dampen their enthusiasm. Most of these Filipinos were highly motivated, with ambitions to climb up the occupational-rating hierarchy. Paulie as with other Filipino recruits believed that hard work and patience were necessary virtues needed before truly realizing the American Dream.

Soon to be realized by Paulie as well as other Filipino stewards was a Western custom of racialized servitude, a traditional practice dictated by the belief that dark skin inheres in natural servitude. As a neocolonial institution in the Philippines, the U.S. Navy also adhered to this worldview in designating the most unsophisticated, unmodern, and undesirable tasks to persons of nonwhite racial stock. The practice of Filipino male domestic service was certainly not unique to the modern navy; the use of Filipino male servants—called "houseboys"—within colonial households was widespread during the American colonial years,[1] a situation in which Paulie's father had served as a houseboy for an American administrator. Indeed, Filipino stewardship can be understood as continuous with the earlier colonial practice of Filipino houseboys, as stewards fulfilled the role of postcolonial male domestic servants in the U.S. military, a remnant of colonial domination. In their exclusion from more technical jobs of the modern navy, the status of Filipino sailors and other minority sailors was arguably traceable to preceding Eurocentric ideas regarding race during the age of Western colonialism—that dark-skinned colonial subjects primordially stood at the outer edges of Western modernity, if not altogether outside it, ultimately justifying their domination and exploitation.[2] What may sound surprising is how long this practice of racialized servitude endured in the U.S. Navy, lasting into the 1970s. Meanwhile, many of the white enlistees who shared the same boot-camp experience with Paulie were to occupy more specialized tasks: sonar technician, electrician, hospital corpsman, machinist, and other modern ratings. Even less-specialized and technically oriented ratings from which Filipinos were largely excluded—such as commissary man, storekeeper, and several others—did not officially entail menial domestic service, let alone the unofficial expectation to serve at the officer's beck and call.

In spite of such unique migratory circumstances, Filipino navy men were not excluded from the welter of migratory themes prevalent among Filipino migratory movements both past and present. Besides colonialism, the theme of Filipino labor as a solution to domestic shortage is readily apparent. Following U.S. colonial occupation, the constitutive migratory labor flows of Filipino agriculturalists, cannery workers, nurses, domestic servants, and navy men would traverse the space initially carved by imperial expansion, the variegated nature of Filipino labor going to the United States following colonization. Still another theme is the transmigrant's reconstitution of identity as hybridized and heterogeneous. While experiencing a profound change after recruitment, often from humble beginnings to a "rich" sailor in the U.S. Coast Guard, Filipino stewards experienced a constant flux in identity upon their occasional visits home followed by their returns to the spatial demarcations of the ship.

Such themes—Western modernity and racialized labor, immigrant labor, fluid immigrant identity—are discussed in this chapter as specifically related to the Filipino steward experience. Specific details are revealed in terms of the contractual obligations, nature of work, and institutional barriers precluding Filipino rating migration in the navy. Importantly, oral testimonies show how entrenched the Filipinos' racial exploitation actually was, in spite of the navy's claims that the steward rating was not exploitative, let alone the claim that stewardship had no bearing on race and/or nationality.

Race, Empire, and the Modernization of the U.S. Navy

As America approached the turn of the twentieth century, expositions that showcased the nation's industrial, scientific, and imperial might were all the rage with the American public. In displays of spectacle demonstrating the country's technological innovation, industrial power, and military might, such expositions drew awestruck crowds exclaiming pride in their nation's newly established international greatness. One such exposition, the Columbian Exposition of 1893 in Chicago, exposed to the public for the first time replicas of the new steel ships of the U.S. Navy, which at the time were replacing the old, slow, and outdated wooden ships rendered obsolete in the modern era.[3] Such vessels would be first utilized in the naval campaigns of the Spanish-American War, as seen with the 1898 Battle of Manila Bay led by Commodore George Dewey, and a decade later would make a highly publicized worldwide tour as America's Great White Fleet, the nickname given for the stark-white paint on the armada's hulls.

At another exposition, the St. Louis Fair of 1903, modern ships transported from the Philippines some spoils of the war displayed at the Philippine Exhibition before an American public curious about their new colony. Included in this traversal of spectacle were colonial subjects from so-called non-Christian tribes of the Philippines, such as the Moros and Igorots, who drew the most fascination from visitors of the fair.[4] This was not surprising, as such premodern aboriginal groups, in their depiction as a people standing outside modern history, stood to affirm not only the crest of modernity achieved by a new colonial power but also *via negativa,* the collective identity of a white American nation, a powerful modern civilization charged by Providence and history with the responsibility to uplift its premodern and uncivilized colonial Others.

Such categories as race, empire, modernity, civilization, and nation as foreshadowed in the Chicago Exposition and the Philippine Exhibition of St. Louis Fair also figure prominently in the navy's modernization efforts that continued into the twentieth century. These same themes were reflected in official naval policy itself as the nation inexorably pursued the course of modernization. No longer an outdated force of "wooden ships and iron men," the U.S. Navy encountered a formidable problem in the endeavor to recruit and train sailors for their modern fleet of sophisticated warships. More than brute strength and physical labor embodied by "iron men" working on wind-powered ships in the Age of Sail were needed; the new sailors had to be trained as technicians and specialists necessary for the technological features of the modern steel ships. The New Navy's enlisted force, it was envisioned, should comprise men with both an educational background and good character, unlike the traditional recruits of the past.

Such demands gave rise to a modernized occupational-rating system.[5] As the military historian Frederick S. Harrod explains, the usual recruitment process of the previous century, which sought men congregating in the seaports, now proved ill-suited. Such men—uncouth, undisciplined, and uneducated—were deemed less desirable in the eyes of the modern recruiter. The typical sailor in the Old Navy was considered incapable of handling the sophisticated technology found within the modern steel ship. Further questioned was the commonplace recruitment of foreign nationals in waterfront areas, an expedient measure in the face of personnel shortage—in fact, by 1890 over 40 percent of enlisted men in the Old Navy were noncitizens (which included Chinese and Japanese).[6]

With America's new status as a legitimate empire in close league with its European counterparts, there occurred a marked effort during the turn of the century to Americanize the U.S. Navy, newly perceived as a harbinger of American civilization abroad. The New Navy, it was reasoned, required enlisted men who not only possessed the intelligence to comprehend and handle their new technical responsibilities but who also demonstrated upstanding character, a desired quality in service of enhancing the navy's prestige overseas. Yet given the lingering domestic reputation of the Old Navy as a low-paying, brutal, and unsafe job befitting unsavory characters, how were naval recruiters supposed to attract desirable recruits into the modern navy?

One solution to this personnel problem lay in shifting the region of recruitment away from the coastal areas toward the interior regions of the country, where the "ideal sailor"—young, white, educated, native-born, of upstanding character—was purportedly found. In the words of a recruiter: "The men we must have enlist largely from a spirit of adventure, a desire to see the world, stimulated by a very considerable amount of patriotic pride."[7] Utilizing modern advertising techniques to attract such men into a life of travel, adventure, and a sophisticated trade, the New Navy effectively changed the complexion of its corps of enlisted men from a multinational assortment of uneducated laborers to that of a mostly white, native-born, and better-educated personnel of patriotic "sailor-specialists."[8]

Relegated outside the navy's modernization efforts and search for sailor-specialists were persons of color, as prevailing assumptions of brown and black inferiority excluded them from technical jobs. Additionally, the New

Navy should predominately comprise white sailors, in accordance with the ideology naturalizing the equation of nation and whiteness. Both African Americans and foreign nationals were not only integrated into the navy's enlisted personnel aboard the ships of the Old Navy but were also permitted to occupy other ratings besides messmen and servants.[9] This would abruptly change in the twentieth century as modernization was underway. Owing to presumptions of both the perceived incapability of African American sailors in the New Navy as with the potential for lack of allegiance among foreign recruits, the modern U.S. Navy changed its views on race and citizenship within its ranks toward exclusion, discrimination, and exploitation.

Recent histories chronicling the plight of African American enlistees in the U.S. Navy have traced this institutional turn from relative inclusion toward systemic discrimination. Richard Miller's account of black navy enlistees in the pre–World War II modernization era, *The Messman Chronicles*, for example, details naval officialdom's vacillating assessments regarding the supposedly inherent racial characteristics of various nonwhite groups among the enlistment. In its efforts to recruit the white "ideal sailor," while abiding with President Woodrow Wilson's order to racially segregate the military, the navy suspended the further recruitment of Blacks by 1919; new policies of rating restriction and segregation were also enacted for the remaining black sailors already enlisted.

This discriminatory policy coincided with the new recruitment of newly colonized Filipino stewards and messmen. Although foreigners, such as Chinese and Japanese stewards, were no longer desired in the modern navy, officials reasoned that Filipino recruits were the perfect race to assume the role of officers stewards and messmen due not only to their status as colonial subjects but also to their supposedly docile nature, a product of Western Orientalist imagination. As Miller tellingly explains: "The Filipino's customary [small] appetites were similar [to Chinese and Japanese] and (stereotypically at least), they likewise seemed to accept certain humiliating working and living conditions that Americans (and later Guamanians) of any color or socioeconomic class typically found intolerable."[10] Indeed, the alleged passivity of Filipino servants would be a recurrent presupposition extending to the later group of Filipino stewards recruited after World War II.

African Americans were thus officially banished from the ranks of the U.S. Navy after 1919. The navy was now envisioned as a modern force composed of educated white enlistees—"sailor-technicians"—whose basic needs would be met by a tractable labor force of colonial subjects. In the New Navy, Filipino sailors occupied a space both within and without: although constituents within the navy's modern space, they remained subject positions constructed from the discourse of Orientalism, thus by definition necessarily outside Occidental modernity itself while consigned to menial unspecialized tasks upon the naval vessels. It would not be until 1932 that African Americans were allowed to enlist in the U.S. Navy because of the perceived imminence of Philippine independence, an event that would complicate the further recruitment of Filipinos due to questions of Filipino allegiance. Even then, resistance among high-ranking officers to reinstate black sailors within the ranks of servitude was quite vocal. The following argument made by Captain (later Rear Admiral) Robert R. M. Emmet surrounding this very issue deserves quotation:

1. As an officer of considerable experience with Officer's Messes, using both Colored and Filipino servants, I feel we ought to hang on to the Filipino till the last. They are cleaner, more efficient, and eat much less than negros [sic]. Negros are capable of being better cooks though even the best require very close supervision or you will find yourself drenched with grease in the cooking.
2. I can't believe that for a number of years to come, the Philippines will rate as a foreign country.
3. Going back to colored men would be a distinct step backward.[11]

Not only does Captain Emmet's argument evince a scheme of triangulation among black and Filipino servants but, furthermore, he arguably also displays a paternalistic veneer in his incredulity surrounding the notion of Philippines self-government, likely due to his perception of Filipinos as remaining outside the modern world.[12]

Yet, indeed, the Philippines was granted independence in 1946, in spite of such conceptions held by the naval captain and others. A brief hiatus in the recruitment of Filipino stewards thus took place during the years following Philippines independence. Article 27 of the Military Bases Agreement of 1947, however, legally guaranteed the reinstatement of Filipino recruitment, and enlistment of Filipino stewards in the U.S. Navy and Coast Guard began in earnest by 1952, with an annual quota of one thousand Filipino steward recruits per year. Due to overwhelming satisfaction with this new domestic-labor force, the marginal quota was doubled to two thousand Filipino stewards per year in 1954. The young men chosen to enlist were in competition with up to one hundred thousand other applicants every year.[13] Given the sheer number of applicants, it is not surprising that the assessment of "luck" is repeated as a mantra by all Filipino retirees interviewed when recalling their recruitment and early life as a navy seaman.

Filipino "Table Navigators"

"You guys are lucky—you guys made it." These words uttered to Paulie Paligutan by his recruiter were ones that every prospective Filipino enlistee longed to hear. The lucky chosen few, after passing the battery of written and physical exams, would then be sworn into the U.S. Navy and Coast Guard and begin their journeys to America. The assertion of "luck" was surely believed by these men, if only judging by their humble station in life just days before recruitment. Sergio Norombaba remembers that out of three hundred hopeful candidates in his group, only thirty passed the exams.[14] When Jesus "Jessie" Reyes was recruited by the U.S. Navy in 1966, he recalls that seventy-five applicants were approved from nearly one thousand candidates.[15] In view of the tremendous odds faced by the average applicant, it is not surprising that Filipinos successfully recruited into the U.S. Navy and Coast Guard were bestowed an elite status in Philippine society. Navy stewards were received in homecomings as members of a privileged social and professional class. Bert Amano explains, "Being in the navy was a big deal at that time. Everybody says, 'Oh man, that kid will be rich.'"[16] Before the journey across the Pacific Ocean began, the recruits had to sign their steward contracts. An official naval document studying growing Filipino complaints by the 1960s reminds its readers of the following facts about Filipino enlistment:

> All personnel in the Steward rating are volunteers. The one major difference between Filipinos and others is that Filipinos are recruited as stewards. No U.S. citizen is recruited as a steward, but rather, comes in as a seaman recruit. . . . *Prior to his enlistment, each Filipino is advised of the duties he is expected to perform.*[17]

Especially among the earlier cohorts, most Filipino recruits did not even know what the word "steward" meant, let alone the duties expected, and they unequivocally claim that it was never explained to them. They simply recall their naval recruiter informing them of their rating as stewards in the navy; furthermore, they were not openly informed by recruiters that their status as noncitizens precluded rating migration. And, indeed, Filipino applicants did not initially care what they would be doing in the navy or coast guard. As Tony Javier remembers: "I was just very glad to sign in and come in the service because I heard about the U.S. and how prosperous they are and all that stuff. . . . I just signed; I really didn't care what is a steward. There's no stipulation, like, 'You have to make beds,' or whatever."[18] Paulie Paligutan signed his contract with no hesitation: "They just tell you how many years you're going to stay in service—four or six. Then we signed the paper that we were going to be stewards. But the thing is, we didn't know what stewards were. I don't care what it is. Heck, I'll sign the thing. Just let me in! Whatever it is, I'll learn it when I get there."[19] Julian Ortiz echoes similar sentiments: "All I know, I got in for six years. All I know is I'm going to the coast guard. I know nothing about a steward; I know nothing about being seasick; I know nothing about pulling a trigger on an M-1."[20] As Ernie Cabanes remembers upon his recruitment by the coast guard in 1955: "They didn't explain it to us. 'Steward'—I don't even know the meaning of it. . . . Just let me in!"[21] Even those Filipino stewards that enlisted during the late 1960s and early 1970s (a few years prior to the Admiral Elmo "Bud" Zumwalt reforms, discussed in chapter 6), many of whom were aware of the menial nature of stewardship due to the revelations of earlier Filipino sailors, did not bother to question their relegation to servant labor. As admitted by Gerardo "Gerry" Silva, recruited in June 1970: "The contract, I didn't even look for [the job description], I'm so excited. . . . I'm ready to go, that's all. I don't care what job it is."[22]

Evidently, the U.S. Navy did not strictly adhere to its directive to explain the steward's work description to every single Filipino recruit, and presumably most new recruits did not care to know it at that time. It seems possible that the navy envisioned a temporary pool of foreign domestic laborers rather than a group of would-be "lifers" that would eventually challenge their occupational segregation at some point. For Filipino enlistees, the possibility of economic upgrade, adventure abroad, and life in America eclipsed any concern about exploitation at this early point. Thus in many ways, a predecessor of an overseas contract-labor force in the Philippines—a contemporary reality of Filipinos laboring in the global economic system—was formed under neocolonial auspices, often without a formal explanation of the nature of work overseas.

Signing the steward contract marked the Filipino's entry within an occupational category individuated by its population of racial minorities, both citizens and noncitizens. As suggested in official documents, the navy, not surprisingly, understood the nature of "contract" in a literal sense: a noncoercive agreement between two or more parties, all of whom are assumed to be free agents. As stated in a memorandum issued in June 1953: "Enlistment in the Navy as Steward Recruit is strictly voluntary and *has no bearing on race, color, or creed*".[23] Despite this claim, however, an analysis of the migration of Filipino stewards in strict terms of voluntarism is ultimately short-sighted, as structural explanations foregrounding the determining effects of colonialism must be considered. In this sense, it is arguable whether Filipinos were truly "free agents" as assumed by navy recruiters. Moreover, the blatant reference of stewardship as having "no bearing on race, color, or creed" demonstrates how naval administrators were able to somehow separate issues of volition from the reality of racial segregation within the U.S. Navy, a separation that clearly lacked any correspondence to demographic reality.

Once reaching American soil for the first time, Filipino stewards were likely bedazzled by the spectacular glint of modern America, as Paulie's narrative describes above. Yet for some, this initial excitement would soon be followed by less-than-pleasant experiences within their new home. Right away, the new sailors were bused to either Alameda (for coast guard recruits) or San Diego (for navy recruits) to undergo basic training. Reyes's recollection of his first experiences in America demonstrates how the brown skin of his fellow Filipino recruits in training camp marked them for differential treatment:

> I could hear [non-Filipino recruits] saying, "I don't understand these people, you know they could hardly speak English." . . . Then, one of the company commanders always said something behind our backs. Subtle things. In clothing stores, they would give whites the better uniforms. We were issued the same dungarees, but we didn't have any jackets when we first came in here. It was cold in Treasure Island, we were shivering in our dungarees. . . . [The whites] were already issued [jackets]. It took almost a couple of weeks before they issued us [Filipinos] winter clothing and jackets.[24]

At first glance, such claims of differential treatment regarding basic proper clothing may strain credulity, yet Jesse's recollection of this matter is not singular; in fact, one major factor for an incident of Filipino labor stoppage at the U.S. Naval Academy in Annapolis (discussed later) was the navy's neglect in providing Filipino stewards appropriate cold-weather clothing while forcing them to walk to the mess hall in the dead of winter. Furthermore, some stewards truly believed that they were denied the same food privileges as other enlisted men, which would be a factor in a labor strike at the U.S. Coast Guard Academy. At times, basic staple necessities, according to oral testimonies, were differentially allocated based on race and/or national origin.

Norombaba, who enlisted in 1960, remembers that upon finally arriving in the United States and finishing boot camp, fresh recruits undertook a new series of examinations during a period known as "indoctrination." All new recruits, regardless of ethnicity or national origin, were required to take the General Classification Test (GCT). This exam gauged the new recruit's aptitude, thus helping him choose his enlisted person's rating—his occupational category in the navy or coast guard. More-specialized ratings included radioman, sonar technician, medical corpsman, electrician, and machinist mate, among others. Unofficially among enlisted sailors, the stewardsman position occupied the lowest position of this rating system due to its servant responsibilities and menial nature. While other recruits were promptly rated according to their GCT performance, Filipino recruits were clearly excluded from other ratings aside from stewardsman, regardless of aptitude indicated in these examinations. Let us not forget the high number of college students and graduates among the Filipino recruits, which would undoubtedly be reflected in the results of the General Classification Test. For Norombaba, this was his first glimpse of discriminatory conditions Filipinos faced in the navy: "I didn't see anybody from our group that were able to go to a different rating than steward. . . . To me, [the GCT] was a bogus classification. If it was supposed to be a classification, you can hold another job besides serving. But they didn't do it, because all of us just went into serving, into the galley."[25]

The official rationale for this blatant discriminatory practice was that Filipino stewards were not U.S. citizens and were thus denied the possibility of movement within the navy's rating system as officially enacted by the *Bureau of Naval Personnel Instruction 1440.5C*.[26] They were told that "classified information" was openly involved in other occupations, and, therefore, as foreign nationals, Filipino sailors could not occupy such ratings for "security reasons." Filipino recruits had no choice but to remain stewards throughout their entire enlistment period. They were *permanent* stewards—or in naval parlance, their assignments in the navy were "non-rotational." Paulie's reflection on this matter indicates that Filipinos did, in fact, realize their dual positions not only as a labor pool of permanent domestic workers denied the opportunity of occupational upgrade but also as source of replacement workers for the navy's labor problems: "We picked up [on the notion that] since [African Americans] cannot be stewards any more, then we are the next victims. And the technical thing of this was we were not American citizens, so it was hard to wiggle out of this state [of nonadvancement]. Even if you know you qualify . . . the first question is, 'Are you an American citizen?' You say, 'No.' If I wanted to be a storekeeper or yeoman—'Well, you cannot handle classified information, you are not an American citizen.'"[27] What was often left unspoken to most Filipinos about the job of the "TN"—the navy's abbreviation designation for stewardsman—was its menial nature.[28] This fact could no longer be hidden after basic training when Filipino recruits promptly began training at steward school. Serving officers their meals was the primary task, yet the TN's service extended much beyond that. Javier summarizes what they were taught in steward training: "In steward training they teach you how to set up the table, how to set up the silverware, how to clean up the room, how to do their beds. It's kind of a domesticated type of job—housekeeping, or something like that. I didn't know that's part of the job. When you think about it, it feels like a woman's job."[29]

As most stewards recall, the *stewardsman* training manual, unofficially known as the blue book, contained detailed instructions on how to serve officers. Apparently there was a need by authors of the stewardsman training manual for a quasi-religious justification in the use of navy personnel as servants, as suggested in the manual's opening paragraphs:

> There have been Stewards aboard American fighting ships since the days of the American Revolution. . . . The steward profession, however, dates much farther into the past. It dates back to the time of the Bible. In the Gospel of St. Luke, the man in direct charge of the household, under the master, is referred to as the steward. He was the man in charge of finances and of food procurement, planning, and preparation. He was responsible for the general comfort and welfare of the entire household. The steward profession continues today, in the Navy and aboard commercial ships and aircraft. Now, as in Biblical times, it includes responsibilities for food and for the comfort and well-being of others.[30]

The stewardsman training manual carefully described specific work procedures for navy servants, such as the configuration of the silverware, arranged in order of use. TNs were instructed to serve on the left and pick up on the right. They were taught to serve in order of rank: the captain of the ship was served first (unless special guests were onboard), the executive officer next, down to the junior officers and supply officer. Stewards were also taught how to fix salads and cook and the proper way to make an officer's bed and clean the officer's quarters. The steward "uniform" on the job was glaringly dissimilar to that of other enlistees—a white jacket and (sometimes) white gloves.

Prima facie, such tasks may not appear as exceedingly exploitative—the steward's job seems not unlike that of a waiter, janitor, or domestic worker. Furthermore, it is important to emphasize that, as reflected in official naval documents, the U.S. Navy steadfastly believed the rating as undeserving of any controversy almost until the rating's demise, all the while refusing to recognize the job as the exploitation of nonwhites. The navy viewed the steward rating as an essential labor category. To naval officers, the perceived necessity of servitude was not only justified in biblical terms as mentioned above; it was also rationalized by the Bureau of Naval Personnel (BuPers) as an integral element in the smooth functioning of the navy's daily operations. To again quote the stewardsman manual: "Men of the Navy who follow the steward profession are responsible for the comfort and well-being of naval officers. . . . By allowing officers to devote their time to the technical affairs of the ship, the Steward Branch contributes to the efficiency and safety of the ship as a whole."[31] Of course, such logic would hold no truth-value after the steward branch was eliminated by the mid-1970s. In the buildup to that very policy change, the semantic ambiguity surrounding the term "steward" would be exposed in naval correspondence debating the pejorative connotations behind the word itself. The divergent understandings between navy men of color and the Bureau of Naval Personnel over this semantic confusion is exposed in the following passage: "The use of 'steward' to describe someone who performs certain service functions is not unique to the Navy and carries no opprobrium per se. It is universally applied and accepted at sea in all naval and commerical [sic] vessels. In fact, the definition of a steward is: 'An administrator, or supervisor; a manager. A person employed on board ship to do the catering, superintend culinary affairs, etc.' In another category, the term 'stewardess' is applied to one of the more glamorous occupations to which a young woman can aspire."[32] Not only is the dimension of racialized labor lost upon the authors of this correspondence but it furthermore suggests a dubious connection between the signifier "steward" with notions of managerial and supervisory responsibilities. Still further, it appeals to notions of glamor that supposedly was found with the gendered labor force of airline stewardesses, a tangential affinity made by virtue of a common experience with travel and adventure abroad while dissociated from the practice of servitude.

Left unsaid in the stewardsman training manual was that considerably more was demanded of them other than what they learned in steward training, duties that redefined the steward's job as akin to a personal servant. The blue book did not contain instructions to fetch coffee, wash the clothes of the officer's family, perform errands for the officer's wife, babysit children, walk the officer's dog, work the movie projectors and serve popcorn after chow, serve at the officer's beck and call, and the like; yet such tasks were precisely part of the steward's unofficial job description. Jokingly, stewards were self-referentially designated as "table navigators," based upon the designation TN, yet Filipino recruits soon realized that their duties extended beyond the tables of the officers' wardroom (the ship's dining area for officers). The knowledge already possessed by African American TNs—that "steward" and "servant" were distinctions without a difference—came to be realized by those who were brought to take their place.

Ensuring the "comfort and well-being" of officers, as mentioned in the blue book, was the overall task of this racialized labor force. In the case of stewardship in the U.S. Navy and Coast Guard, it is instructive to analyze this labor not as "productive" labor but, rather, as "affective labor." Such labor, also referred to as "immaterial labor,"[33] describes labor performed outside the capitalist mode of production within industrial society; immaterial labor's function is to supply services intended to affect both the emotional and physical state of the recipient—for example, labor associated with the work of servants, maids, valets, food servers, flight attendants, and others. In the case of naval stewards, Filipino sailors were restricted to jobs meant to ensure the comfort and thus the mental and physical well-being of naval officers through the steward's performance of valet-type duties: cleaning, taking care of wardrobe, serving meals, and so forth, not to mention servant labor performed at the officer's beck and call. Affective labor, which also describes both the unpaid work of housewives performing household chores and the paid labor of women domestics, was clearly seen as a priority among navy policymakers, because the steward position remained in existence for most of the modern navy's history. As chapter 5 shows, the elimination of Filipino servants from the navy would be met with considerable protest on the part of some naval officers and policymakers who enjoyed these perks belonging to the naval officer.

To be sure, most Filipino recruits at first did not mind the work of the steward. Interviewees remarked that they initially responded to their new responsibilities with enthusiasm. For it was not only their means to escape the poverty of the Philippines but also their gateway to realize their dreams of prosperity in America. Traveling east to America still looms as an ineradicable memory suffused with elation; Norombaba remembers about his first experiences in America: "It was great! Our eyes were wide open. [I thought] 'My God, this is fun!'"[34]

Such moments of frisson slowly began to vanish, however, as Filipinos realized their new positions within a new neocolonial space, one that functioned to sequester them within novel locations of marginality. Specifically, Filipino stewards labored solely within what the blue book referred to as "officers' country": the living and eating spaces of officers within the ship. Officers' country was the exclusive domain of officers and their dark-skinned servants tending to their comfort and well-being; that is, only the highest and lowest of the naval hierarchy were found within this particular enclave, while other enlisted men were generally excluded. Due to the Filipinos' assignments as servants in officers' country, other ethnic groups, especially Caucasians, readily associated them with positions of inferiority. Recalls Bert Amano:

> My first encounter that I was a minority class of people was my first time in the galley, in the mess hall. . . . You can feel it . . . that they were much

superior class of people, the whites. I guess it's because they know we were native Filipino, and all manual labor was performed by Filipinos . . . so I guess that was their impression, that we were not educated and all that. But most of us were college students. We were aware what was going on in current events . . . versed in political issues, not only in our country but all over the world. . . . We were told to pick up the food as fast as we can. . . . They were herding us like a group of prisoners.[35]

Thus Filipinos identities were formed anew within a deterritorialized space where their "existence" as servants was misperceived as their "essence." Although leaving behind the spatiotemporal boundaries of their nation, these Filipinos were unable to escape beyond the trappings of neocolonial space.

Upon finishing steward training and beginning formal work, Filipino stewards could not help but notice the conspicuous absence of Caucasian stewards in officers' country. "When we got in, the Blacks were already the high-ranking stewards, and the newcomers—the Filipinos—were the lowest," recalls Paligutan.[36] Norombaba has a similar recollection: "Right on my first duty station, on the USS *Van Voorhis*, that's when I noticed that all Filipinos and blacks were the ones in the wardroom."[37] Although interviewees of this study do not recall seeing white TNs, Caucasian stewards, according to naval rating statistics, made up a small fraction of the steward population. However, future naval studies of their rating systems (to be discussed) indicated that the steward rating tended to repel white recruits due to its stigma of servile labor; in fact, even the rare white recruit volunteering for the steward rating was usually turned down. The overall assumption held by navy officials, it seems, was that the steward rating should remain a nonwhite one.

Soon, the novelty of life away from the Philippines began to dissolve. As the servile nature and drab predictability of steward work cast a pall over their everyday lives, some began to regret their decision to join the navy. Enduring the indignities of servitude was perhaps tolerable if the possibility of promotion existed, yet in the case of these Filipinos, their contract restricted them to menial servant duty for the duration of their service period. For many interviewees, this fact coupled with their newfound inferiority within the navy served as frontal assaults upon their dignity. The shorthand label "stew," often used by junior officers before issuing their commands, eventually became despised by Filipinos as a form of derogatory name-calling. Lucio Pontanares recalls this colloquial insult most hated by Filipino navy men: "'Hey stew!'—are we dogs?—'Give me a glass of orange juice.' Because of our lack of status we had to obey. Unselfish obedience you've got to know. They're superior to us; you've got to follow."[38] Julian Ortiz also describes the necessary response of servile deference: "You got to fix their bunks, you got to clean their toilets, you got to clean their space. And from time to time, they might call you and say, 'Hey, young man, bring me a cup of coffee over here!' And you say, 'Yes, sir, here's your coffee.'"[39]

Disenchantment would transmute into resentment, especially as Filipinos became aware of the impossibility of advancement. Ortiz's recollection of this dilemma distills the frustration they felt: "My first two years of being [a] steward, I didn't mind doing the job . . . until I was convinced myself that I could do other jobs. . . . That's when my job as a steward was getting sour. But I couldn't do anything at the time because I wasn't a U.S. citizen."[40] Meanwhile, other enlisted white men and some African Americans were hardly impeded in their movement up the occupational ranks. Paligutan's bitterness over this glaring inequity is still palpable: "You see these white boys, they come aboard the ship with two little stripes, and then about a year and a half, they're already second-class petty officer! And you've been there four years and don't make anything out of yourself. So you become disgruntled. . . . Why should I shine shoes? I don't feel like doing this anymore."[41]

Indeed, for these mostly educated and ambitious Filipino men, the humble nature of their jobs suspended the belief of America as a source of overabundant wealth readily acquired through hard work. It punctured the myth (perpetuated by some disingenuous Filipino sailors themselves upon returning home) that all Filipinos in America lived a life of extravagance and comfort. Filipinos in the U.S. Navy occupied an elite position in Philippine society; according to the scholar Yen Le Espiritu, the salary of a Filipino enlistee placed him among the top quarter of his country's wage earners.[42] The attainment of status, however, was ephemeral, as it lasted only until their ship embarked for America. Upon leaving their country, identities had to be reconstituted within a neocolonial space ensuring their peripheral status. A realization had by Pontanares after years of steward labor underscores the reality of Filipino naval servitude in the past and present: "I was frustrated! My goodness, I did not want to join the navy to become a servant. Day in and day out, plates and plates and plates, wash the dishes, clean the wardroom, mop the floor, shine the shoes. To myself I said, 'So this is the navy that our Filipino forerunners went through?' Exactly."[43]

As previously mentioned, a sizable number of Filipino recruits were either college students or already held college degrees. Thus it was not uncommon that the lowly foreign stewards were consulted by higher-rated enlisted men and even ranking officers in matters involving accounting and writing. Norombaba's remembrance of this is quite vivid: "I had officers that are coming to me for spelling. These are officers who don't know how to spell simple words, and I was so upset. God damn! You're an officer, and you come to me to spell this simple word?"[44]

Interestingly, Timothy Ingram, a journalist writing for *Washington Monthly*, suggested that the tradition of stewardship made navy vessels analogous to "floating plantations."[45] To be sure, one can take issue with Ingram's hyperbolic usage of the plantation analogy, since Filipinos were certainly not driven by the officer's lash. In point of fact, the Bureau of Naval Personnel required officers to treat their stewards with decency; this imperative was imparted upon officers in their everyday contact with stewards, as related in the *Administration of Officer's Messes* manual: "Since [stewards] are constantly in rather close contact with officers and have frequent occasion to be in the wardrooms and in officers' rooms, there is a tendency to become too familiar with them, or perhaps, at times, to be brusque with them. *An officer should always be tactful* in his dealings with stewards. If an officer feels a complaint is in order, or disciplinary action necessary, he should deal directly with the mess treasurer of who is in charge of the stewards."[46]

Quite a number of senior officers, in fact, grew attached to their Filipino servants, sometimes treating them as sons, and often that feeling was reciprocated. Reyes remembers: "Most of the senior officers treated us right, especially the captain, the commanding officers of ships. They were really nice to us and they consider us part of [their] family."[47] Thus, the imperative to treat their stewards with decency was mostly adhered to by senior officers according to the testimony of most interviewees. This was in contrast with some junior officers, similar in age to Filipino stewards, who tended to be overdemanding, exploiting their newfound privilege of having servant labor by calling stewards not by their names but by the generic label "steward" (or worse, the shorthand "stew"), which Filipinos hated. Rey Pellos explains, "The senior officers were really nice because they've been through the system. . . . But the junior officers, they are the rotten part of the apple. . . . They kinda looked down on us—'Do this! How come this is not done yet? What's a matter with you, can you not understand?' Because you have this accent . . . you're hard to understand. . . . It's degrading. I felt belittled a lot of times."[48]

Among themselves, Filipino stewards imputed a sense of enhanced prestige upon those able to secure the coveted positions as stewards for captains and admirals (in naval colloquialisms "captain's boy" and "admiral's boy"), as these positions designated them among the best at the job. It also led to not only close personal relations with the highest-ranking officers of the navy but also various perks gained by this close relationship, such as less work ashore (laboring for only one person) and more liberty time, professional recommendations, "protection" from the complaints of junior officers, and others. Javier, who served as a captain's boy, used his privileges among sailors higher in rate: "The captain treats me very well. On liberty time, if others hold me [from] liberty, I just tell them, 'The captain said so,' then they let me go."[49] As Silva, a former captain's boy for Captain Arthur Hodder on the USS *Vancouver*, describes his elevated status, "[Being a captain's boy] was good for me because of the good privileges with the CO [commanding officer]—you're close [with the CO], you're untouchable."[50] Nonetheless, in spite of the lack of a precise homology between Ingram's "plantation" and naval ships, the comparison properly invokes the image of a labor relation beyond the customary employer/employee dichotomy. According to the interviewees in this study, the affective labor provided by Filipino stewards meant that they were at the beck and call of the officers whom they served, sometimes until "taps" (lights out). Reyes clarifies this in his distinction between steward duties onshore and offshore: "[On the ship], pretty much you're under their disposal until ten o'clock, which is taps. . . . Especially on the ship, the more they demand of you because you cannot go anywhere. It's actually better when you are assigned onshore because at least at the end of the day you can go home. . . . [But] not on the ship—you're pretty much at their beck and call twenty-four hours."[51]

The desire for the affective labor expended by stewards meant that their typical workday's timeline would not coincide with most other enlisted men, whose workday ended during the late afternoon (unless assigned on duty or on watch). Federico Bona found this detail particularly troubling:

> The one thing that really irked me was . . . being a steward, our time was completely different from the rest of the crew, because we have to clean up and serve the officers. After [other enlisted men] ate their meal, unless they have collateral jobs, they are free. They eat, they kick back. But for us stewards we [still] have to serve the officers. When they are kicking back, we were still serving the officers. . . . So we finish maybe about 7 p.m.; meanwhile, the rest in the crew in general, they work until 1600 then they eat. . . . After that, they watch movies.[52]

Yet even onshore, some officers required their stewards to extend their services beyond the official end of the workday. An experience recalled by Teodulo "Doloy" James Coquilla describes how the exploitation of Filipino servant labor by the occasional demanding officer might be conducted, in this case being denied his right to liberty after work and being replaced with serving the officer's family: "After your job, you can go on liberty, but some asshole officer [would say]: 'No you're not leaving.' You operate the movie, you make popcorn, you make coffee. Especially when there's a family, the wife's there, the children come, and you are there like a fucking houseboy or maid, taking care of the children, making sure you clean up. So before you know it, because the movie is usually two hours, it was already ten o'clock, then you clean up."[53]

Javier's experiences with serving junior officers' wives and girlfriends similarly underscore this point. By simple virtue of being designated the enlisted man on weekend duty, it was further expected that he should not cease in catering to the wishes of his superiors: "At night, if I have duty, I have to stay onboard. . . . [The junior officers] bring their wives or their girlfriends on board, and I have to serve them. See? They expect me to serve them because they're ODs [officers of the day]. So, what I do is go ahead and give his wife or girlfriend what [she] wants. . . . I serve them that night. That's one thing that sticks in my mind—I have to serve his girlfriend or wife."[54]

Pontanares was a steward for a navy admiral—an admiral's boy. His recollection at once evokes feelings of pride, for he was serving the highest-ranking officer in the navy, and of bitter resentment in the knowledge that he was being exploited by even the youngest family members of the admiral's family. "You got all the dirty jobs. Jobs that [are] not appropriate [for others], they let you do it. Like if you're assigned to the quarters of the admiral. You're proud, but you are the servant to the whole family. . . . They treat you like a servant, really. "Hey, could you wash my socks?" "Hey, Poncey . . . go get the dog for me." The little boy [ordered me]!"[55]

Similarly, Coquilla's stint as a captain's boy led to the officer's exploitation of steward labor; in this case, Coquilla exposes his ambivalence over his station as a captain's steward: "There was one commanding officer of the minesweeper that was so nice to me. He would ask me to help the wife [with] the children . . . and there were several times when he asked me to go with him to the house and take the kids with the wife to the park. . . . Because I feel that being a friend with the captain, there was respect also in my part because when you work for the captain or XO (executive officer), the other Filipinos would [respect] you the most because I was a captain's boy."[56]

The above observations regarding onshore versus offshore domestic servitude as well as the veneer of paternalism characterizing the officer/steward relation allows us to draw similarities with slave and servant relations of the past. Of course, Filipinos stewards were not physically enslaved in their role as domestic workers; yet in terms of a paternalist ethos, Filipino stewards, being relegated to labor in officer's country away from most enlisted men, tended to develop closer relations with their officers, not unlike house slaves (in contrast to field slaves) with their masters, as well as other colonial and contemporary contexts involving domestic servitude. While out to sea, officers and the stewards at their behest found themselves working closely together from the earliest hours of the day until taps. This was less likely with onshore duty, whereby a steward could free himself of the officer's demands at the end of the workday and leave the ship. Similar to other slave and servant societies, stewards able to leave the confines of servitude at the end of the day eventually forged bonds of identity with other Filipino stewards, which would be crucial in their efforts to resist the oppressive constraints of naval stewardship. All these factors would coalesce in the eventual decision to end restricted ratings for minority sailors. By the early 1970s, the highest-ranking naval officer, Chief of Naval Operations Elmo "Bud" Zumwalt, was compelled to initiate the end of Filipino permanent stewardship based on these dual factors: the institutional rigidity he faced that impeded his paternalistic efforts to promote the rating of his Filipino stewards and the consequences of resistance strategies that many Filipino stewards exercised. As discussed in detail in chapter 6, the celebrated Zumwalt reforms of race restrictions were initially spurred with the intersection of the paternalist officer and servant relation and the persistence of Filipino resistance.

To add to these exploitative practices, Filipino stewards were occasionally fed meals that were less expensive than those of the officers. As stated, Filipino stewards were mostly sequestered from the other enlisted population during the workday, including their dining activities. Filipinos quite often dined in the wardroom after serving the officers, which meant that, at times, the stewards would be fed cheaper rations compared to officers. Recollections of being fed cheaper food or the officers' leftovers were not uncommon among the interviewees. Even the simple request for rice, an inexpensive staple, was sometimes denied to them. Pontanares remembers one of his first lessons in respecting the boundaries between officer and steward: "When I was new as a steward, I served officers in the wardroom. I was on the LST [landing ship tank] . . . and after I served them, there was steak leftovers on the platter. . . . I got one of these steaks, and I was eating it. And [an officer] said: "Hey, you're not supposed to eat that steak—you're not an officer!" What can I say? I cannot say anything."[57]

While the race relations between senior officers and Filipino stewards were generally professional and friendly, it was not always the case with regards to white enlisted men. To be sure, not a few Filipino stewards remark that anti-Filipino sentiment did not infuse all relations between Filipino and Caucasians; in the case of Paligutan, for instance, southern white enlistees on his ship readily accepted him as a friend even while displaying virulent antiblack racist behavior. Reyes remarked that, once escaping steward duty, he was able to interact with more whites: "Of course, there are a lot of good white people, especially when I changed rating to storekeeper. . . . They take you wherever they're going to liberty port."[58] Yet while the majority of subjects in this study did not feel victimized by overt racism perpetrated by white enlisted men, some experienced the opposite, readily recalling steady incidents of racial insults directed toward them by white enlistees—sometimes playful, other times pernicious. Perhaps most egregious was the epithet "monkey" commonly hurled at Filipinos. Not only were Filipinos sailors conceived as standing outside Western modernity but they also were furthermore described through signifiers that connoted a condition of being "less than human." Jaime "Jim" Ebalo explained: "Not the officers but [white] enlisted men, they are calling us monkey—they don't like us. After 1950, I got used to it, they're still calling me that. I don't fight with it, but usually my friends in the navy, we go to the bar. . . . My co-Filipinos then at the time, they're always in trouble at the time in the bar. . . . [The whites are] calling them monkeys. Some guys don't like to hear that, so they're going to fight—there are bottles flying all over the place!"[59] Coquilla had similar recollections of racial antagonism between Filipino and white enlisted men: "With the white people, they call us . . . 'You brown monkey, go home!' . . . They call us brown monkey, especially [those] from the deep south, from the boondocks. . . . Because they haven't seen a Filipino [before], they call us brown monkey . . . There was an exchange of bad words. . . . Sometimes there's a fight. We wait until the guy stepped into the parking lot, then we gang up on him."[60]

Relations between Filipinos and black stewards and messman were generally amicable, according to interviewees, due to their predicament as members of the lowest-rating branch. When Filipinos began integrating within the steward branch by 1952, African Americans held the higher authority within both the messman and steward branches. By the 1960s more and more black sailors were escaping mess-duty assignments for other ratings, and by the late 1960s some rose up the ranks to even become warrant officers. Some newly recruited Filipinos felt more comfortable with black sailors due to their work proximity as well as a mutual recognition of their imposed inferiority. Javier remembered his initial realizations of racial hierarchy during his first deployment on the ship: " I think at that time I was more close to the Blacks than the whites. . . . My thinking was that the white race are more superior than the Blacks. . . . That's why I stick with the blacks. I feel more comfortable at that time. The Whites, they put me down, and other stuff."[61] Similarly, Reyes remembered how he felt more comfortable with African Americans in his initial experiences in the navy: "In my first duty station, there were two black men in our steward division. . . . We were friends, I kinda aligned with them because the color of our skin."[62]

Off the base, the treatment of Filipinos was unpredictable due to their liminal standing outside the black/white binary. Paligutan's recollection of his confusion surrounding his race when needing to use the restroom in the segregated south illustrates how the inescapable issue of race often pursued Filipino sailors upon venturing outside the gates of the naval base. In Paligutan's case, he was told by a townsperson that he was not "colored" and therefore allowed to enter the "whites only" area. For other Filipinos, however, one's racial category was deemed as not so clear-cut. In Javier's case, the assumption that his brown skin shielded him from the institutional racism of Jim Crow proved to be a mistake. When driving from St. Petersburg to Miami, Florida, with a white friend during liberty, the two sailors decided to stop at a restaurant for a quick meal. Once seating themselves, Tony was surprised at what followed:

> We ordered some food, and the waitress was looking at me. . . . The waitress told us, "Understand that I'll be able to serve you [his white friend] . . . because you're white, and I'm not going to be able to serve him [Tony]." . . . I really feel bad, I was really going to go after [her], but my friend said, "No, Tony, just don't do it." I was really, really mad. . . . In the Philippines, when an American comes in, they treat him like a king. I wasn't expecting to be treated like a king, we're just getting hungry, and I just want to eat. And my friend, he was a good friend, and he didn't even eat. We didn't order, we just left.[63]

Alongside the racial inferiorization of Filipino sailors lay a gendered dimension that deepened their sense of subordination. Javier's earlier remark of steward labor as woman's work highlights an important aspect with regard to the Filipino steward's self-esteem. The scholar Evelyn Nakano Glenn, in her book *Issei, Nisei, War Bride*, discusses how Japanese American women laboring as domestic workers faced problems of finding satisfaction in work considered unchallenging, as well as problems in maintaining their self-esteem and independent identity in a position viewed to be inferior by others.[64] In the case of these Filipino stewards, a gendered dimension is added to the "problem of self-esteem," as these men who generally embraced a masculine ethos were consigned to jobs many considered as "woman's work." This particular aspect of the TN's job was part and parcel of the Filipino servant's reconfiguration of identity: the experience of emasculation by some amid a homosocial space suffused with hypermasculinity. Sometimes referred to as "boy" (as found in the informal appellation of admiral's boy or captain's boy),[65] the lowly steward held a position that determined his placement at the base of a pyramid of masculinity, as rank and rating corresponded with male power.

Interestingly, what was lost within the enclaves of the naval warship or the home port would be recuperated with the sailor's return to his homeland. For not only was the menial nature of their jobs not known by most at home but the sailors would also demonstrate their economic power through their conspicuous spending; they would flaunt their manliness through their U.S. Navy uniforms, signifiers of the elite status as well as hypermasculinity; they easily attracted the attention of beautiful women with their economic standing and occupational prestige. Some stewards, feeling ashamed of their lowly status as domestic workers, would often hide the servile nature of their daily job to those at home while sometimes exaggerating the appeal of the U.S Navy and America. Before his own recruitment, Silva recalled some his navy friends hiding the truth of Filipino subservience: "Some of them tell me the truth, and some of them they don't tell me the truth, and I find out later on that they are stewards. I don't know why they are ashamed to show [what they do] in the navy. . . . Maybe they are ashamed."[66]

Yet for some Filipinos, the passing years spent at the navy's bottommost rung, serving their superiors without rating promotion, compelled them to reassess their masculine identities beyond mere emasculation. Javier recalled the patience, discipline, and humility necessary to endure long-term stewardship within the masculine spaces of the naval ship forced him to reevaluate his own sense of manhood: "Anything they do to me, I became more of a man. I woke up. It made me more of a man because I could deal with this stuff. Now I'm older, I can be a better man that I used to be."[67] As echoed by Pontanares, "I give the navy twenty-two solid years. All I wanted . . . [was] not to be a great man but to be a real man, so to say."[68]

What the U.S. Navy expected from these postcolonial subjects was responses of alacrity and docility—did not these Filipinos themselves realize their own good fortune in being employed by the U.S. Navy? A common justification put forth by the navy officials for the practice of Filipino domestic service was exactly this economic quotient: the earnings of Filipino men serving in the U.S. Armed Forces were significantly higher than most college graduates in the Philippines. As described, it was often the case that not only would their economic lives be suddenly transformed but their social statuses as well. Articulated to the sailor's masculinist performativity evinced during trips home, it is not surprising the most Filipino stewards chose to reenlist despite their exploitation overseas. The tradeoff seemed worth enduring if for such fleeting moments during homecomings, where they were idolized as hometown heroes, conspicuous consumers, and manly pioneers of the greatest country in the world.

Just as contemporary global labor migration from the Philippines results in remittances sent back home to families (ultimately contributing to about 10 percent of the country's gross domestic product [GDP]), so, too, did most Filipino sailors faithfully send money to their families as economic aid. By the late 1960s Javier was married to a Caucasian American and had three children, yet he had to work a night job at a restaurant just to support his family while maintaining remittances sent to his father. "Out of that seventy-eight dollars, I had to send back to the Philippines twenty-five dollars. Because my father didn't have anything . . . imagine that? [interviewer: Most Filipinos were doing that?] Yeah, because we were brought up that way, we have to take care of the older ones, take care of the whole family as much as we can."[69] One of Pellos's motivations to join the navy was this moral imperative that incidentally boosted one's social standing among others: "After talking to some of the guys who were trying to [be recruited], they always say, 'Well, this guy went to the navy and look what he is now, he's rich, his family is getting rich, because he was in the navy.' It's really luck. My family felt lucky because they knew that when I get to America, I would be able to help them. And I did, for many years I sent money."[70]

As one can imagine, the receipt of this money was a financial largesse upon conversion to the local economy; as with today, the result was usually a dramatic rise in conspicuous consumerism and outward signs of financial elevation for these families—quality education, better meals and clothing, luxury goods, and even the purchase of homes. While this cultural practice common in societies acquainted with abject poverty was mostly tied to familial obligations, it is also true that acts of economic providing boosted the sailor's standing in society while demonstrating his ability as a provider to potential marriage partners; he was conferred the status of a "hero" in his familial and social circles, not unlike, on a larger scale, the public heroification of overseas foreign workers by the Philippine state today.[71]

Thus the practice of remittances sent to families certainly played a role in the sailors' decisions to reenlist as servants, despite their growing resentment and loathing directed at the nonending steward career. According to Filipino interviewees, the only escape routes from permanent stewardship available to Filipinos was marriage to an American citizen, deployment in actual combat duty (which entailed granting of citizenship for foreign nationals), or the support of a sympathetic officer willing to make a special request for rating upgrade. The third option, however, was not exactly easy for stewards, since as a whole, officers enjoyed their steward privileges. In fact, it involved a delicate balancing act between being a mediocre steward and an exceptional one—mediocre stewards could not expect enthusiastic support from officers, while excellent ones were deemed highly valuable. Pellos explained: "There are some exceptions. . . . If your officer backs you up, like say, you're working for the admiral—an admiral's boy—you confront the admiral and say, 'Hey, Admiral, I want to change my rate,' he can pull some strings. But if he likes you, he won't do that, he'll keep you. . . . [If] you get *too* good servicing them, they'll keep you."[72]

While passivity and resignation may have been their initial responses, many Filipinos reached breaking points in their toleration of discriminatory work conditions. Most, however, realized a return to the Philippines after their service term meant being mired by economic uncertainty. Nonetheless, their frustrations required some kind of alleviation. Amano summed up the Filipino steward's yearning for a solution: "Some of the officers really treat you like you are the 'help'—you are just kind of a 'helper.' . . . You are nothing but a maid, or a janitor, which is difficult for me to admit because I think of myself as better than a darn janitor . . . a basic 'clean-up guy.' I can do better with this my life. I had on my mind: 'I've got to get way from this.'"[73]

Wittingly or not, the solution to their predicament necessarily involved the overturning of official naval policy intact since the U.S. Navy's creation. As discussed in the following chapter, while such a goal may have initially seemed unattainable in the minds of Filipino stewards, this fact did not prevent them from resisting their secondary positions as the navy's "chambermaids for the braid"—a term used by African American stewards and messmen, reflecting their servile labor performed for their superiors.

"What Is to Be Done?"

As the U.S. Navy embarked upon the modernization of its fleets, it relegated racial minorities—conceived as situated in the exhaust fumes of modernity's historical path—to menial positions, as seen for example in the steward rating created to provide naval officers with a supply of personal servants. Filipino enlistees, unlike Americans, were recruited solely as steward recruits, regardless of aptitude, education, and natural abilities. The navy, in the meantime, denied that race had any bearing on the steward rating—an unbelievable assertion given its conspicuous composition of mostly Filipinos and African Americans. Filipino stewards confronted the draconian naval regulations solely applicable to their racial and national group—the prohibitions against rating migration, stationing at their homeland, and even marriage, not to mention the servile duties they had to endure without promotion. Such restrictions would shatter their idealization of America, their belief in naval meritocracy, their dignity, and, for an alarming number of Filipino sailors, their mental well-being. For these men, the dividing line between servile labor and meaningful work was drawn not by aptitude or education but by race and nationality; to use the words of Pontanares: "Because of my skin and my 'being' as a Filipino . . . to me I interpret that as 'insignificant human being' to the navy."[74] The perennial question continually posed before the oppressed, "What is to be done?" would soon enter the minds of these men.

CHAPTER FOUR

Tales of Resistance

After basic training, Paulie Paligutan performed his first steward duties at the U.S. Coast Guard Academy in Connecticut and then at Annette Island, Alaska. Soon after, he found himself stationed in the Deep South, a place fermenting with racial strife as the nation's inexorable struggle for civil rights pressed forward. Since his recruitment, he became painfully aware of the discrimination that persons of color faced in the U.S. Navy and Coast Guard. Although the military had been desegregated under Harry S. Truman's presidency, vestiges of de facto racial separation nonetheless remained intact aboard naval ships, as racial groups adhered to a decorum based upon a perceived natural separation of the races. White prejudice was readily apparent in the interaction—or lack of—between white enlisted men and African American sailors. Yet curiously enough, Paulie became fast friends at this new station not only with a number of white enlistees but also with the few black sailors stationed aboard. Perhaps it was his lack of personal experience with American race relations that caused him to wonder why these same white sailors did not harbor feelings of distrust and dislike toward him as they sometimes displayed toward African Americans.

Once stationed at the base in Panama City, Florida, he at last witnessed the workings of Jim Crow society, something he had until then only heard about. While the color of his skin did not estrange him from whites aboard the ship, he still wondered what would happen should he venture into town. When he first strode through the streets of Panama City, it was clear to him that his naval uniform served to allay the curiosity of passersby provoked by his "racial uniform." On that very day, a particularly eye-opening incident occurred. Looking for a public restroom at a bus terminal, he noticed two separate facilities: one for whites, the other for "colored." Unsure of which restroom to enter, he politely asked a white lady behind the counter for proper direction. "Well, are you black?" she asked impatiently as she pointed to the white facilities.

Although initially intimidated to speak to whites during his first year in America, by now he felt more confident in his English-speaking ability and social skills. He was proud of the fact that he was developing a convincing American accent after just a few years, especially compared to other fellow Filipino sailors. He eagerly adopted many of the masculinist practices he observed to be typical of white sailors—using slang, swearing, drinking excessively, and pursuing women during liberty. There was nary a protest from him regarding his new nickname "Paulie" bestowed to him by his white shipmates, an abbreviation of his surname. His white buddies, many of them from the south, would invite him to the bars during the weekend, where they would drink heavily, dance with local women, and occasionally get into trouble. He was soon anointed the best dancer among their group, which meant that he would be a key to meeting the local women. His first ventures to the bars in town, however, did not fail to draw attention from some locals. While most white women did not seem to mind dancing with him, he could sense the constant surveillance undertaken by some of the white local men. During one night out in town, a rowdy troublemaker tapped him on the shoulder on the dance floor. "Where are you from?" he asked in a belligerent manner. "The Philippine Islands," Paulie answered. "Where's that?" the man continued, seeking to cause trouble. Thinking fast, Paulie suddenly blurted out: "Hawai'i." Somehow, this seemed to work in disarming the rowdy local.

From the beginning, Paulie noticed that the sole African American sailor on ship, Harold, was more or less isolated from the otherwise close-knit group of enlisted men. Paulie worked every day with Harold in the galley, and a friendship developed between them. Eventually, Harold invited him to the bars on his side of the town, boasting of all the women he would introduce to Paulie. At this point, Paulie made a decision he would regret in his future years. Although he considered Harold a friend, he also knew that fraternizing with him at the black part of town would cause his white friends to abandon him. Although Paulie did not reveal the reason behind declining Harold's invitations, he believed that it was something that was tacitly understood between them. During the numerous times the crew would disembark the ship for liberty, he recalled, the paths of the men would eventually diverge at a certain point: Paulie and his white friends heading to the "white" area of town, while Harold walked alone to the "colored" area.

A commonality Paulie and Harold shared was their daily predicament as the only stewards aboard their small ship. Harold seemed not as fatalistic about his subservient role as Paulie initially was. As the months turned into years, frustration began to mount, eventually reaching the point whereby Paulie found it harder to feign the cheerful disposition he had outwardly displayed for years. He observed early on that newly recruited whites would advance through the ratings system very quickly while most nonwhites wallowed in menial labor. At first he was willing to accept this conspicuous inequality. As years of subservience passed, his patience eroded inversely to his increasing impatience, and the realization that he was cut adrift from the American dream gnawed at his conscience. By 1961, six years after his recruitment, Paulie's toleration reached a threshold. One morning he decided to no longer don the steward's white smock—a garment he now interpreted as signifying his differential inclusion within the navy, instead wearing just the enlisted man's uniform. The officers certainly took notice to this but decided to ignore it, as they had become quite fond of Paulie. Since a reprimand from an officer never came, Paulie's daring act started to become routine, to the quiet dismay of his superior officers.

Accompanying this act of intransigence was a marked change in Paulie's attitude, as an air of disobedience replaced his earlier enthusiasm. And with each passing day, the officers' patience with Paulie began to wear thin—most officers believed that Filipinos in the U.S. military were lucky to be there, especially when considering the Filipino's premigration lives in the Philippines. While Paulie did not forget his great fortune in coming to the United States, he nevertheless felt he deserved much more than a lifelong career of domestic servitude.

Filipino stewards in the navy and coast guard share a communal knowledge: as a response to their exploitation, passive acts of resistance were forged in order to ease their frustration and abuse from the occasional overdemanding officer. Some Filipinos regularly committed such acts as cooking distasteful meals, spitting on the officers' food and coffee, putting asbestos in their sheets, and so on. While Paulie had admittedly committed similar acts through the years, he now felt that they no longer quelled his frustration. His growing display of discontent in front of the officers, an act that could lead to serious consequences, now seemed an involuntary response to the servile job from which he found no exit. Days later, he purposely destroyed a lock latched onto a locker, for which an officer finally reprimanded him for "destruction of government property." He then ignored his responsibilities as the enlisted man "on duty," leaving without clearance for liberty. Such acts of disobedience could no longer be ignored by the officers, and an inevitable disciplinary meeting loomed between his superior officer and himself. When that day came, Paulie could not mask his bitterness before his commanding officer as Paulie tried to explain the reasons behind his growing disobedience.

Several days later, Paulie was having a lucky day catching fish when he suddenly glimpsed Lt. James Randall doing the same across the way. Strange, he thought, for he had never seen him fishing before. He also noticed that Randall was not a very good fisherman—perhaps this explained why the lieutenant was gradually making his way toward Paulie's lucky spot. Eventually, Randall approached him, asking permission to share his spot. After a few minutes of small talk, the lieutenant told him: "You know, Paulie, I just received notice of an opening for trainees in the commissary rating. Would you like me to put in a good word for you?" His words caught Paulie by surprise, and at once he began to wonder how this could happen, for he had never seen a Filipino commissary man before. Nonetheless, he responded enthusiastically, and the lieutenant said with a grin, "Consider it done!" Paulie was overcome with elation rarely felt since his first years in America. As he watched Randall suddenly turn around and head back to the ship, Paulie realized that the lieutenant never intended to go fishing that day.

As Paulie's narrative shows, Filipino stewards experienced daily a pronounced liminality characterizing their experiences as postcolonial subjects, marginalized servants, and foreign Others. As this chapter describes, Filipino sailors constantly found themselves "in betwixt and between" the more determinate spaces of their host country—whether racial, spatial, or national belonging. Even as their ships docked in their home ports, their liminality was hardly mitigated. Unmoored from the safe harbor of their native country, they were often unable to find comfort and security within coethnic enclaves (since for single sailors, the ship was often considered home). Furthermore, they were unassimilable within the prevailing black/white racial dichotomy during the civil rights era. While the nation heaved from the historical aftershocks of institutional slavery, Filipino sailors found themselves as a new exploitable labor force upon "floating plantations," to use the journalist Timothy Ingram's phrase. How would their positionalities be determined relative to white sailors and black sailors? What avenues were available for Filipinos to protest their subjugation within the U.S. military? Would their invisible struggles be recognized at all, and if so, how much attention would these struggles garner from the navy's top brass in light of highly visible black protest?

Filipinos were able to develop a multifaceted system of resistance—a form of "counterhegemonic resistance"—in spite of their caricaturized image as passive workers governed by economic logic. This system encompassed not only smaller acts of nonconfrontational resistance familiar to past peasant and slave societies—foot-dragging, feigning obedience, feigning illness, destroying property, and so on—but this resistance also involved active measures of vocal opposition and complaint, desperate pleas directed at the admirals, captains, junior officers, and chaplains whom they served, and even illegal labor stoppage. Such actions deconstruct the essentialization of Filipino sailors as passive subjects laboring as servants in quiet resignation. Notwithstanding the U.S. Navy's focus upon defusing the tensions between black sailors within the "White Navy," the emergence of Filipino steward resistance techniques proved its effectivity, as the navy's top officials could no longer presuppose "Filipino passivity" as an essential Filipino trait. Thus, the Filipino sailors' methods of resistance, variants of which are described within Paulie's recollections above and in the testimonies revealed below, were ultimately effective in sending a message to the highest command of the world's most powerful military institution, the U.S. Navy.

In the Interstices of Race, Nation, and Citizenship

Paulie's ordeal within the Jim Crow South during the 1950s and 1960s was illustrative of the Filipino sailor's experience caught in the interstices of "home"—in this case, "home" being a naval vessel constantly patrolling the oceans and seas of the world while occasionally at rest within its port of station. During this historical period, such American naval ships traversed the globe as part of America's self-proclaimed mission to protect the Free World, although ironically embodying the reality of institutional racism within American society writ large while resembling neocolonial societies in miniature. Indeed, one wonders how Paulie and other stewards conceived of home while aboard these warships, especially since the overwhelming majority of them did not consider a return to the Philippines as an attractive option.

As foreign Others, Filipino servicemen found themselves outside the nation's conventional racial dichotomy, a space all too familiar in the history of Asians immigrating to America. The primacy of the black/white binary at this time was especially foregrounded due to postwar racial anxieties approaching a dénouement after centuries of African American oppression. Confronting the sins of its racist past, America was caught in the turbulence of racial strife as African Americans rose up to defy their subordinate positions excluding them en masse from all levels of American society. The impact wrought by this social revolution yielded cracks and fissures upon the foundations of Jim

Crow segregation, although the reality of institutional racism would remain standing for decades.

Since the nation's history of civil rights struggle predominately operated within the black/white paradigm, Asians in America were mostly positioned outside the boundaries of civil rights discourse. Indeed, as far back as the debates surrounding the Fourteenth Amendment (a century before the modern civil rights era), Asians had been largely eclipsed in the national struggle for racial equity, resulting in blatantly anti-Asian immigration and naturalization laws, not to mention extralegal discrimination, racial violence, and mass internment.[1] Hence, a moral equivalence was not yet drawn between black struggle and Asian oppression, due largely to the deliberate erasure of Asians within the American imagined community. This reality was occasioned by a racial imaginary designating the Oriental and Occidental worlds as mutually exclusive, as earlier discussed regarding America's metaphysics of race. It would take considerable time before the plight of Asians would be accorded equal urgency with that of black struggle, as the steady influx of different ethnoracial groups within the United States eventually provoked the reconsideration of "nation" beyond the black/white disjunction.

Indeed, the institution of the U.S. Navy was not impervious to civil rights politics; not a few black sailors during the post–World War II era were swept into the growing tide of black racial pride, which in some cases initiated acts of defiance rather than deference toward their naval superiors. Serafin "Cabby" Cabral remembers this time well. Recruited in 1963 during the height of the civil rights era, Cabral recalls the palpable tension aboard the ships at this time. Increasing numbers of black sailors began to openly protest the lack of work equality aboard navy ships. He comments, "During this time [the sixties], there were stories of riots on ships. You could feel it. There was a lot of tension between blacks and whites."[2] Teodulo "Doloy" James Coquilla similarly remembers that the place of Filipino stewards aboard naval ships was determined largely by black protest:

> When all the Filipinos were ready for the job, they took all the blacks away [from the mess] and put them on the deck force, fixing the ship, handling lines. Because you know why? I find out, the idea was to pull the blacks to the deck force because the blacks were already complaining when MLK [Martin Luther King Jr.] started make noise, Medgar Evers, Julian Bond, all the black people in the south, when [John F.] Kennedy was president at the time.[3]

Such high-level racial tension as attested by retired stewards was less pronounced between Filipinos and other ethnicities. In fact, some Filipinos felt caught in-between the growing racial conflicts aboard navy ships, as demonstrated in Paulie's narrative above.

In the context of the navy's systemic racial discrimination, the protest activities of African American sailors must be recognized as a precursor to Filipino steward protest, paving the way for a culture of resistance to be forged by the latter. As mentioned, black sailors demonstrated their willingness to undertake mutiny during the infamous Port Chicago incident. Later, in 1944, a thousand black Seabees staged a hunger strike at Port Hueneme, California, to protest racial bias in promotions and quarter assignments.[4] And, indeed, during the postwar era, African American contempt for the navy's relegation of black sailors as stewards—"chambermaids for the braid," as they called it—was demonstrated by the simple act of refusing to enlist or reenlist despite the expanded effort by the navy to recruit more African Americans during this period. In 1956 African Americans represented 9.5 percent of navy enlistees, and this figure would drop appreciably to 3.1 percent by the early 1960s.[5] Interestingly, as a solution to overcome the problem of black defiance and lack of passivity, the navy decided to focus African American recruitment in the southern states in the belief of a supposed predilection toward accepting white supremacy and positions of subservience.[6] Such beliefs, however, were eviscerated with the reality of the resistance of southern blacks to their subordination. The desired trait of "Filipino passivity" by officers can only be explained by its lack among many African American sailors during this time.

Notwithstanding the powerful impetus propelling the civil rights movement toward racial reform, it is erroneous to assume that the gains of desegregation and equal opportunity would at once be transposed upon the conservative navy. Witness, for example, the prolonged consignment of African American sailors and other racial minorities to subservient roles well after the civil rights act of the mid-1960s, not to mention the paucity of African American officers for years to come. Indeed, the military as an institution should in some cases be considered sui generis—apart from the legal and political institutions that govern the citizenry inhabiting the space of nation. Although obviously a state institution itself, the military as a "disciplinary regime" operates according to its own set of rules, its own judicial system, and its own racial and gender hierarchies.

The category of "labor" in the U.S. military, for instance, should not be construed along the exact meaning and practice as commonly associated with industrial capitalism, demonstrated for instance with earlier Chinese migrant workers laboring for railroad companies in the West or with Japanese farm laborers in Hawai'i's plantation economy. Such labor diasporas were pulled to U.S. territory with U.S. capitalism seeking to expand profit margins through the extraction of cheap labor from Asian immigrant workers. Clearly, the capital/labor dichotomy does not apply in the case of Filipino servicemen laboring as domestic workers for naval officers—the U.S. Navy is obviously not a capitalist enterprise, although arguably playing a historical role in safeguarding U.S. capitalist interests overseas. Rather, the modern navy's duty within this imperial context was to spearhead U.S. imperial designs and protect American vital interests primarily in the Pacific region—to turn this ocean into an "American lake," as originally envisaged by late nineteenth-century imperial architects such as Capt. Alfred Thayer Mahan, U.S. Senator Henry Cabot Lodge, and then Assistant Secretary of the Navy Theodore Roosevelt. Absent the division between the social classes of capitalists and workers, the notion of labor within the navy's status hierarchy must be recast in historical analysis. Indeed, with regard to the racialized labor of navy stewards, the notion of "affective labor," as previously discussed, is a more useful category in this particular analysis; here, the emotional well-being of officers was in principle the ultimate concern in the labor of stewards, entirely unrelated to the goals of maximum productivity and profit generation associated with the employer-employee relation of industrial capitalism.

Suffice it to say, the lowly steward rating dominated by ethnic minorities evinces the navy's historical practice of systemic racism. Notwithstanding Truman's Executive Order 9981, issued in 1948, which declared that the nation's armed services must observe the "equality of treatment and opportunity . . . without regard to race, color, religion or national origin,"[7] the U.S. Navy intentionally dragged its feet in implementing the effort to realize a more egalitarian state of affairs within its occupational hierarchy. While in some respects ahead of the nation in the movement toward wholesale desegregation, the navy's willingness to provide equality of treatment and opportunity for Filipino sailors proceeded at a glacial pace. The affective labor provided by Filipinos was evidently deemed highly valuable by the navy—again, a value not based on the Marxian "abstract labor" but, rather, upon the luxury and comfort that officers enjoyed as a perk due to their superior rank.

As described earlier, the impossibility of upward rating mobility in the case of Filipino stewards turned on the fulcrum of national belonging. While African Americans pressed their claims for equal work opportunities, Filipinos were institutionally constrained in similar efforts for reasons linked to citizenship—situated outside the civic membership of the American nation, they were officially classified as "aliens" working for a national institution and thus were not as protected from the possibility of mistreatment as the U.S. citizen. Not unlike earlier Asian foreigners who labored in the fields, mines, and railroads of the West, Filipino sailors were easy targets of exploitation due to their peripheral statuses. Yet, a unique liminality surrounds the case of Filipinos nationals in the U.S. Navy and Coast Guard: they were not required to possess a Philippine passport or a U.S. work visa before their entry into the United States (unlike earlier Asian laborers requiring national passports). They were expected to swear an oath only in connection to their service to the U.S. Navy—allegiance to the nation itself apparently was not stipulated. To further underscore their liminality, Filipino recruits were disallowed from voting and participating in any Philippine elections; this meant that they were disenfranchised entirely in their own homeland. The national in-betweenness of Filipino sailors in the U.S. military is well captured by Ray L. Burdeos's observation: "The Philippines had no means to protect us because we were serving the U.S. military and had signed a pledge of allegiance to it. We could not vote in U.S. elections because we were not U.S. citizens, nor could we vote in the Philippines. We felt like exiles caught between two countries."[8]

One can only wonder how to classify such Filipino nationals in both a theoretical and historical sense. Caught in the interstices between two nations, Filipino sailors found themselves positioned in a zone of in-betweenness not only with regard to place but also with regard to citizenship, race, and even labor. Thus, their positions within the narrative of Asian American history must be considered for its uniqueness, if only due to such radical liminality characterizing their immigrant experience. Unlike most earlier and later Asian immigrants in the geographical American west, many young Filipino bachelors began to consider the ship as their actual home, a "place of settlement" that never was truly settled geographically but in constant movement throughout the world—the next step beyond the historian JoAnna Poblete's conception of the "U.S. colonial" migrating from colony to colony.[9] Upon finding their placement within the spatial demarcations of the ship, these servants (usually very few in number) were surrounded daily by a predominately white population in racial tension with its marginal black population and were prevented from forming ethnic enclaves ashore due to the radically migratory nature of their labor as well as the prohibition against marriage; their neocolonial subjectivities were in a state of constant flux with their incorporation as postcolonial servants aboard looming symbols of colonial power and global hegemony—American naval ships—only to be reconfigured again once visiting their native homeland. Yet, as the next two chapters discuss, the leaders of the world's most powerful navy would be forced to take notice of the "weakest" element within its own ranks.

"Weapons of the Weak"

"What the heck can you do? Refuse them? You are in the military, you'll be in big trouble."[10] Julian Ortiz's reminder underlines the apparent futility of active resistance toward the navy's restrictive policies against Filipino recruits. While a few Filipinos decided upon a return to the Philippines over an occupation of servitude, most did not consider it a viable option. Similar to earlier Filipino agricultural laborers who did not rush home with the passing of the Repatriation Act of 1935,[11] these recruits understood that dire economic prospects awaited them in the Philippines; furthermore, their sense of pride prevented them from packing their bags. For most, however, a threshold of toleration was inevitably reached, and for some of these Filipinos, the practice of counterhegemonic resistance—whether active or passive—became inevitable responses undertaken in the reconstitution of their identities as active agents.

The higher education level achieved by many of the Filipino stewards, as described earlier, helped raise awareness of their exploitation related to the navy's "servant problem," not to mention their immediate comprehension of how their liminality served to garner servility while precluding mobility within the rating system. Federico Bona's memory of the stewards' in-betweenness (in this case, with regard to citizenship) reflects his keen observation skills even as a newly recruited steward:

> I was a UP [University of the Philippines] student, so in our thinking, we were radical, so it didn't sit well with me. . . . How come it's only blacks that were stewards, and then we were taking over? Because the system was changing, it was the civil rights movement, so I knew it was going to change but in a slow way. That's why the blacks were going to other ratings, the blacks were working where they wanted to work. . . . Somebody has to take over their place, so that's where we came in as Filipinos. . . . [Stewardship] became redundant. When you're aboard the ship, you're doing the same kind of work every day. The work of quartermaster or electricians mate, it's interesting. . . . So I tell [the officer], "Sir, can I change my rating?" They say, "Are you an American citizen?" "No." "Well, what you can do [is] put in time. After you put in time to be an American citizen, then you can reenlist then. . . . Whatever you're qualified for you can get it. Or you can marry an American citizen, that's another way." . . . That's what they tell us.[12]

And those Filipinos who were not college educated also understood that knowledge was a formidable weapon in their practice of counterhegemonic resistance. Although Ortiz's education did not reach beyond secondary education, he proved to be a leader possessing the acumen enabling himself and others to formulate strategies of resistance.

> I was one of the rebellious kids. . . . I was beginning to read the books about rules and regulations. I understood what they call "One Man's Rations"—they have to give equal portions. . . . So one day, I said to the young Filipinos, "Hey, we are serving them steak, how come we only have chicken wings?" . . . I said, "Look, guys, they have to feed us better. According to this book, we should have equal portions." . . . Man, I wanted to taste the steaks . . . but they were not feeding us the right food. So I was the first one onboard the ship to make a complaint. And I was at first joking to the commissary officer: "Sir, we gotta have steaks like you guys. Otherwise, no steaks, no work!" And he comes back at me: "Okay, Ortiz, no work, no pay." [laughs.][13]

The officer's retort, although given in jest, was in reality the serious truth faced by Filipino stewards. Collective strikes in the military are strictly prohibited.

The initial passivity of Filipinos, alongside their enthusiasm and occasional obsequiousness, is not exactly an overstatement. While sentiments of passive resignation may have lasted months, if not years, a significant number of Filipino stewards eventually refused to accept their secondary status without protest. Commanding officers increasingly found themselves giving audience to direct complaints by Filipino servants. Many stewards found an avenue of protest through their navy chaplains.[14] A solution to their predicament was mostly met with the reality of their signed contracts that legally restricted them to servitude.

One response was to eventually discard their pretense of docility and fatalism and to begin carrying out acts of disobedience, sometimes to the outer limits. For Paulie Paligutan, this tactic was a response deemed inevitable after six years of nonadvancement. It began one day when he decided to no longer don the obligatory white jacket of the steward, eventually leading to a slippery slope of other acts of insubordination—disobedience, destruction of government property, and taking unauthorized liberty. Finally reprimanded by his commanding officer, Paulie expressed to him the source of his disobedience: "I'm sorry, Captain, I'm not really a bad man—I'm a hardworking guy. I know what I'm doing. The problem is that I cannot make anything out of myself because of my rate. . . . I've been here six years in this outfit, didn't make third class at all. How can I expect to look ahead and have a family if I'm going to be like this all the time?"[15]

Frustrations mounted as these Filipino stewards faced not only the impossibility of changing rates but also the occasional overdemanding and even abusive officer. While it is important to emphasize that most interviewees felt they were treated decently overall by their superior officers (which, as a reminder, was a directive sent to all naval officers), a few officers, nevertheless, seemed intent on treating stewards as "insignificant human beings," to use the earlier words of Lucio Pontanares. This led to subtle acts of revenge. Ortiz narrated one:

> This dude from the south—a warrant officer—he loved to call me "stew." ... And I said, "Sir, it's Ortiz." ... I got a little mad about it. I told the XO [executive officer], "Sir, I request that you inform the officer to call me by my name instead of 'stew.' My name is Ortiz, not 'stew.'" ... I was a young rebellious "stew," man. ... I was serving soup at sea; the ship was rocking, and I was mad at this guy. I was serving scalding soup ... and purposely poured it on his lap. I said, "Oh, I'm sorry." The XO knew I'm mad, and he kind of smiled.[16]

Stories abound of how these stewards were able to exact "revenge," however subtle, upon officers bent on mistreating Filipino stewards. Unsuspecting abusive officers did not realize that dirty socks were used to make their morning coffee or that dirt from the steward's shoe was mixed in their breakfast jelly on toast. An officer's insensitivity and occasional cruelty sometimes resulted in uniforms, hats, and shoes thrown out the ship's porthole; asbestos placed in their bed sheets; or steaks seasoned with saliva. Of course, not all stewards participated in these acts, and some ruefully acknowledge that these may have been improper responses to their mistreatment. Such incidents, nevertheless, served as communal knowledge for these Filipinos, as these actions were attempts to restore their sense of dignity while exacting revenge toward deserving officers.

Doubtless, cultural miscommunication and misunderstandings played a role in heightening the occasional tensions between Filipino stewards and naval officers. In Filipino culture, for example, one's age is an important prescriptive index on how persons comport with each other—older age commands respect, and failure to observe proper decorum related to this social dynamic leads to shame (called "*hiya*"). Furthermore, excessive arrogance is often viewed as a character flaw. Throughout this study, many stewards expressed an often respectful—and sometimes paternal—relationship with senior officers and described the opposite of younger junior officers. One factor likely influencing this opinion is the perceived attitudes displayed by junior officers once discharged from officer training—stewards remember them as brash, arrogant, and more inclined toward exploiting their servants, a new perk some of the junior officers likely relished and abused. Some stewards mentioned that junior officers originally from the south were especially abusive. Native Filipino cultural norms played a role in elevating Filipino resentment held toward overdemanding junior officers, many of whom were similar in age if not younger. Tony Javier explains: "Sometimes it made me kinda frustrated and mad because these young officers are kinda demanding. . . . They think that because they're the officers, they could demand too much. They are about my age when they get out of the [naval] academy or [officer's] college. . . . But the senior officers, like the captain and XO, they're kinda mild. . . . they're older."[17] Furthermore, as related by Jerry Silva, it is likely that cultural misunderstandings caused inappropriate gestures committed on both sides:

There are some officers that are not good in dealing with a steward, they call you like that [makes a beckoning sign with index finger]. Filipinos, you don't want to be called this way. . . . It's embarrassing, you're degrading them. . . . But here in America it's nothing. . . . They call you like this, "Hey stew!" [makes same finger gesture]. Filipinos, they get mad, the next time you gonna see them, they gonna spit something in the food. I heard about it, but I didn't do that.[18]

And as we shall see shortly, Filipino sailors stationed in the U.S. Coast Guard Academy would have difficulty with their role as servants for midshipmen straight out of high school, a contributing factor leading to work stoppage.

Servant tasks were often expected to be performed not only for the "comfort and well-being" (to use a BuPers phrase) of the navy's highest ranks but also for their families and friends: the madame (the admiral's wife), the children, and visitors. Salvador Floriano, an admiral's steward during the early 1950s, summarizes his stint:

FLORIANO: Like I said, it's prejudice. . . . When the admiral is on land, they brought us with [his family] and work for them [and] the madame. . . . Besides, we cannot go in the front door, [stewards] have to [enter] the back door. . . . You have to clean up the house, take care of the uniform, and serve the family, and also [serve] when they have parties.
INTERVIEWER: You had to serve the madame?'
FLORIANO: Oh, naturally![19]

The position of "admiral's boy" was considered the highest status of the stewardship rating; as stated in the stewardsman training manual: "Only top-notch Stewards and Stewardsman can qualify." Hence the ambivalence in the stewards' attitude surrounding the assignment: those recognized as the best stewards were assigned to the admiral's quarters and enjoyed some aforementioned advantages of being the admiral's boy, yet this distinction also entailed the expansion of their servant duties when onshore. Opposition to the admiral would certainly entail harsh punitive consequences, so Filipino tales of resistance are noticeably less prevalent among admiral's stewards. Some acts of defiance—however small and seemingly futile—were, nonetheless, committed, as recalled by Salvador Floriano:

> I know one guy . . . when they let him wash their clothes, he said [to me], "Okay. I'll throw the panties of the madame away." . . . And one of my friends—we were in the flagstaff, working for the admiral—this guy, when the admiral is gone, he wears the suit of the admiral! I said, "What the hell?" That son of a gun, he's something else. [laughs heartily.][20]

In the case of admiral's steward Jaime "Jim" Ebalo, an outright display of refusal before an admiral and his family led to punitive measures that still today he interpreted in racial terms. Ebalo earned a reputation as a top-notch steward due to his tireless work ethic, fastidious attention to detail, and willingness to undertake extra measures to ensure the comfort and well-being of his superior officers. Such attributes resulted in the elevation of his status within the stewardsman rating to an admiral's boy, and, indeed, Ebalo would serve several admirals during his twenty-year stint in the navy. Yet, even Ebalo would not permit the officer/steward relation to trespass beyond certain self-designated boundaries. In his case, this meant refusing to serve the admiral's multiple family members, which multiplied his daily tasks beyond necessity. To quote Ebalo's understanding of this job: "Working for [this] admiral's family, he has one daughter, one son, the wife. The admiral's a two-star, the wife's gotta be four-stars, you understand what I mean? [laughs]." Ebalo regularly worked onshore at this admiral's housing. The admiral and his family readily expected him to perform duties akin to a domestic housekeeper: cleaning, washing clothes, serving, and even gardening. At once, Ebalo refused to be exploited as a family servant. After refusing to wash the family laundry, he was promptly admonished by the madame. Ebalo recollected: "She asks me why I didn't do it. 'I'm sorry, Ma'am,' I said, 'but I joined the navy to take care of the admiral, not the whole family.' [For the] admiral, I'll do everything but not the whole family." The penalty Ebalo paid for his perceived insolence and insubordination before the "four-star madame" was quite steep. He vividly described it:

> Two weeks after that they transfer me to the BOQ [bachelor officer's quarters], they take me out of the admiral's quarters. I was there June. . . . They waited for January to transfer me. Why did they [wait so long to transfer me]? I don't think they liked me, because in transferring armed forces at the

time, BuPers instruction black and white don't transfer personnel [during] those kinds of bad weather, all the snowy months; no transfer except on spring time. . . . And they transfer me in January. You can think of how that admiral's racism about my race . . . how bad he is, he don't care that [I'm] gonna get killed transferring. I was asking my car to be shipped out. . . . They didn't approve it, they wanted me to drive it to Rhode Island. . . . They sent me to the smallest ship in the navy, in the roughest duty you ever had. It's just like a speed-boat size, and you go across the Atlantic from Portugal to Canada. They call this DER—destroyer escort radar ship—because we sonar the submarine, we radar the airplane. . . . If you go to sleep, you have to strap your body from your knee up to your waist, . . . otherwise you'll fall down. That's a rough duty. They put me in that kind of a situation, so I said, "I already have a bad record."[21]

Ebalo's punishment for disobeying the admiral and his wife, it seemed, lasted for several years, and by 1962 he was ordered to report to Washington, DC, where he was told he would serve as a steward for Secretary of Defense Robert McNamara. Ebalo's excellence on the job led him from the secretary of defense to the actual White House, where he was part of a Filipino crew of stewards working for the Lyndon B. Johnson administration. Interestingly, once cast adrift from the rigid hierarchy of the U.S. Navy with his new duties among civilians, Jim feels that his self-esteem was somewhat restored due to the more dignified treatment demonstrated toward him and other Filipinos:

I really didn't mind working for people like that. . . . It's real nice to work [for them] because [I] got the experience for my first four years in the navy, you work in the wardroom, they call you, "Hey, steward! Hey, steward!" . . . But when I start working for those people, they call me by my last name. Sometimes they ask me my first name, I said "Jaime," and then they call me James.[22]

In some cases, Filipino stewards resorted to extreme measures as a way to vent the mounting pressure and frustration provoked by permanent stewardship. These sailors, whether by nature or nurture, acquired the stereotypes as being hot-headed and volatile when upset. According to Rey Pellos, acts of violence became common among those Filipinos with volcanic tempers, something perhaps unimaginable to them during their earlier elated moments upon recruitment. Inclinations toward violence were likely acted upon when correlated to the steward's growing discontent with steward duties. Pellos commented: "There are some stewards that had been in trouble because they punch the officers. It does happen. They've been away from home, they're lonely, then you're going to be treated like this. . . . Especially in the Norfolk area, the south. There are a lot of problems with the Filipinos among themselves. When they go out, they fight. Because they're already upset with the job, then they get in a fight with the officers, then they got out, they drink, and you look at them kind of wrong, and they punch you out.[23]

In the case of Coquilla, nine years of steward duty without promotion in rate led him to consider the wildest fantasies of escape routes:

> During the days that I was steward for nine years, I was bitter. I hated it. . . . There was a time when we planned to rob a bank in Richmond, Virginia. . . . There were five of us, we [would] use two cars to rob the bank in Richmond, Virginia, go to the gas station and set the cars on fire, then go to the next gas station and set that car on fire, . . . until we get to Norfolk, Virginia, and then hijack a plane going to the Philippines. Yeah, that was our plan. . . . I was frustrated. Nine years, I was a steward![24]

The frustration of Filipino stewards and mess attendants reached a crescendo at the U.S. Coast Guard Academy in New London, Connecticut. Tasked to serve the cadets, many Filipinos, wearied and frustrated after years of servitude to their superior officers, felt the sting of indignity deepen further since they were now serving midshipmen—"boys" fresh out of high school—which, along with their native cultural norms, only exacerbated the stewards' lowered self-worth. Adding insult to injury was the fact that they were denied their simple request for rice to be included in their rations. This was construed as unreasonable, because rice was an inexpensive request. This last straw struck a responsive chord. The greater concentration of Filipinos at the academy—Javier estimated that between seventy-five to one hundred Filipinos worked as stewards and mess attendants at that time—formed a semblance of "race consciousness" among them.[25] Ortiz, also stationed at the coast guard academy at the time, did not slacken in his role as a "Filipino headache," a designation he earned from his commanding officer due to his rebellious streak, as he became a leader in fomenting revolt against their inferiorization. As he recollected: "One day, we decided we don't want to serve the cadets. We were mad, we were tired of being a steward. . . . So we decided, 'Hey, let's walk out of here.' . . . It [had] something to do with the food, too, because sometimes they just served us the leftovers. . . . Whatever was the cheapest one to feed us."[26] Thus it happened that one day in 1960, midshipmen at the coast guard academy woke up to discover that there were no Filipino stewards and mess attendants to serve them breakfast. News of the display of disobedience soon reached the admiral's ears. Javier had a vivid recollection of how the issue was resolved:

The admiral of the base comes in and says, "What's happening, boys?" And some of us says, "Well, Admiral, all we wanted is to have rice with our meal. That's our request. . . . We're not used to the mashed potatoes, or whatever you have that day. All we want is rice." . . ."What else do you need?" "Well, Admiral, that's all we wanted." . . ."Okay, boys, you go back to work, and I promise you you're going to have your rice. But if you don't go back to work, I promise you I'm going to send you back to the Philippines." And so . . . we have the rice for lunch. Not only do we have the rice, they assigned one cook just to cook the kind of food we like.[27]

According to several interviewees, similar incidents of disobedience and work stoppage occurred at the U.S. Naval Academy in Annapolis, Maryland, where many of those already deemed troublesome among the Filipino navy men were sent to work.[28] This deliberate practice of sending the more rebellious stewards to stations considered least tractable must have been realized by navy officials as a regrettable misstep, since it only spawned a critical mass of Filipino TNs willing to take extreme measures in protest of their subordinate positions. Jesse Reyes, who was recruited in 1966, remembered hearing upon arriving to America as a fresh recruit such stories of a labor strike from other Filipino stewards "I heard stories from Filipino stewards that served [at the naval academy] that at one time they got into trouble because three hundred of them decided simply to strike. . . . They were all reprimanded and eventually told to go back to work. So I guess they were given leniency instead of nonjudicial punishment, NJP—this is three days' bread-and-water. . . . Most of them got leniency."[29]

The outspoken Ireneo "Rene" Amano, who would later become a journalist in Tacloban, Philippines, proved to be a leader in his willingness to organize Filipino labor stoppage at the academy. Recruited in April 1962, Rene followed the footsteps of his older brother Bert, who was recruited by the U.S. Coast Guard seven years earlier. Although he was soon to graduate with a degree in political science from the University of the East in Manila, Rene's yearning for adventure led him to submit a request for recruitment by the U.S. Navy—as he remembered, "I was dreaming of America, land of the free, land of honey and all that stuff . . . [ever] since I was practically in high school. I really wanted to go to America . . . kind of an adventure. You know how young people are."[30] Surprised to receive a calling-card, he headed to Sangley Point to take the exams and interviews, a process that, for a young Filipino desperate for a chance, acquired the reputation as a formidable barrier to their passage to America. Yet, luck continued to follow Rene, as he was one of sixty-four chosen to be recruited out of a pool of roughly eight hundred hopeful Filipino men that day. Once leaving to America, Rene's hard work and dedication were instantly recognized by his superiors. His natural intelligence combined with his drive to excel led Rene to achieve the distinction of Honor Man upon graduating from recruit training—the only Filipino among this small group of distinguished enlisted men at the top of their class. He remembers proudly how their accomplishments were featured in a San Diego newspaper with a photograph on the front page and how distinguished he felt when it was his turn to receive a bouquet of flowers from the commander's wife during the graduation ceremony. The path of Rene Amano as a U.S. Navy man seemed bright indeed.

It was at the graduation ceremony that he first discovered that his career path was not one of open possibilities but of limitations. Since his accomplishments earned him the distinction of Honor Man, he was conferred with the status of seaman apprentice (SA) after graduation, while other Filipinos received their expected TN status. Rene was soon told that regardless of his SA rating, he would not be allowed to enjoy the privilege that his fellow Honor Men had in claiming the best ratings available among the newly graduated. Rene recalled his first encounter with disillusion:

> Why am I in this school for stewards? I was supposed to be a seaman apprentice—all were white, I think I was the first Filipino. I was an SA, not TN. That's when I first found out that I could change my rate later on. . . . There was rebellion on my mind: "Why not now!?" So I understand that it was [because I was] Filipino, that's it. This was my first disappointment. They told us everyone is equal in the U.S. Navy. I felt that this [was] not equal. I just kept it to myself.[31]

Putting his disappointment aside, Rene decided against acting upon the impulse of "rebellion in his mind." Instead, he decided to dedicate himself toward achieving nothing short of excellence as a navy sailor, feeling confident that the navy's celebrated meritocratic system espoused by his superiors would catapult him to the top echelon of the enlisted ranking-and-rating systems. And, indeed, his hard work seemed to reap instant dividends, for it was not long before he was rewarded the coveted position as a captain's steward—or, "captain's boy." Rene describes this tenure as the best possible world for a young new Filipino recruit in the navy, partly due to the paternal relation with high-ranking officers:

> For five, six years, I was a captain's boy, so my work was solely for the commanding officer or the captain aboard the ship. Among the stewards, it's a distinction from the others . . . [a] distinction I got [in comparison to] to the ordinary steward. It was domestic work, like in the hotel. . . . My last commanding officer, he was going to D.C., [and] there were times when he dropped me off at this house. He fixed me up in their residence. He treated me like a son.[32]

Rene was to eventually discover that the place of Filipinos within both the U.S. Navy and American society itself was an indeterminate one, where at times they were wrongly situated within the Procrustean standard of America's black/white racial dichotomy while at other times singled out according to the peculiarities and exoticism of their race, skin color, and Orientalized cultures. As with many Filipino sailors at this time, Rene felt trapped in a zone of indeterminacy, especially when he occasionally ventured outside the naval base, where his "Oriental" appearance sometimes attracted long stares. This was impressed upon Rene quite early, when he decided to obtain a driver's license upon completing steward's training in California. While filling out the driver's license application, a response was required for one's racial background. Not sure what to insert, Rene decided to write "brown" as a response. This led to a category confusion between him and the examiner:

> When the examiner called me up, [he asked,] "What is this 'Brown'?' [I responded] "Sir, I'm not White." "You are not White . . . but you are not Black." "No, I'm not." "Young fellow, if you want your license, there's only two classifications in this office—you're either black or white. So write down 'White,' otherwise you won't get your license." I was surprised, you know!"[33]

Once inside the naval yard or aboard the ship, however, Filipino sailors resumed their assigned positions as racialized servants. While such consigned spaces caused no category mistakes among navy officers and enlisted men, it was, nevertheless, a zone of in-between-ness that Filipinos occasionally attempted to reterritorialize. Attempts to reestablish cultural practices of their premigration lives in America seemed elusive due to the strict regimen of military life. Even the issue of food preferences for the Filipino stewards was typically greeted with scorn and disgust, at worst, or indifference, at best. As with the "striking" coast guard stewards in the academy, attempts of reterritorialization through the cultural practice of native-food preparation and sharing among themselves were generally discouraged if not outright disallowed, notwithstanding the absence of an official prohibition in navy regulations. Similar to the recollections of other Filipino sailors, Rene's memories of attempts made by Filipinos to cook native food, often clandestinely, are marked by both amusement and resentment:

> Sometimes we tried [to prepare Filipino food] aboard ship, but the commanding officers won't allow it. When we were in Florida on our way to Cuba—the Cuban crisis—we were fishing, and the Americans, after picture-taking [of the fish], they throw it back in the water. The Filipinos, they keep it; they hide it in the steward room. Maybe around 11 or mid-

night, we were cooking the head—*tinola* [a native soup]—and they got wind of it. The colored steward went down and said: "I smell something, what the hell are you cooking?! God damn, throw it away!" You can't do otherwise, we throw it overboard. The captain was pissed off! "If you want to eat fish, you fry it!"[34]

After a prolonged period of hard work, dedication, and occasional bouts of servile behavior, Rene arrived at a point in his career where he felt he could no longer hold his "feelings of rebellion" in abeyance. Sent to work at the naval academy, Rene encountered other Filipino stewards and messmen who harbored similar feelings of disenchantment with the navy's practice in institutional discrimination. Talk among the exploited workers grew from whispers of resentment to collective discussions of organized action. Rene felt that in this case, a cleavage existing between those advocating action and those in favor of inaction precluded the galvanization needed for a collective effort of revolt. Recalled Rene: "We talked about [work stoppage] during days off; some of the Ilocanos thought, "Well, maybe we cannot do anything about it." But for us who went to college, [the discrimination] was revolting to us. We were looking at [many of] the African Americans—they haven't even finished high school; and the white Americans were just high school kids. It was revolting.[35]

When winter arrived, Filipino stewards were ordered to walk in their steward uniforms from their quarters to Bancroft Hall, where they served food to the midshipmen and naval cadets. This draconian regulation only enflamed the stewards' feelings of revolt: why were they not allowed to wear a jacket, they angrily wondered among themselves, during the cold trek to the hall, especially during the harsh mid-Atlantic winter? When efforts to complain to their superiors fell upon deaf ears, some Filipinos decided to go "over the hill"—military slang for unauthorized absence (or AWOL). Rene remembered: "So we went over the hill, not really as a group—I think individually we started missing our work, and they charged us for AWOL maybe two or three times. They sent us sometimes to the brig. I was known there as a leader because I was the most vocal. I told the superior [officer], 'Maybe it would be better for us if we had some kind of transportation from where we live to where we work . . . during the winter.' Well, they keep on saying that, 'Yeah, we will tell DC.'"[36]

When promises for the improvement of work conditions failed to materialize, Rene decided against putting a halt to his acts of disobedience. By this time, his feelings about America and his career in the U.S. Navy, he intimated, were irretrievably shattered. Thus, he pursued his course of disobedience with a twin agenda: to not only protest the unfair and unreasonable regulations imposed upon Filipino sailors but also to hope that excessive AWOLs would lead to his discharge from the navy and ultimately a return to his native country.

Rene's open contempt of navy regulations resulted in a summary court martial, sending him to a six-month sentence at a military prison in Portsmouth, New Hampshire. In the brig, its sobriquet "the castle," he decided that his insolence was no longer necessary, and Rene was sent home to the Philippines two weeks short of his full sentence due to his exemplary behavior. He remembered: "I was a model prisoner when I was in the brig. 'Amano, you are a good guy, why the hell are you going over the hill? You are an intelligent sailor.' I said, 'I was expecting more than what I was getting.' I was expecting that I would be treated within my qualifications, because I know that I could improve given a chance. I'm always a model, even in prison—that's ironic, huh? [laughs.]"[37]

Rene's heroic actions and unjust punishment were not in vain. While serving time, he received a letter from a fellow Filipino sailor stating that within six months the navy promised to build new barracks for stewards and messmen, ones that were close to Bancroft Hall. After serving his sentence, he was sent back to the Philippines in handcuffs, and his plane made a stop in California (he believes it was Los Angeles, although he's not entirely sure). Upon disembarking the plane, he was surprised to be met by a small group of Filipinos. He distinctly remembers a placard inscribed, "We're proud of what you've done!"

The Subaltern Speaks

As revealed in this chapter, Filipino sailors agency readily expressed themselves as agents of counterhegemony through various strategies of defiance.[38] Yet likely due to the peculiar phenomenon of invisibility surrounding Filipinos in America, such acts of resistance were unrecognized within the larger historical narrative of the civil rights struggle. Until now, these acts were previously known only to the stewards themselves as well as naval officials who would receive reports of Filipino discontent. As the following chapter details, Filipino intransigence would enter the awareness of navy officials already engrossed in public-relation problems involving race. A decisive factor in the navy's and coast guard's reconsideration of their "Filipino servant problem," Filipino resistance would indeed play a significant role in the elimination of racialized servitude within the occupational ranks of the U.S. Navy and Coast Guard.

CHAPTER FIVE

The Navy's "Filipino Servant Problem"

After six years of servant work, Paulie Paligutan was sent to Groton, Connecticut, in 1961 to receive training for his new rating as a commissaryman (the navy rating for cook). While his new rating was not considered specialized, and despite the fact that he was still consigned to the kitchen galley, Paulie was, nonetheless, enthusiastic about his promotion. Not only did his promotion free him from the most menial tasks of the coast guard but he was also promoted to the rate of third-class petty officer (3PO) and received an increase in pay.

Furthermore, he now qualified for certain benefits that were denied to stewards, one being the government-subsidized transportation of dependents to the United States. This meant that Paulie, now in his early thirties, could begin to consider marriage. Let us recall that the U.S. Navy only recruited single Filipino men without dependents. This "bachelor society" of Filipino sailors, consigned to servant duties and unable to form families in the United States (unless their wives were American citizens), found it increasingly difficult to withstand such indignities without finding an outlet for their pent-up frustrations.

After four months of training, Paulie the commissaryman was assigned to Staten Island, New York, home of the cutter USCG *Mackinac*, whose duty was to patrol the Great Banks of the north Atlantic in order to monitor the movements of icebergs. At his new station, things were now different: he was not among the first sailors awakened in order to prepare the officers' breakfasts, nor was he expected to clean the officers' wardrooms, shine their shoes, and scrub their latrines. With his new rate he was now authorized to dictate orders and delegate duties to fresh recruits assigned to the galley.

His promotion took him six years to reach, unlike the typical year or so it took for the promotion of a white recruit. Paulie now decided to place this history of inequity behind him and resume his exceptional work ethic, a trait associated with him since boot camp. As he recalls many years later, he was never averse to hard work, no matter how menial, so long as there was a chance for a promotion based upon one's abilities and work ethic.

Good fortune struck again only one year after his assignment to the *Mackinac*. Reassigned to Yorktown, Virginia, at the U.S. Coast Guard Reserve Training Center, Paulie was a commissaryman in the galley of the base, tasked with feeding the base's population of reserves in training. After half a year of duty in Yorktown, Paulie was notified that he was eligible for promotion to second-class petty officer. He was quite stunned in hearing the news—while it took six years to rise above the lowly TN position, it only took a year to be promoted to second-class rank by virtue of merit. After years of donning the steward's white smock, by 1962 he now had two stripes—signifying his rate of second class—emblazoned on the sleeve of his uniform. This higher rate was something quite rare for Filipinos in the U.S. Navy and Coast Guard at that time. Upon encountering other Filipinos in the base, he could almost anticipate their inevitable surprise at the sight of his two stripes, something that always made him feel proud not only as a sailor but also as a representative of his own ethnicity, whose men were beginning to be recognized by the navy for demonstrating industry and intelligence on the job.

His new rating opened the door to another fortunate episode. As the years passed, the excitement that accompanied the freedom of bachelorhood in America began to wane with his growing desire for marriage and family. As with many other Filipino sailors, Paulie pursued and dated Caucasian women throughout the years. Yet in the back of his mind, a notion crystallized that, unlike some of his Filipino buddies, he would not marry an American woman because of cultural difference. Aware of a cultural gulf between himself and a Caucasian woman, he wondered if he would meet someone in America who would fully understand and accept his foreign Otherness. He also worried about the possibility of divorce; among Filipinos, the social stigma surrounding the separation of spouses was so great that no actual divorce laws existed in the Philippines. After years of bachelorhood in America, Paulie wished for an extended period of time in the Philippines in order to find a wife. It was common knowledge that Filipinos were not typically stationed in their homeland.

Paulie's fortuitous ascent to the rate of second class enabled him to escape this stricture and again achieve good fortune in his life. Due to his rating, Paulie was able to secure a commissaryman position in 1962 at a LORAN (long-range aid to navigation) station in Palawan Island, Philippines. By now, Paulie felt that the recent reversals of fortune were less a result of chance. This was a change of life philosophy for him, one that he would often exclaim even during his twilight years though the adage: "If it's yours, then it was meant to be."

Life as a Filipino sailor in Palawan was hardly strenuous, he recalled, since the station consisted of less than twenty men with limited daily duties. The rest of the day on this tropical island was spent eating, drinking, or going to town where, as the only Filipino in a U.S. Coast Guard uniform, he drew the admiring glances of the locals. During this time, Paulie often thought about a woman from a small town of Oras, a place nearby his childhood barrio. Cecilia was from a more prominent family of town, a daughter of a successful merchant. Growing up in the barrio, Paulie, even in the most mundane matters of provincial life, was often reminded of his humble class origins. The professional, educated, and merchant classes of town, however small, were held in high esteem, and their elevated status commanded a decorum of deference in their routine comportment with other townspeople: they were not expected to wait in any lines, were served the best food, and were sold the best products in the market and established personal relations with the local clergy. And the young women from the higher class habitually ignored the amorous attentions of men beneath them. Like others from his lower social class, Paulie grudgingly observed such boundaries throughout his early life. Cecilia was a beautiful young woman whom he always admired from afar, a distance drawn by social decorum. Now, with his elevated status as a sailor in the U.S. Navy, he knew that these barriers no longer mattered.

Now that Paulie was stationed in his home country, he could begin to inquire about Cecilia. He discovered that she was a successful teacher, a graduate of one of the best teaching universities in the nation, the Philippine Normal College in Manila. She had decided to return to the town of Oras upon graduation, bringing with her the latest theories of pedagogy to her backward home province, where teaching methods were still based upon the crude Spanish-based methods of rote memorization and the routine use of physical punishment inflicted upon slow learners. Paulie was happy to hear that Cecilia had not yet married, although she was courted by several bachelors of eligible standing, including a prominent attorney who later became the region's congressman. By simple virtue of his status as a U.S. Coast Guard sailor, Paulie no longer felt intimidated to court her, no longer wary of the shame that accompanies the transgression of social boundaries. With his feelings for Cecilia rekindled, they fell in love and were married in Manila in April 1963, afterwards moving to Palawan Island, where they would stay until his transfer to a new station in America. Decades later, when asked to recount his courtship of his wife, Paulie was fond of punctuating the story with the following playful image: "You see, when I returned to the town of Oras, I put a U.S. dollar on my forehead, and my wife said 'yes.'"

During his last months at Palawan Island, he was asked to make a speech for the grade-school graduation at a local town called Culion. Like his own hometown barrio, Culion was poor, comprising struggling peasant farmers whose backgrounds were similar to his own. Admittedly, he felt uneasy, for he had no experience at such things—never did he imagine he would be viewed as a paragon of success by others of similar background. When addressing the graduates, Paulie spoke of hard work, optimism, diligence in one's studies, and the fortitude required for success. As he spoke, he knew in his heart of hearts that such conventional pieties were sometimes not enough for an impoverished kid from the barrio in the provinces. Recalling how good fortune intervened at key moments in his life, he now felt that the ubiquitous Tagalog phrase *bahala na* ("come what may") was not merely a folk expression explaining life's hardship. It could be that one was fated to leave behind the vicissitudes of hard life in a poor country. "If it's yours, then it was meant to be."

Under normal circumstances, Paulie's humble occupational promotion to a navy cook might seem unremarkable and would hardly garner praise, let alone elicit such an elated response from the person being promoted. As Paulie's recollections demonstrate, this meager promotion beyond the steward rating led to immediate upgrade in other areas of his life, eventually allowing him to pursue the American Dream. Most Filipino stewards at this time, however, would not be recipients of similar good fortune, therefore remaining fettered to permanent servitude.

For some Filipinos, the suffering of serious mental illnesses, such as depression, paranoia, and even psychosis, was the consequence of their unique predicament, which prompted the U.S. Navy to investigate the disproportionate rise of mental illness among Filipino enlistees. For others, acts of resistance would become routinized in their efforts to escape from permanent stewardship.

Especially by the 1960s, the rising tide of Filipino protest—through channels formal and informal, strategies passive and active—compelled the navy's top command to address this mounting problem within its internal race relations. Not only was it necessary to address the accusations of segregation, exploitation, and discrimination emanating from African American enlistees but the navy also could no longer ignore the controversy surrounding its practice of servitude performed by brown-skinned domestic workers from a former colony. This chapter argues that a decisive factor in the navy's change of race-based practices was forged by the efforts of the oppressed themselves. That is, while some marginal journalists and outside critics—in assuming a role as a voice for the voiceless—may have roundly condemned the navy for its practices of Filipino servitude aboard "floating plantations," and while the spirit of racial reform during the 1960s certainly contributed to liberalization efforts, official navy documents show that the navy's servant problem was eventually accorded enhanced focus due to the groundswell of Filipino protest that percolated up the chain of naval administration. While not describing the specific details of Filipino protest (as detailed in this work) and while proposing a variety of solutions to such complaints, these official documents directly recognize Filipino discontent regarding their circumscribed positions. The candid reports of Filipino disenchantment with permanent stewardship would hardly be apparent within these official documents if not made public by Filipino stewards to their superior officers via a broad array of protest. Filipino sailors, notwithstanding their marginality, were hardly passive and fatalistic as often presumed not only by many of the officers that they served but also even by those observers trying to raise awareness of these sailors' plight. Filipino stewards during the civil rights era managed to transcend their near-invisibility and contribute to the termination of racialized domestic labor in the navy. Once freed from the constraints of servant duty, Filipinos sailors would demonstrate that their capabilities extended considerably beyond their duties as "table navigators," and many would rapidly ascend in the navy's ranks, similar to Paulie's narrative.

A Misdiagnosis

To typical observers at this time, the sight of racial Others—Filipinos, African Americans, and to a much-lesser degree, Samoans, Latinos, and Chinese—undertaking the entirety of menial tasks aboard navy warships would hardly raise eyebrows, since a connection of nonwhite skin with menial labor was naturalized in the American worldview since the beginnings of U.S. history. The racialization of labor was justified in terms of white superiority. As mentioned in the introductory chapter, America's racial "metaphysics of absence" shrouds the presence of racial minorities in a naturalized state of noninclusion and invisibility. In material terms, a corollary to this belief is the historical existence of racial minorities to the lowest positions of the socioeconomic stratum. Part and parcel of the metaphysics of absence is its connection with essentialist beliefs about racial Others. It confounds their "existence" as workers of menial labor with an ahistorical "essence"; that is, racial minorities *existed* as laborers performing the most menial and lowest-paying work due to a supposed *essential* quality of inferiority they shared, thus serving to justify their lowest station on the economic ladder. This practice has its beginnings with African chattel slavery in the early seventeenth century, later manifested with Chinese laborers in the nineteenth-century West and Latino/a and Filipino agricultural workers in the following century, not to mention African American sharecroppers and domestics in the Jim Crow South. Although dying a slow death in our contemporary world, this belief in America essentialized as white still has its adherents today.

The gradual denaturalization of this linkage between race and menial labor during the twentieth century is owed in large part to America's largest minority population—African Americans—in their struggle to dismantle de jure and de facto discrimination in American society. Their galvanized efforts to confront the "problem of the color line"—whether economic, political, or social—reached a new crest after World War II, the consequence being a slow yet discernible transition in mainstream white attitudes regarding the unjust treatment of nonwhites. This opened the door for other marginalized groups to advance their claims toward economic, political, and social equality.

Granted, other factors served as dissolving effects upon America's racial divide during the period of this study. After the horrific cataclysm of World War II, the U.S. state faced an unavoidable dilemma regarding its race relations engendered from within and without. To begin, the universal indictment of racism and "overtly-racist societies"—to use the historian George M. Frederickson's term—was sparked in the aftermath of a destructive global war waged against Nazi fascism attempting to eradicate Europe of its Jewry and other ethnic minorities.[1] The unprecedented level of annihilation was at once staggering and sobering, proving the capable extent of nationalist-fueled racism's reach. With the war's end, the ensuing decolonization of global territories formerly held by now-enervated European empires elevated the visibility of non-European decolonized populations on the world stage, as former colonies became newly taxonomized as the Third World. What is more, the U.S. state was forced to confront the sins of its racist past and present due to political pressure wrought by the war of ideology with the Soviet Union. Why should the darker-skinned decolonized nations of the Third World enter the orbit of the "free world," given that it denies freedom to its own persons of color? In the face of Moscow's condemnatory stance toward American institutional racism, statesmen and policymakers realized that such charges could not be met with indifference and quietism, especially as they aimed to convince the Third World that the United States deserved the mantle of "leader of the free world." The hearts and minds of darker-skinned people throughout the world could only be won by narrowing the manifest gulf between American principles and performance. One can plausibly argue, therefore, that the U.S. state's role in ending legal segregation in the south was driven in a significant degree by pragmatic—more so than moral—concerns.[2]

Such political exigencies, however, should not overshadow the historical role of minority groups in paving the way toward the bottom-up reform of society's race relations. Just as earlier slaves of African descent played a pivotal role in shaping the outcomes of emancipation and the American Civil War in spite of their state of bondage,[3] so, too, did the exercise of agency among disenfranchised African Americans and their supporters lead to the overturning of *Plessey vs. Ferguson* and the dismantling of Jim Crow structures. Outside America's national boundaries, similar world-historical events were unfolding as the colonized "wretched of the earth"—to borrow Franz Fanon's well-known phrase—began to extricate themselves from the yoke of European colonial rule. It is important to conceptualize Filipino steward rebellion within this world-historical context writ large: with the increase of such acts of resistance coinciding with the diminishing toleration of racial discrimination, the ripples of protest would reverberate from the bottom up, forcing the highest level of government to lift oppressive constraints that heretofore circumscribed their movements.

Despite our present recognition of the role of "subaltern agency" in institutional change, the neutral observer at the time might have failed to recognize its applicability to Filipino sailors, precisely insofar as the culture of resistance forged by them was not visible outside the parameters of the naval setting. Even the most overt displays of collective protests, such as that led by Rene Amano in Annapolis discussed in the previous chapter, were known by only those immediately involved. Indeed, in October 1970 muckraking journalist Timothy H. Ingram astutely connects the official nonrotational rating policy of Filipino servants to both naval security issues and Filipino passivity:

> [A] key phrase that keeps Filipinos in their place is "security necessity," which is used in current Navy regulations in regards to ratings which normally require access to classified information. Such ratings are closed to Filipinos, as security clearances are not granted to foreign nations. . . . The Filipino steward program is justified by the Navy on many of the same grounds used to justify the old bracero farm program, in which foreigners were also recruited to do work involving tasks that menial and degrading for which there was a supposed shortage of American labor. The defense is that Filipinos like this kind of work. They are satisfied with their lot. They are glad to be stewards.[4]

Yet, in the next breath, Ingram posits his belief regarding the Filipino steward's supposed acquiescence:

The Filipinos themselves are unlikely to pressure the Navy for reform. They generally regard obligations of friendship as inviolate matters of honor and rarely question authority. Recently, a steward gave the typical response for the lack of protest: "I can't complain. No one forced me to join. But it's too bad I can't get training I can use." Even if they were inclined to activism, Filipinos are foreigners in the military service. They have no vote and no congressman, and they would have a difficult time forcing democratic reforms up the chain of command.[5]

Ingram cannot be entirely faulted in his assumption that Filipino sailors were unlikely agents of reform, owing to their lack of visibility within mainstream society. Similarly exploited racialized labor groups were typically much larger in number, practiced unionism, and were, therefore, more visible in their organized protests. The glaring misconception in Ingram's article, however, lies in his erroneous characterization of Filipinos as disinclined toward protest and activism due to specific cultural factors. Had Ingram investigated this issue more deeply, he might have uncovered a culture of protest—as disclosed in this work—forged and sustained throughout the stewards' period of service in spite of outward appearances of fatalism and passivity. This fact leads one to question whether Ingram, notwithstanding his good intentions, had likely adhered to either the Orientalist stereotype of the "docile native" or the assumption of the constraining power of Filipino cultural norms. Filipino resistance described in this work shatters both beliefs.

Mounting complaints by Filipino stewards from the mid-1950s through the 1960s—whether direct complaints to superior officers or navy chaplains, whether passive or active—led to naval officialdom's realization that it could no longer look askance at the navy's servant problem, and preliminary investigations into the probable causes of Filipino discontent were thereafter conducted. Coinciding with Filipino discontent—and, perhaps, more alarming to navy administrators—was the high rate of reported cases of mental illnesses suffered by Filipino stewards. Studies conducted by naval psychiatry frontally acknowledged the reality of Filipino discontent and racially connected feelings of oppression within the navy. Moreover, they suggest a causative link between race-based servile work and lack of rating advancement with depression, psychosis, and paranoia experienced by a significant number of Filipino sailors, who as a whole suffered higher rates of mental illnesses compared with other enlisted men during this time of study.

In an *American Journal of Psychiatry* article in January 1967, the authors, Lt. Donald Duff and Cdr. Ransom Arthur, postulated the likely connection of the prominence of hypochondria and paranoia among Filipino sailors, with cultural factors including traditional values, customs, and child-rearing practices. Recognizing the "cultural shock" experienced by Filipinos upon entering the navy, the authors note that attempts were made beginning in the training period to "maximize rapid acculturation." Yet at the same time, stewards were positioned as marginal not only in rating but also in both spatial and racial terms—thus likely sources of dissonance. In Duff and Arthur's words: "As stewards, the Filipinos in the Navy have daily contact with officers but, of course, the contacts are of the briefest, most circumscribed kind. At sea the stewards' division lives and eats together. On liberty there is usually little mixing with their American shipmates."[6] Thus, the attempt to rapidly acculturate and integrate Filipinos ultimately produced a form of psychological dissonance given their daily encounter with the segregated inner workings of the navy.

The authors then argue that despite such efforts of acculturation, it was accepted as "axiomatic" by traditional naval psychiatry that Filipino patients were not amenable to psychoanalytic treatment due to a supposed divide between worldviews. Misunderstanding flowed in both directions in the assumption that such a gulf not only prevents successful treatment by navy physicians but also precludes the patient's conceptualization of his illness in Western psychoanalytic terms. Viewed through the lenses of postcolonial analysis, an apparent—if unwitting—critique of psychoanalytic theory is leveled by the authors at naval psychiatry's failure to address what turns out to be the social structure of colonialism and its determining effects upon native subject-formation. Duff and Arthur explain:

> It has long been axiomatic in naval psychiatry that Filipino mental patients presented a stereotyped clinical syndrome in which hypochondriasis and paranoia were prominent. It was equally axiomatic that meaningful two-way communication between physician and patient did not appear to exist. The eager young middle-class American psychiatrist and naval officer, with a *Weltanschauung* shaped by the concepts of a Viennese genius [read: Sigmund Freud], and the patient from another culture, which is mixture of Occident and Orient, did not appear to get anywhere in their mutual task of healing the patient. However far the acculturation process might have gone . . . it had not extended to the patient's conceptualizing of [his symptoms] . . . as all belonging to one disease entity, paranoid schizophrenia.[7]

The author's characterization of Filipino culture as an admixture of Occident and Orient is noteworthy, doubtless referring to the indelible imprint of colonial epistemologies upon the Filipino's own Weltanschauung, although the authors in the last instance fail to deconstruct this colonial dimension in broad measure. Rather, the authors submit Filipino liminality as an etiological factor, not only in spatial terms (i.e., racial segregation within an otherwise homosocial space of the naval warship) but also in terms of the psychic territory of the Filipino sailor supposedly occupying a limbo between East and West. The authors, wittingly or not, are destabilizing the universalist and totalizing pretentions of classical Freudianism by postulating the likely role of social structures—the colonized spaces both social and psychological—in the formation of subjectivity. The taken-for-granted axiom of Filipino mental illness held by naval psychiatry, an axiom toward which the authors cast their doubts, is the recognition that previous efforts of "rapid acculturation" induced since the recruit's training proved to be futile in shaping the native psyche's amenability to psychoanalytic treatment.

The authors stop short in their consideration of factors involving the explicit racialization and colonization of Filipino subjects in their investigation of Filipino mental illness. Rather, they advance the hypothesis that it is native culture in and of itself that explains their apparent resistance to psychiatric treatment. The apparent uniformity of symptomology found among Filipino sufferers of psychosis, whether Filipino stewards in the U.S. Navy or clinical patients in the Philippines, has led the authors to make this totalizing claim. While unsettling the universalist pretentions of classical Freudianism, Duff and Arthur's analysis remains dehistoricized and decontextualized in its view of native symptomology.

As they search for clues within native culture, the authors highlight two central points: the emphasis within Filipino culture of familial collectivity over individualism, and the Filipino culture analyzed as a "shame culture." As discussed in their report, these two characteristics supposedly intertwine in the quotidian life experiences of the typical Filipino. As the young toddler grows older, for instance, values of filial obedience and familial responsibilities are often imparted through practices involving shaming, teasing, and ridiculing the child; at the same time, the child is taught to repress feelings of anger. Upon entering school and joining social circles outside the family, "collectiveness" and "shame" continue their prescriptive influences upon social behavior. Striving for adequacy rather than excellence is an often-chosen path due to the possibility of shame and ridicule from individuals within one's social circle—"to excel is to shame one's friends," the authors claim.[8] Such cultural norms, they argue, contribute greatly to the native trait essentialized by outside observers throughout this study—a putative state of Filipino passivity and lack of assertiveness.

As with many observers of Filipino culture, Duff and Arthur discussed two cultural practices often cited as governing the interpersonal relations of the Filipino social world and contributing to Filipino passivity. These are "*utang na loob*" (internal debt) and "*hiya*" (shame). Utang na loob extends significantly beyond debt repayment for services, the authors suggest, as it prescribes an individual's commitment to parents and family as the highest form of debt obligation. As they mention in relation to filial duty: "Life is an unsolicited gift and thus the basis of a debt which cannot be repaid." Hiya bears upon the life of the Filipino individual with equal weight. To shame oneself and thus one's family is a cardinal sin in native culture. Relevant to the particular discussion of Filipino sailors is the bringing of shame upon the individual's bilateral family should he fail to repay utang na loob or to achieve a particular goal or accomplishment. Duff and Arthur extend this connection between utang na loob and hiya to suggest the implacability of shame in penetrating the psychology of the Filipino: "The individual is burdened with the gravest obligation to repay a debt that one can never repay. The failure to do so brings deep shame."[9]

As applied to the case of Filipino sailors, the authors speculate that such aforementioned cultural inheritances combined with their sudden immersion within the rigid environment of a foreign military interact to produce the onset of psychosis by those already predisposed to mental illness: "The Filipino in the Navy is faced with acculturation problems while doing servile work and maintaining close ties at home with all the implications of responsibility based on *utang na loob*. Some incident or life crisis such as the arrival of a new and tyrannical petty officer or perhaps some physical illness such as influenza might prevent the individual from fulfilling his obligations. This failure to meet obligations and to attain his goals might give rise to feelings of inadequacy, impotence, and *hiya*, or shame, accompanied by anxiety."[10]

Proceeding in an analysis tinged with the phraseology of Freudianism, the authors suggested that traditional culture wields an influence upon how Filipinos respond to shame and inadequacy engendered by conditions such as the tyrannical petty officer. Assertiveness and anger, the authors remind us, are emotions and actions repressed since early childhood; this manifests itself in the Filipino sailor's perceived response of passivity in dealing with such psychological tensions. The authors put it:

> A culture which discourages open expressions of anger and boldness as well as individual initiative makes an active attempt at mastery difficult. Activity . . . may lead to a transgression of the superego, which will be followed by guilt, a need for punishment, depression, and further anxiety. The patient's upbringing . . . predisposes the Filipino to a passive attempted solution to the problem of shame, inadequacy, and mounting anxiety. The patient may use a classic, passive method of handling feelings of inadequacy, namely, somatic complaint or hypochondriasis.[11]

Duff and Arthur furthermore suggest that "somatic complaints" are likely understood by Filipino patients as sui generis, precluding the possibility of conceptualizing their own episodes of somatization in terms of mind-body connection. Instead, the Filipino patient is supposedly inclined to interpret bodily pains in native nonmedical terms, such as "*pasma sa ugat*, a chronic disorder marked by vague pains, numbness, perhaps weakness, etc., treated by the *arbulario* [native herb doctor]."[12] The attempts by naval psychiatrists to explain these as symptoms rather than actual illness causes only deepening feelings of shame and inadequacy, since what the patient is told ("you are not physically sick") conflicts with his own cultural understandings of sickness. The authors' ultimate speculation is to suggest that therapeutic interventions by a psychiatrist familiarized with these native concepts should serve to lessen the gap between healer and patient.

The mere suggestion of premodern native concepts of disease and their cures, such as pasma sa ugat and arbulario, indicates the authors' insistent stance regarding the intermediary role of traditional culture in creating an epistemic gap between Western-educated physician and the "benighted" colonial servant. To be sure, Western observers would be gravely amiss in averting their analytic gaze away from culture. However, the authors' Orientalist presuppositions lead them to overstate the putative distance between the worldviews held by the naval medical official and the Filipino steward. When asked about premodern views concerning illness and cures, the respondents of my study categorically rejected such views as superstitious and uneducated. Most of these Filipinos had obtained at least some college education, if not full degrees in areas such as commerce, premed studies, and political science and, thus, held rather sophisticated views about the world upon entering the U.S. Navy, sometimes more so than their American counterparts. Traditional practices involving faith-healing and treatment by an arbulario (referred to as a "quack doctor" by one subject) were associated by interviewees with "backwardness" and a "provincial mind." It is not implausible that a handful of Filipino sailors may have believed in non-Western views of medicine; however, the authors' have seemingly assigned too much currency to native premodern metaphysics as mutually constitutive with the typical Filipino sailor's epistemology. Stated otherwise, the authors may have presupposed Filipino patients as remaining too positioned outside Western modernity (despite their earlier observation of Filipino worldview as an admixture of Occident and Orient), a slanted belief likely traceable to skin color.

While Duff and Arthur's study of mental illness suffered by Filipino sailors begins auspiciously in its focus upon rapid acculturation, Filipino marginality, and servile duty leading to psychosis, its conclusions regarding the cultural gulf between Filipino and the West are vastly exaggerated. The Philippine university, consciously structured and imitative of the American university system, provides its students with a cosmopolitan view of the world not unlike those in the West. Child-rearing practices might indeed bear influence upon the lack of assertiveness of Filipinos, yet as proven in this study, a culture of protest employing a full range of practices—from small gestures of resistance to insubordination and even organized strikes—was forged and developed. From a microperspective, indirect demonstrations of protest, rather than overtly direct action, describe one form of "passive resistance," whether exercised by African American slaves in the south, Asian plantation workers in Hawai'i, or Filipino sailors aboard navy vessels. And as the examples of steward "strikes" in Annapolis and New London show, so, too, were Filipino sailors not averse to protest their oppression through labor walkouts, notwithstanding a walkout's strict illegality in naval laws. For some, a heavy price was paid due to their acts of protest, as in the case of Rene Amano, who was discharged, served time in the brigade, and then was promptly sent back to the Philippines.

Duff and Arthur had no evidence of outward assertiveness demonstrated by Filipino sailors, only passivity and docility; this belief was a likely factor steering them toward the hypothesis suggestive of an etiological connection between mental illness and native culture. In spite of their Orientalist inclination, however, the authors at least acknowledge the psychological tension induced by "rapid acculturation." This particular observation shares striking parallels with earlier Western ethnopsychiatric studies of native psychological illness suffered by colonial subjects whose etiologies ascribe "deculturation"—the imposition of modernity upon premodern psyches—as a primary causal factor of native psychosis. Yet, such findings have been exposed by Fanon and others as myopic due to the irrevocably ethnocentric starting point. It is not the case that the traits associated with native mental illness are reduced to atavistic brain structures; rather, they are signs of resistance.[13] In relation to Filipino resistance, the higher prevalence of hypochondriasis, for instance, is fused to their efforts to resist their daily subjugation. The postcolonial critic Ania Loomba underscores this Fanonian insight: "Laziness, for example, is the 'conscious sabotage of the colonial machine' on the part of the colonized."[14] As Fanon reminds us in his own inimitable way, it is more the case that colonized minds are "overdetermined from without" rather than "from within."[15] That is to say, in the case of Filipino sailors as racialized subjects within an imperial navy, their particular subjectivities were determined less by inner psychic forces in the Freudian sense than by the systems of meaning imposed upon them by dominant Western culture, meanings indissociably linked to dark skin color, or in Fanon's own language, the colonized "racial epidermal schema."

Confronting the "Filipino Servant Problem"

Contrary to the journalist Ingram and the naval psychiatrists Duff and Arthur, whose Orientalist views and tin ears misinterpreted Filipino "silence" as lack of resistance, the Bureau of Naval Personnel (BuPers) at this time found that it could no longer disregard the rising chorus of protest emanating from the navy's marginalized spaces occupied by Filipino servants. An unintended consequence of an earlier policy to remedy African American discontent, Filipino protest was now deemed a "problem" in numerous naval official documents circulating by the early 1960s. As will be shown within various official naval documents, the navy's "Filipino servant problem,"[16] while emerging during the age of racial reform, was a direct result of Filipino protest and resistance, as stewards exercised their agency in the struggle to escape the confines of permanent servant labor.

The servant problem, as well as proposed solutions, was framed in a variety of ways within the naval documents. For instance, some discuss the problem of Filipino nationals in the navy primarily as an administrative matter and largely remained silent regarding the injustice behind its racialized labor institution. In an official navy letter, "Recommendation: Keep Filipino Input at Minimum," the author(s) acknowledge an emerging problem surrounding Filipino stewards in the U.S. Navy—the unanticipated rise in requests for both rating transfers as well as stationing in their homeland of the Philippines. Interestingly, the circular letter frames the problem as primarily a bureaucratic concern rather than a racial one. For one, the author(s) remark that such problems correlate with the enlargement of the navy in its size and its advanced weaponry, both conditions related to the Cold War: "As the Navy grows, so must its administrative work grow. As advanced means of warfare are brought into use in a time of increased technological progress, greater security measures are necessary."[17] Foreign nationals, in this case Filipino citizens, were prohibited from obtaining security clearance, the very rationale that precluded their rating migration. The emphasis is placed on the bureaucratic burdens created by Filipino rating and transfer requests that could not be accommodated due to increasing security issues.

In administrative terms, the document recognizes the increasing requests by Filipino sailors to be stationed in their homeland as a growing burden: "Most Filipinos desire duty in the Philippines, and as there are but 66 billets, competition for the same is keen. At the beginning of this year's Seavey, 220 Stewards requested overseas shore duty in the Philippines in lieu of Continental Shore duty."[18] The document further notes other administrative and logistical burdens, such as family transfers to the United States, travel costs involved in assignment to and from the Philippines, and the widening of bureaucratic details required by the U.S. Department of Justice for foreign nationals in the armed forces. Such burdens might have been legitimate concerns to the Bureau of Naval Personnel; however, conspicuously absent from this analysis is any expression of concern over the racial dimension behind these problems. Rather, the document merely describes the problem as a "distribution problem" owing primarily to issues of security and administration, not to issues of racial discrimination.

The letter details, "Although these foreign nationals (Filipinos) sign a statement at the time of their enlistment to the effect that the Steward branch is to be their Navy career pattern, over 600 requests are received annually in the Bureau of Naval Personnel, primarily from non-rated Filipino TN/TR's for a change in rating."[19] Again, nowhere is it speculated that such requests for a change in rating outside positions of steward service are manifestations of Filipino discontent with their secondary status, as a struggle to escape servitude. Nor does the discussion delve into matters relating to requests for transfer to their homeland as a partial escape from their marginalization both afloat and ashore (let us not forget that part of the allure in joining the U.S. Navy, initially at least, was formed by a sense of adventure; the toll of permanent stewardship seemed to erode the desire to live adventurously overseas for some). Presumably, these unmentioned details regarding Filipino discontent are tacitly understood by readers and/or, perhaps, deemed incidental.

The letter ends with the likely causes behind the burden of rating-transfer requests from Filipinos:

> Despite the fact that clearly set forth restrictions on the assignment of foreign nationals to programs requiring security clearance, numerous requests have been forwarded to the Bureau of Naval Personnel for such transfers. . . . There appears to be two primary reasons that generate these requests: a. poor advancement opportunities at all pay grades in the Steward petty officer structure . . . b. the educational and experience level of *some* better educated Filipinos who are all enlisted as TR (steward recruits).[20]

Importantly, this statement corroborates the likely role of the more educated Filipino stewards in protesting their relegation to steward duties to their superiors, an action that previously emphasized by the oral testimonies within this study. It also appears to once again sidestep the social issue of racial discrimination while framing this circumstance as an administrative matter.

Other documents implicitly recognizing Filipino resistance address the racial dimension of the steward problem in a more frontal fashion, although most of the proposed remedies outlined in these correspondences are surprising in their superficiality. That is, some of the solutions put forth for consideration fail to consider the elimination of servile duties delegated to the steward position—it appears that the privilege of steward service traditionally awarded with superior rank was deemed too attractive to let go. With increasing internal protest and public scrutiny, the Bureau of Naval Personnel realized that such privileges now hung precariously in the balance and that at least some changes seemed imminent.

One possible strategy put forth was to attract Caucasian recruits into the ranks of the steward branch. As far back as 1961, a memorandum addressed to the chief of naval personnel is quite revelatory, as it discloses a discriminatory recruiting policy that had to be eliminated before a proposed white integration. As written in the document: "The present restriction, *established verbally* under the previous Chief of Naval Personnel, against converting Caucasians to TA [steward apprentice] at the Recruit Training Centers be immediately rescinded."[21] This measure clearly posits an existent practice prohibiting white recruits from entering the steward branch upon recruitment, one that necessarily had to be lifted should Caucasian integration be pursued. Stated otherwise, no White Americans were recruited as stewards. This likely means that the very small fraction of white stewards during this time were themselves voluntary rating transfers. Moreover, it suggests the practice of disallowing white steward recruits as not written or official but verbal and, thus, unofficial. As a reminder, recall from a previous chapter the navy's official stance regarding race and stewardship: "Enlistment in the Navy as Steward Recruit is *strictly voluntary and has no bearing on race, color, or creed*."[22] The verbal restriction mentioned in this letter evidently contradicts the navy's official stance. It offers an answer regarding how the racialization of domestic labor within the navy materialized while drawing affirmative conclusions regarding its desirability by naval officialdom.

Despite such efforts to racially integrate the rating branch, the image of the steward rating proved to be a problem. Not only was the racial profile of the rating a likely deterrent for some white recruits but also the connotation of servility proved too great. A later report indicates, "Caucasian input is falling far short of providing necessary input to SD rating, e.g., from July quota of 88, only 19 volunteered. . . . SD rating has an aura of servility, especially at entry levels, which makes it unattractive to most—Caucasian, Filipino, and minority groups."[23] As the decade passed, the continuing drop in black enlistment combined with Filipino steward recruitment led to even more disparate ratios between Filipinos and other ethnicities. A comment from a naval officer involved in this discussion, while expressing an unwillingness to integrate the rating, recognized that the "single source" of naval servants was now an apparent problem: "I do not entirely concur with the . . . recommendations concerning the Filipino and Caucasian input into the SD rating. However, in view of the existing virtual single source supply of Stewards, it does appear that some Caucasian input, on a trial basis, may be desirable."[24]

Another proposal to initiate the recruitment of Caucasian stewards as a remedy for racial imbalance suggests its launch as a "carefully monitored" experiment. As with other proposals, it argues that the stigma of the rating, being attached to servility, had to be overcome. As stated by a BuPers memo circulating in June 1968: "One of the best methods of increasing the input of Caucasians in the steward rating is to enhance the "image" and general desirability of the rating. This does not involve the use of gimicks [sic] but rather an aggressive public information campaign starting at the recruiting level to emphasize the positive aspects of the rapidly expanding and lucrative food service occupation."[25] The apparent strategy undertaken here is to emphasize to white recruits the transferable skills acquired as experienced stewards to the lucrative food industry after navy service. However, the rating's preexisting image of servility prevented this strategy from working, as Caucasians remained averse to performing those tasks traditionally delegated to minorities despite the navy's information campaign.

The more popular proposal appears to be integration in the opposite direction—to simply merge the rating of stewardship with the higher rating of commissaryman (populated by Caucasians and African Americans), largely in recognition that the former title carries a pejorative valence that the latter does not. One official document with the rather cumbersome title "Summary of Pertinent Facts Related to Changing the Title of the 'Steward' Rating and Making It a Service Rating of the Commissaryman Rating" acknowledges the "image problem" connected to stewardship. The following quote clearly shows the extent to which Filipino complaint and protest captured the attention of navy officials, leading to this study:

> The Steward Branch has the image among many Asiatics as being a discriminatory structure and is indicative of American racial prejudice. Allegedly, Filipinos feel that they have secondary status by being permitted to enlist as Stewards only, for six years instead of four, and resent the prohibition

against being married upon enlistment. Additionally, the contention is made that the image created by the title Steward is demeaning in that it conveys the connotation of a "servant" or "flunky." Another impression is that those in the rating either can't qualify for another rating or that the assignment to the rating is of a punitive nature.[26]

The report provides a very brief history of the U.S. Navy's stewardship position, noting that the duties associated with the position extend back to 1797. It then mentions that the recruitment of Filipino citizens after Philippine Independence in 1946 was established as official naval policy by 1952 following negotiations between both nations (although the report fails to mention the politics of race motivating the navy's recruitment of Filipino citizens, passing over in silence the history of racialized labor behind the stewardship rating). The report acknowledges that as early as 1958—a mere six years after the policy's implementation—attempts were made by navy officials to deal with the emerging Filipino servant problem, undoubtedly stemming from the growing recognition of Filipino complaints. There is a neutral gloss to the study—the author(s) neither deny nor admit that the naval (unofficial) policy regarding the steward rating inheres in racial discrimination. At this point, for instance, there is no recommendation for naval officials to investigate the plausibility behind the belief of "American racial prejudice" attached to the rating; there is no analysis of Filipino protest over the "punitive nature" of their jobs. Indeed, as implicitly suggested in the report's brief history of stewardship in the navy, a clear presupposition by the author(s) exists that the traditional duties associated with stewardship should not be immediately abolished, whether due to its perceived necessity or to its traditional place in naval organization.

The objective of the report is to address the recommendation that the *title* of steward—not the duties—be eliminated altogether, while the duties associated with the rating be moved under a different title. To quote the report itself: "Because of the bad 'image' created by the population representing the Steward rating and the demeaning, ignominious connotation of the title 'Steward,' the following recommendations are made: 1. Change the title of 'Steward' to 'Commissaryman 2. Make the Steward Branch a service rating of the Commissaryman rating." The report performs an astute analysis of both supporting and opposing factors behind this policy change. Noteworthy in this discussion is the navy's defense in the retention of the steward rating: the steward's job has been around since "Biblical times" and is in common use today in other industries: "The title 'Steward' and the performance of their functions is not unique to the Navy. Stewards are found aboard buses, airplanes, and ships." Furthermore, the report emphatically reminds its readers that Filipino recruits in the steward rating were all volunteers: "Prior to his enlistment, each Filipino is advised of the duties he will be expected to perform."[27] Yet as shown in previous chapters, the oral testimonies of Filipino sailors demonstrate that strict adherence to this recruitment protocol was more often than not unfollowed, especially with the earliest Filipino volunteers.

The opposing factors against the policy change predictably point to the superficiality of the proposal. To begin, the report acknowledges that a simple change of the title while not eliminating the tasks performed by Filipino sailors is merely a short-term remedy masking a deeper social problem: "Should such a service rating materialize, Stewards would still be detailed as such, so such an administrative course of action would be nothing more than a smoke screen or a cover-up for something which . . . the Navy is trying to sweep under the rug." Furthermore, it is pointed out that Caucasians occupying the CS (commissaryman) rating might resent the presence of former servants newly integrated into their ranks: "If the proposed merger were effected, the morale of the personnel in the CS rating might be adversely affected, for . . . this stigma would be extended to the personnel in the CS rating . . . (and) they would be guilty by association."[28] This statement clearly demonstrates a concern over the possibility of Caucasian demoralization while recognizing that simply changing the title is replacing one social problem with another.

The worry behind this proposal being perceived as a "smokescreen or a coverup" reflects the navy's concern with its public image regarding its race relations during the 1960s. Based upon information found in other official documents in correspondence about the Filipino steward problem, it is quite evident that the U.S. Navy was attempting to shield from public scrutiny the negative image surrounding its practice of racialized labor. Some firmly believed that there was nothing disdainful about a mostly nonwhite servant labor force while they still worried about the image it projected to the outside: "If the image of the Steward and the duties performed are held in distain [sic], this attitude must come from *outside the Navy*, for all personnel in the rating are volunteers, know the rating title, and the duties performed before entering the rating."[29] Again, this has been refuted by early Filipino steward recruits who maintain they were not told by recruiters that they would be permanent personal servants. In another memorandum, the Bureau of Naval Personnel suggests that the policy change should be publicized as an attempt to merely restructure its entire food-service approach rather than addressing a social problem, thus diverting outside attention away from the issue of racialized labor: "That assuming adequate publicity, it will be made evident that the

Navy is taking action to analyze the whole functional area of food service and is not "zeroing in" on the Steward rating alone. This approach would also tend to minimize, if not eliminate altogether, any connotation that we are being pressured into a review of our policies relative to the Steward rating specifically. It would also provide a rational basis for making any desired changes."[30]

The navy fully recognized that the presence of brown-skinned servants among its lowest rating was a glaring publicity problem amid the high tide of liberalism during the 1960s. As explicitly stated in the above quote, the navy wanted to avoid the public appearance of being "pressured"—whether by Filipino stewards, outside critics, or both—into reexamining its servant problem. The desired effect was to maintain an appearance of administrative restructuring, not a deliberate effort at personnel reform provoked by moral opprobrium from within and without.

The concern with public image was connected not only with domestic issues during the civil rights era but also internationally during the Cold War. As earlier discussed, the U.S. state worried about its national image before the international community as it fought a pitched ideological battle with the U.S.S.R. Accusations of racism emanating from Moscow could not be countered as crudely propagandistic, for it was in plain view that the self-appointed leader of the Free World, in its historical past and present reality, did not extend its precepts and practices of freedom and equality toward its own racial minorities. The stewardship tradition in the navy was just one instance of this time-honored practice. Furthermore, the state institution of the U.S. Navy and its race-based policies shared a history with private capitalism's racialization of menial "cheap labor," a practice also deeply embedded in American history.[31] Many of the official navy documents addressing the steward problem display a defensive posture in reaction to communist condemnatory rhetoric. Navy officials indeed recognized that the steward problem itself may very well serve as fodder for North Vietnam propaganda during the Vietnam War; as expressed in one official Navy document: "America has been accused of racial prejudice and bias by Asians, particularly in Vietnam. Racially segregated entertainment facilities exist there as in other Asiatic areas. *North Vietnamese propaganda that identifies the steward branch with this unfavorable image probably exists.*"[32]

While some documents reflect the authors' skepticism of the steward-rate change proposal based upon its superficiality, others evince a discernible measure of incredulity toward the notion of stewardship being connected to racialized labor. T. E. White, director of mess management facility, implies in a memorandum that while the steward rating indeed comprises mostly non-

Caucasians, this fact has no necessary connection to discriminatory rating policy. White argues: "The fact that the steward's rating is non-Caucasian continually amazes everyone who is interested in this very important segment of the Navy. Well over 100 American Caucasians try to enter the rate each year but are rebuffed at Great Lakes and San Diego." In White's reasoning, minority presence within the steward rating should not be explained by the supposed negative perception held by Caucasians about its servile nature. The fact that whites themselves (however small in number) have served as stewards in the past and continue to seek entry into the rating, according to White, is a counterargument to the charge that stewardship is relegated to minorities due to racial discrimination. Obscured from this controversy, he points out, is that Caucasians have actively sought positions within the rating only to be "rebuffed" from entering. A conclusion drawn from this observation, he seems to believe, is that Caucasians must not deem the job as belonging to "servants" and "flunkies." White maintains that it is naval bureaucracy itself that has ossified the rating as a minority one—as mentioned above, a verbal policy followed at recruit training centers disallowed Caucasian entry into the steward branch. White argues: "The rating name and structure is not the reason why American citizens did not seek the rating. The reason is that BuPers has attempted to keep this a non-Caucasian rating." To further reinforce his argument, White decides to include personal statements in his memorandum from non-Filipinos (including a rare white steward) regarding the attractiveness of the steward's job due to its supposedly meritocratic structure for all races. Among White's chosen comments below, since the last testimony is marked as "Caucasian," it is reasonable to assume the other comments were taken from African American stewards.

> SDC Charles H. Reed, USN: "I made Chief Steward in 1967 and I feel I have more opportunity to make E8 or 9 than ever before." SDC Harry C. Hickson, Jr., USN: "The steward's rating structure is open and any man who will open his books and study can make his rate. I am proud to be a young Navy Chief, I made the rate in 1967." TN Eric A. Mahnerd (Caucasian) stationed at Dallas with a B.S. Degree in Speech and English from Mankato State College: "I enjoy the working conditions of a Navy steward and find it an interesting and challenging job."[33]

Contrasting White's argument that the steward rating was not discriminatory as proven by prior examples of white sailors interested in the steward rating, the authors of other memorandums express a felt need to increase the presence of Caucasian sailors into the rating as a corrective to the reality of discriminatory practice. The best way for this to happen was through the enhancement of its image and desirability among white recruits through the use of a vigorous public information campaign. The selling point: that stewardship prepared the white sailor for a lucrative postnavy profession in the expanding food-service industry. This strategy, moreover, could effectively disarm those inclined toward complaint regarding the menial aspects of the job. As stated in the memorandum: "For those who do not intend to make the Navy a career, the experience gained by serving in a wardroom or in the general mess could be a valuable stepping stone to a profitable food service career. A knowledge of the above facts will also help preclude such complaints as "being sold a bill of goods" by the new steward who reports aboard and is initially assigned some of the more menial tasks in the wardroom."[34]

The solution advanced in this document advocates not only the aforementioned merger of stewardship and commissaryman but also recommends the formation of a new serviceman apprenticeship in addition to the already existing fireman and seaman; this new category would include Filipino sailors within its ranks. As the authors express: "[The new apprenticeship] would obviate the contention that there is discrimination in the relegation of a racial group to one rating, as well as possibly reducing future requests for changes of rating from Filipinos." At another point in the memo, the authors argue that "the principal advantage derived is the removal of the 'segregation' label from the SD [steward] rating and its combination with another group performing similar tasks"; additionally, it "may serve to heighten the sense of job identification."[35]

A noticeable trend when studying BuPers correspondence relevant to the Filipino servant problem is the navy's concern about the Filipino servant problem increasing incrementally through the passing years. During the early 1960s, the problem was acknowledged obliquely, ultimately framed as a bureaucratic burden. Through the ensuing years, one detects the growing urgency behind the servant problem. By the late 1960s, it was frontally addressed as a social problem whose urgency could not be ignored, as stated in the correspondence below: "The steward rating is afflicted with several crucial root problems which impact in many areas outside the rating itself. It is a chronically sick rating, now dying from the bottom, stagnated at the top, and racially unbalanced. Of greater concern is the stigma of menial duties, and charges that stewards are simply personal servants for navy officers, with unsatisfactory racial and colonialistic overtones."[36] The urgency redolent in these two sentences is hardly found in earlier official documents. As seen in a different memorandum: "I believe we are on the threshold of a crisis and need to face up now to some of the shoals ahead on our present course. The fact remains that the connotations of servility presently associated with the SD rating are incompatible with social attitudes of today."[37]

It is revealing that growing realization of the "colonialistic" nature of stewardship directly relates to Filipino stewards; as the excerpt acknowledges, Filipino complaint, it is evident, has reached the attention of naval officials-cum-reformers.

With the proposed elimination of segregated mess duty, the navy's next concern was to pursue the civilianization of its mess-related duties within its shore facilities, as other military branches had already done. The hiring of contract messmen was the beginning of the end of mess duty performed by enlisted men, although certainly not abolished upon naval ships overseas, where no civilians were permitted. In a *Navy Times* article, published March 10, 1971, in anticipation of such change, civilianization was announced to its readership as a solution that was administrative—not racial—in nature: "The end of mess cooking means that each year, 180,000 non-rated sailors will be freed for more important jobs and for the fleet up to three months or more earlier."[38] Yet, it appears that even the civilianization of mess duty did not mean that the navy had finally found an egalitarian basis for its most undesirable jobs, as suggested in the same article: "Many women are in the messman program, a large number of them military-dependents. The part-time nature of most of the jobs makes the work ideal for mothers who have children in school. 'Women are a major factor in the improvement of service,' says Mr. James Zucco, who monitors the contract messman project for NSO [Navy Subsistence Office]. 'A gal tends to clean up as she goes along while men are inclined to let it wait and do it all at one time.'"[39]

The Myth of Filipino Passivity

The years of servile labor did not spawn a fatalistic outlook for many Filipino sailors but, rather, increased their zeal in their struggle for equality. Indeed, the cumulative result of their acts of resistance, as described earlier, would be the overturning of official naval policy regarding discriminatory rating policy, a change hardly anticipated by early naval policymakers in their reduction of Filipino recruits as foreign workers abiding by an economic logic dictating upward mobility at any cost. Lost in this reductionism was the capacity of Filipino sailors to press their claims toward more equitable inclusion, to participate in a counterhegemonic culture of protest that would culminate with the change in the navy's policy regarding servant privileges to naval officers, a tradition that hearkened back to the very beginning of

U.S. naval history. Thus, contrary to earlier misleading depictions of Asian workers in America as passive victims of exploitation, Filipino sailors were living counterexamples to such narratives of passive victimization. As shown within archival findings discussed in this chapter, the result of this disobedience led the navy to finally seek a solution to its Filipino servant problem, a predicament involving issues of unofficial racial discrimination, exploitative labor, abuse of authority, and Filipino insubordination, as well as growing outside criticism.

CHAPTER SIX

Achieving the American Dream

One day while aboard his ship, Paulie Paligutan overheard a first-class petty officer complaining about his impending appointment to the Philippines. Home to the biggest military installations outside the United States, the islands served an important logistical function during the Vietnam War, a conflict then escalating with each passing year. An idea formed in Paulie's mind. Still missing his homeland, Paulie made a proposition to the first-class petty officer: why not trade assignments? The white sailor, openly expressing trepidation at serving in a war zone, happily accepted the proposal. Paulie now found himself back in the Philippines in 1968, although the tradeoff meant being sent to Vietnam.

These were turbulent years in America's history, marked by antiwar protest, student revolt, racial turmoil, and generational friction. Especially after the 1968 Tet Offensive, the United States was immersed in a war whose public support began to unravel. Due to the divisive political nature of the war, there were two Americas at this time: "Amerika" and "America—love it or leave it." Furthermore, Paulie and his family were living in a society undergoing a sea change in its racial relations. With the passage of the civil rights acts, American society began its atonement for its racial sins of the past as expressed in the expurgation of legal segregation. Even the nation's most cherished institutions, such as the U.S. military, were affected by the systematic dismantling of U.S. segregation. Under close scrutiny by outsiders, the navy's public relations recognized its own race-based policies had now reached their terminal point.

Despite the monumental importance of the navy's and coast guard's changes in policy, Paulie's agonizing over the lack of upward promotion had since withered away after his promotion with the help of now-Captain Randall, a man he considered as his benefactor. Paulie was now a first-class commissaryman, a rare thing among Filipino sailors. At the same time, however, it was precisely this promotion in rating that brought him to the open seas of Vietnam, in combat against an Asian people proclaimed as the enemies of freedom and democracy. Despite the brutality of war on the ground, Paulie recalls his stint in Vietnam in terms of adventure and at times even leisure. The main tasks of his ship, the USCG cutter *Blackhaw*, were to patrol the waters and rig buoys. Skirmishes and firefights periodically erupted between his ship and the Viet Cong, although this was hardly a daily episode. The enemy that fired upon them was rarely seen, rendered invisible by the thicket of the surrounding mangroves. The "navy" of North Vietnam, he humorously recalls, hardly deserved the name, since it comprised rickety outriggers manned by men in shorts and sandals, armed with primitive weapons. Clearly, the most brutal fighting was taking place not on the seas but in the rice fields, hamlets, and small villages of the inland regions of the country.

It would be many years later that Paulie would discover that his two-year stint in Vietnam was not as inconsequential as he initially believed. For it was during his stay at the navy station in Cat Lo, Vietnam, that he was exposed to experimental chemicals and herbicides sprayed over the landscape. The purpose was to defoliate the surroundings of the "invisible enemy" and deprive them of cover while forcing rural populations to flee toward urban areas, thus depriving them of rural support. Agent Orange was a deliberate form of chemical and herbicidal warfare whose effects would be felt by both friend and foe. Decades later, Paulie suffered from chronic diabetes and other illnesses causally related to Agent Orange exposure, and the Veterans Administration conferred him with a 100 percent service-related disability. Yet despite acknowledging the etiological connection between Agent Orange and his diabetic condition, the U.S. government waited until 2004 to award compensation.

After his service in Vietnam, Paulie's next assignment was in Baltimore, Maryland, in June 1970. As a new immigrant in America, Paulie's wife, Cecilia, was mostly deprived of the dreams and expectations she initially held of American life—the accoutrements and material possessions she associated with the so-called affluent society of Cold War American society. Early in her life, Cecilia had a cosseted upbringing due to her status as the youngest child. The status quo that characterized her life as a teacher of higher status (teachers are esteemed in Philippine society) to that of a sailor's wife in America was upended. Her new life in America centered on the responsibilities of marriage and motherhood, as well as unexpected financial austerity punctuated by prolonged episodes of loneliness when her husband was gone for months at a time. Alone in a strange country, she began to question the prevalent naïve belief held by most Filipinos that America was a place where all the problems of life were solved.

Now with a family of four children, Paulie felt it necessary to seek housing outside the naval base, and in the town of Glen Burnie he was able to find a decent-sized house in a quiet neighborhood. His return from combat duty in Vietnam, however, did little to efface the mark of foreign Otherness. As they were still settling into their new house, Cecilia received a disturbing phone call while her husband as at work. An anonymous caller with a menacing tone warned her that "Japs" were not allowed in their neighborhood and that their house would be burned down if they didn't move out. Frantically, Cecilia called her husband at work. The anonymous threat to burn his new house and harm his family was met with sincere concern by a commanding officer, who assured Paulie that the matter would be handled. As more threats followed the next several days, Paulie began to consider moving out of Glen Burnie back to the security of the naval base. Suddenly the phone calls stopped. A few days later, a friendly neighbor mentioned to him a "strange event" that just happened in the neighborhood: a group of investigators went around several blocks interviewing neighbors about a certain "urgent" situation. "Do you know what this was about?" the neighbor asked. Feigning ignorance, Paulie realized that these mysterious investigators were the likely reason why the racist threats suddenly ended.

Paulie and Cecilia decided early on that their children were going to be fully "American." For them, this entailed a specific approach to the way they would raise their children. Their native language of Tagalog was never taught to them. Although certain native values and cultural practices were inculcated from the beginning—Catholicism, extended family (compadrazgo), and filial obedience—both parents were hardly critical of specifically American attitudes and behavior their children learned and displayed via their interaction with other American kids. In fact, two meals during dinner were often prepared: Filipino dishes for the parents, American ones for the children. For Paulie and Cecilia, assimilation was understood as the loss of native culture, a necessary price to pay—or so they assumed—in order for the children to become fully American.

Paulie's rejection of a more "hyphenated identity" for his children is perhaps more understandable if one remembers the institutional obstacles and individual prejudices he particularly faced as a first-generation immigrant. He reasoned that if success is to be obtained in America, then the impediments he himself faced as a stranger in American society—the barriers of language, culture, worldview—must be removed as much as possible. Indeed, for Paulie, his new American dream was for one of his sons to ascend to the rank of officer in the U.S. military. He tried to impart this early upon his eldest son, buying him books about famous generals, driving him to visit the U.S. Coast Guard Academy in New London, and encouraging him to excel in school. After his earliest years in America shining shoes for officers as a steward, he dreamed that one day a white enlisted man would shine the shoes of his son, an officer in the U.S. military.

During the last years of his life, Paulie Paligutan claimed that he was not disappointed that the American Dream he envisioned for his son never materialized. This was because his son ended up writing a PhD dissertation about his father's years as a steward in the U.S. Coast Guard. Perhaps *this* was his son's fate in America. "If it's yours, then it was meant to be."

Due to the efforts of a sympathetic officer, Paulie was able to expand his range of experiences in the United States compared to his earlier plight as a steward. For his promotion not only allowed him to request stationing in the Philippines (which was denied to most stewards) and thus experience combat duty in Vietnam but, more important, it opened a new avenue in his life with the ability to marry and raise a family in America. As mentioned, Paulie's fortune was more the exception than the rule—the majority of Filipino stewards would have to persevere until the navy's eradication of the steward rating, an accomplishment precipitated by Filipino resistance.

The initial attempts at solving the servant problem considered recourses beyond the actual lifting of rating strictures placed upon Filipino nationals in the U.S. Navy and Coast Guard. Initially perceived (or perhaps more accurately, disguised) as an "administrative" problem rather than a racial one, a number of policymakers at the top command apparently maintained a posture of relative indifference regarding the obvious racial dimension involved, for, as mentioned by the historian John Sherwood, "admirals adored their Filipino stewards and could not envision a Navy without them."[1] It would take the headstrong ambitions of a young, liberal Chief of Naval Operations, Admiral Elmo "Bud" Zumwalt, to will the initial problem-solving efforts of naval officialdom into formal policy. Unlike his predecessors, Zumwalt did not avoid the fact that the navy's personnel problems were glaringly racial. Due to his efforts, Filipinos were granted the freedom to move into other ratings other than mess-related duties by 1973—no longer would Filipino navy men be consigned to sailing second class.[2]

The end of race-related discrimination of Filipinos in the U.S. military opened doors of opportunity as immigrants in America. In spite of the radically migratory nature of their early lives aboard war vessels, these Filipinos were eventually able to gain citizenship, serve in Vietnam, raise families, and enjoy the status advancement, material acquisition, and relative economic security that many feel would not be possible had they not enlisted in the U.S. military. Restitution for their virtual servitude, for the most part, is not on their minds during their retirement years. Indeed, for many Filipino sailors settling in the United States, it would be the formation of family and the chances available to their children that serve as the best restitution for their early struggles as servants in the U.S. Navy and Coast Guard.

Zumwalt's Reforms

In his autobiography, Zumwalt recounts a key episode early in his naval career that led him to reconsider the navy's treatment of minorities. As with all commanders of navy vessels, Zumwalt enjoyed the luxury of personal service provided by a Filipino steward. Zumwalt thought highly of this young sailor due to his exemplary hard work and enthusiasm. Like virtually all Filipino navy men, the frustrated steward longed for rating advancement, prompting him to ask Zumwalt for help. Without hesitation, the young naval officer contacted the Bureau of Naval Personnel (BuPers), only to confront unnecessary resistance and red tape. This surprised and eventually dismayed the young officer, and it was only after applying a considerable amount of unanticipated pressure and extra work that Zumwalt succeeded in securing the Filipino steward a rating outside of stewardship. Later, upon transferring his command to another ship, Zumwalt experienced similar difficulty in his attempt to help still another deserving Filipino steward with advancement, again entailing extraneous effort that was "embarrassing and uncalled for," to use his own words.[3] This only reinforced a growing suspicion that the navy's discrimination of minorities was much deeper than he initially believed it to be. In the future, the "Admiral of Naval Reform" would readily single out such episodes involving hard-working yet resentful Filipino stewards as epiphanic: "[It] taught me a healthy contempt for bureaucracy and for institutional racism in the Navy."[4]

Driven by such experiences reflecting the reality of institutional racism within his beloved navy, Zumwalt eventually gained recognition as a zealous reformer who eliminated deeply entrenched racial discrimination once being appointed chief of naval operations (CNO) in 1970. His sweeping reforms encompassed not only the eradication of institutional racism but of institutional sexism, as well. Moreover, Zumwalt gained notoriety in his attempt to liberalize the navy's attitude and policies toward enlisted men, a move that accorded with the spirit of the age during the 1960s and 1970s.

Zumwalt's life narrative describing his liberal upbringing and his rapid ascendancy within the navy's ranks provides more than a clue as to why such changes should not be surprising. Born and raised in Tulare, a racially mixed town in the San Joaquin Valley in California, he grew up with and made friends with a considerable number of minority children. His parents, both medical doctors, were apparently quite progressive in their outlook on race and imparted such views to their children. Zumwalt would openly profess throughout his career his core belief that skin color had no relevancy whatsoever in his judgment of others.[5]

During World War II, Zumwalt demonstrated ample evidence of bravery and leadership, while his exceptional intellectual ability was evinced when serving under the wing of Secretary of the Navy Paul Nitze after the war. Such exceptionalism led Zumwalt to the top of the navy's chain of command once promoted as full admiral and eventually chief of naval operations at the atypical young age of forty-nine. Earlier, Zumwalt shared Nitze's vocal opposition to American intervention in Indochina;[6] by 1970 he found himself in charge of the nation's naval forces entangled in a conflict that seemed more and more unwinnable not only militarily but also in terms of popular support at home.

The rising antiwar sentiment converged with the navy's well-known conservative reticence toward institutional reform in precipitating a very serious personnel problem, which, in turn, contributed to a public-image problem for the navy. With increasing pressure emanating from outside scrutiny as well as plummeting reenlistment rates, then Secretary of the Navy John Chafee realized that a fundamental rethinking of the naval career was necessary; he recognized that Zumwalt's liberal outlook, younger age, and administrative skills made him a prime candidate to institute radical changes in the effort to leave its more encrusted traditions behind. To quote Zumwalt: "[Secretary Chafee and the Nixon administration] wanted a non-aviator as CNO for the first time in nine years, and . . . they also wanted someone younger than the norm in order to help bring the Navy 'into the modern age.'"[7] The phrase "modern age" is revealing: evidently the U.S. Navy, perennially marching behind the other military branches in terms of reform, finally decided that it could no longer ignore its internal dysfunctions.

As CNO, Zumwalt famously issued a series of official pronouncements that later became known as "Z-grams." These were messages addressed to the entire fleet, whose purpose was to address four fields of reform: personal behavior—such as dress, grooming, and so on—in order to align the navy's policies with the social mores of the time, operational schedules that would allow sailors to spend more time with their families, delegation of more opportunities and advancements for enlisted men, and most important, the eradication of the navy's "silent but real" discriminatory policies based upon race and gender.[8] Given the liberal slant of these reforms, it is not surprising that Zumwalt met considerable resistance from the navy's more conservative personnel, some criticizing them as "ZWIs" (Zumwalt's wild ideas—an acronym originating from his command in Vietnam) that purportedly served to fragment the navy's authority structure rather than improve it. These conservative barriers failed to stem the admiral's tenacity in pushing the tide of reform during the early 1970s. Paramount concern, he believed, should be focused upon the navy's personnel problem over its military capabilities, a problem that could be easily addressed through lifting the unnecessarily draconian policies lending evidence to the navy's image problems. Zumwalt describes his viewpoint: "Here were patriotic men who understood the need to fight and who fought very well, men of the kind the Navy most needed to attract and keep, who were ready to quit because of the high-and-mighty tone the Navy took toward their personal habits and tastes and their individual needs."[9]

On November 10, 1972, Zumwalt issued the well-known Z-gram 57, a directive addressing the "the elimination of the demeaning and abrasive regulations" pertaining to the enlisted man's personal behavior. Traditional policies applying to personnel grooming and dress were changed in toleration of cultural currents of the times. Suddenly, a change was evident in the typical navy man's appearance—longer hair, sideburns, mustaches, and beards were now allowed, and "modern" civilian clothes were no longer prohibited. While to some, such reforms bordered on triviality—or, in the navy's own phrase, "Mickey Mouse"—Zumwalt was keenly aware of how such reforms could work wonders on morale due to earlier similar experimentation he had conducted while commanding a ship. Against the wishes of some atop the naval high command, Zumwalt actively sought out public channels to announce his reforms, a move that eventually landed him on the cover of *Time* magazine. The strategy of widespread media exposure, he believed, was considered vital in spreading the word of a new "mod navy" that has moved beyond its image as a "humorless, tradition-bound, starchy institution owned by and operated for the benefit of white males."[10] Indeed, with his increasing visibility in the public eye, it was plain to see that the admiral was setting an example by wearing his sideburns at the longest length allowed by his own navy regulation.

Zumwalt's reforms reached beyond the establishment of the navy's "new look"; more important was his determination to institute a "new complexion" of the navy's personnel. That is, the reform-minded admiral, in his intention to make the navy conform to society-wide changes occurring in America, was determined to eradicate the institutional discrimination faced by minority groups within the navy. Statistics at this time showed that African Americans constituted 5.5 percent of enlisted personnel and a paltry 0.7 percent of officers.[11] Such measly numbers were indeed attributable to the largely negative image of the naval career held by African Americans: a thankless job as a "chambermaid for the braid." Further official investigation and study into the navy's racial problems, overseen in large part by a bright and talented African American officer, Bill Norman, led the admiral to conclude that black discrimination was much deeper than he initially believed—evidently, black mistreatment went beyond the demeaning nature of the jobs, prevailing in practically all aspects of African American life in the navy.[12] Details known to all black navy men—discriminatory work conditions, de facto segregation, white disrespect of the rare black officer, the difficulty of black navy men in finding housing outside the base, the cultural neglect of blacks in their preferences (music, clothing, grooming products, etc.) within naval stores, among others—lent support not only to black negative perceptions of the naval career but also to Zumwalt's uncommon stance that the navy's personnel problems were more pressing than its military ones. As Zumwalt now saw it, racial reforms, a consideration managing to elude priority since the navy's very inception, should no longer be confined to the navy's bottom drawer.

Zumwalt's goal to eradicate African American discrimination required another prior change in the navy's rating policy, according to Norman, Zumwalt's righthand man during such reforms. Norman felt strongly that before such broad sweeping changes being discussed between them could be implemented, a particular policy change needed to precede all others, as explained by historian Sherwood:

> In essence, Norman wanted to test the seriousness of the new CNO's commitment to equal opportunity by making two very significant demands of his potential boss. First he wanted Zumwalt to commit himself to weekly meetings with Norman. Second, he wanted Zumwalt to slay one of the Navy's most sacred cows—the predominance of Filipinos in the steward rating. . . . Because of Filipinos' renowned efficiency and skill as messman and stewards, many of the Navy's admirals adored their Filipino stewards and could not envision a Navy without them. Maintaining a racially segregated rating, however, could not continue if Zumwalt was serious about reforming equal opportunity in the Navy.[13]

Norman rightfully judged the segregation of Filipinos within the steward rating, notwithstanding the "adoration" supposedly manifest in the admiral/

steward relation, as symptomatic of a larger problem of systemic discrimination and segregation.[14] Thus both reformers reached common ground in their goals of eradicating naval policies entailing the differential inclusion of Filipinos within the U.S. Navy—a necessary condition before more wide-sweeping racial reforms were to take place.

Guided by a newfound zeal furnished by Norman's experiential knowledge and research findings, Zumwalt's firm insistence upon racial reform became official with the issuance of Z-66, "Equal Opportunity in the Navy," on December 17, 1970. Twenty-two years after President Truman's command to desegregate the U.S. military, Zumwalt put into motion not simple reform but institutional change. The unprecedented approach found with Z-66 is not exactly located with the proposals to eliminate discrimination while recognizing the needs of racial minorities in the U.S. Navy;[15] rather, it is found with Zumwalt's insistence upon a specific date—set at January 15, 1971—by which such goals were to be realized. Described by Zumwalt as the "most heartfelt" of all his 121 Z-grams, the document expresses his sincere concern for the plight of minority sailors while underscoring the urgency of institutional change, often tinting his remarks with personal sentiment. In Z-66, Zumwalt addresses the myriad of everyday problems faced by minority sailors: occupational discrimination, housing discrimination outside the base, lack of minority representation, neglect of black cultural needs, and so forth. Importantly, the admiral specifically emphasizes the need for "communication avenues" among all minority groups to be established with the goal of minimizing friction among different ethnic groups. This entailed the firm commitment of naval bureaucracy to handle the specific issues and problems pertaining to racial relations, an unprecedented move that set apart Zumwalt's changes from earlier naval attempts to deal with internal race matters. Immediately in January 1971, Norman was appointed director of the CNO advisory committee on race relations and minority affairs, a ground-breaking committee tasked with the duty to "evaluate, coordinate, and advise" the CNO on "all matters concerning race relations and minority affairs policies and programs in the Navy."[16] As described by Sherwood in his book *Black Sailor, White Navy*, the claim of "sweeping reform" is deserving, for it led not only to the navy's commitment of racial equality but eventually toward policies of affirmative action.

Admiral Zumwalt's staunch effort to finally abolish the practice of minority servicemen "sailing second class" (to use his own term) forced the navy to conform to the letter of the law regarding the desegregation of the U.S. Armed Forces proclaimed by Truman's Executive Order 9981 in 1948. That it took more than twenty years for the navy to catch up with the other branches of the military reflects a reticent attitude and stubborn resistance in the face of progressive change. Zumwalt's Z-66 effectively collapsed the institutional boundaries that were erected within the navy whose purpose related to racial compartmentalization. Zumwalt's last sentences of Z-66 echoes his vision of a new navy: "Ours must be a Navy family that recognizes no artificial boundaries of race, color, or religion. There is no black Navy, no white Navy—just one Navy—the U.S. Navy."[17]

Epilogue

An antiquated tradition, one that the navy clung to even in the civil rights era, was finally amended. Now bolstered by unexpected pressure from the Philippine government,[1] Filipinos were permitted to enter other occupational ratings by 1971. Immediately upon implementing the new policy, Filipino nationals served in fifty-six of the eighty-seven ratings available for enlistees.[2] The steward rating itself would soon run into the shoals. External criticism emanating from Philippine government officials complaining of the exploitation of Filipino citizens would persist through the first half of the decade. Domestically, the U.S. Congress would encounter the steward problem as a national issue. In Senate meetings, the prominent Wisconsin senator William Proxmire critiqued naval officers as such: they "get up in the morning to put on clothes pressed by stewards, shoes shined by stewards, all laid out in proper order. They eat at home with food cooked by stewards and then are driven to work or elsewhere by these same men."[3] Proxmire did not omit, furthermore, the fact that racialized steward labor left the navy subject to charges of overt racism and imperialism.[4] Such criticism left the navy no seeming option but to terminate the steward rating by December 1974. A new rating, mess management specialist (MS), which combined the duties affiliated with messmen with commissaryman ratings, was launched, minus the duties self-described by the navy as "hotel duties" affiliated with naval stewards.

Most of the subjects in this work rose swiftly up the occupational hierarchy, eventually holding positions of greater responsibility and authority. Paulie Paligutan, for example, eventually rose to the rate of senior chief, becoming accustomed to giving orders rather than receiving them. Although Bert

Amano's earliest tasks as a steward were to clean the officers' wardroom, decades later he would be allowed privileged access to the officers' living spaces, rising to the rank of warrant officer before his retirement. These Filipinos chose to dedicate their professional lives to the U.S. Navy, in spite of the discriminatory conditions they initially faced.

In their retirement years, these men reflected upon their early times of struggle with an admixture of nostalgia and humor, although vestiges of frustration and resentment occasionally caused their voices to quaver or pulses to quicken. For these men the best form of "revenge" existed in the future—their children's successes in America would be proof that their struggles were worth enduring. Paligutan often held this thought while shining officers' shoes: "Since I was a steward, my first aim, if I have a son [and] if he's smart enough, I'm going to send him to the academy, so that somebody will shine his shoes. Because I've been shining shoes for a long time."[5] Decades after their unrespected positions as navy servants, these Filipinos stressed to their children the virtue of education as a key to life with less struggle. Paul Maestre remembers being unable to hold back tears upon hearing his son's name announced at his college graduation ceremony, especially remembering his own early life of sacrifice in America.

Notwithstanding Tony Javier's description of the steward's tasks as "kind of a woman's job," these men were able to "recuperate their masculinity" as they were finally enabled to move into specialty ratings. Javier realized later in his life that he was a "better man," since he was able to endure the indignities of the job.[6] To once again quote Lucio Pontanares's remembrance of his navy years: "I have no regrets, really. I am vindicated of all these things I did. I give the navy twenty-two solid years. . . . All I wanted . . . [was] not to be a great man but a real man, so to say."[7] Yet, if greatness is measured not only by the attainment of a life far surpassing expectations but also in playing a crucial role in effecting institutional change in America, then these men embody the very definition of greatness.

Notes

Introduction

1. Gary Okihiro, *Columbia Guide to Asian American History*, 7. For a history of this settler immigration group, see Marina Espina, *Filipinos in Louisiana*.

2. Jynnah Radford and Abby Budiman, "2016, Foreign-Born Population." Pew Research, www.pewresearch.org.

3. Conceived during the pinnacle of European imperialism, the Western ideology of Orientalism views the world as divided into two compartments—the East (Orient) and the West (Occident)—while positing essentialist and unchanging stereotypes about the Orient. These stereotypes apply to supposedly ahistorical Oriental gender traits—such as the submissive, seductive Oriental woman and the effeminate, passive Oriental man.

4. In this context, I use the term "metaphysics" in a particular sense found in traditional Western philosophy: the positing of an unchanging "essence" to a particular thing—or to use Aristotle's phrase, "being as such." In essential terms, past lawmakers, commentators, and historians defined the "racial being" of the United States as a white nation. In the service of ascribing a racial essence, the homology of America and "whiteness" naturalized the historical presence of Asians (and other racial minorities) as an absence. Of course, such attempts to locate essential and ahistorical qualities of America predate the contemporary view of nations as social constructions—"imagined communities" to use Benedict Anderson's well-known term.

5. The term "reclamation" in the scholarly production of histories has become shorthand for a methodological approach whereby the scholar purports to uncover the "buried" histories of past peoples heretofore ignored, forgotten, or marginalized by mainstream tradition. Despite its crucial importance, the project of reclamation is not immune to criticism, specifically insofar as the term presupposes a degree of objective solidity to a "buried past" of historical discourse—thus, the elision of what

remains "suppressed and irretrievable," according to the scholar Laura Hyun Yi Kang. See Kang, *Compositional Subjects*, 90–91.

6. Yen Le Espiritu, *Home Bound*, 5.

7. Although economics is an inescapable dimension in U.S. expansionism, this work rejects economistic interpretations of expansionism, but instead interprets expansionism as an overdetermined historical phenomenon involving cultural, political, and racial aspects as well.

8. Gilbert G. Gonzalez, *Guest Workers or Colonized Labor?*

9. Pierrette Hondagneu-Sotelo, *Gendered Transitions*.

10. Espiritu, *Home Bound*, 25. While Espiritu appropriates transnational theory as a conceptual tool, she cautions scholars of the danger in decontextualizing immigration from structures of global inequality, such as colonialism and globalization.

11. Catherine Ceniza Choy, *Empire of Care*.

12. Dorothy Fujita-Rony, *American Workers*.

13. For region-based studies of Filipino American communities, see Dawn Mabalon, *Little Manila Is in the Heart*; Rick Bonus, *Locating Filipino Americans*; Espiritu, *Home Bound*.

14. JoAnna Poblete, *Islanders in the Empire*.

15. Choy, *Empire of Care*, 11.

16. In his "benevolent assimilation" proclamation issued in December 1898, President William McKinley formally announced the intention of the United States of seizing control of the Philippines, thus establishing the islands as ceded territory. The term itself conceals the imperialistic nature of American intervention while couching colonization as an act of good will. American rhetoric framed benevolent assimilation as a civilizing mission whose intention was to uplift Filipinos toward the highest ideals of civilization.

17. Bonus, *Locating Filipino Americans*. The process known as "reterritorialization" is a vital component of transnational immigration studies, whereby immigrants engage in restructuring the spaces of inhabitation primarily through their material culture; reterritorialized space is often cited as one where immigrant agency is restored.

18. Paul Gilroy, *Black Atlantic*, 16. I owe the theoretical connection of naval ships with Gilroy's "chronotopes" to Steven McKay, in his essay "Filipino Sea Men: Identity and Masculinity in a Global Labor Niche," found in Rhacel Parreñas and Lok C. D. Siu, *Asian Diasporas*, 63–64.

19. While the term "deterritorialization" has become polyvalent as academic jargon since its original conception (Deleuze and Guattari), in this work it is utilized in a more straightforward sense: economic, social, and/or cultural transcendence beyond spatial boundaries, especially those of the nation-state.

20. E. San Juan Jr., *Philippine Temptation*, 105.

21. Fujita-Rony, *American Workers*, 91–95.

22. Proceso Ada Paligutan, interview by author, 2003. The tape and digital recordings of all interviews of all interviewees are in the author's possession.

23. Kale Fajardo, *Filipino Crosscurrents*, 77.

24. Robyn Magalit Rodriguez, *Migrants for Export*.

25. Valerie Francisco-Menchavez, *Labor of Care*.

26. This particular claim appropriates the Foucauldian notion of "technologies of power" situated within the colonial milieu, a disciplinary regime functioning in the "interpellation" (to borrow an Althusserian phrase) of the colonial native—that is, the formation of colonial subjects via their responsive actions toward colonial ideological apparatuses. Interpellation, however, was not an inexorable process—it is not suggested that Filipino colonials as rational agents lacked the capacity to resist such technologies of power.

27. Parreñas, *Servants of Globalization*. The second edition, published in 2015, of Parreñas's book includes a new chapter on male domestic workers in Rome and Los Angeles. For another study of the labor diaspora of Filipina domestic workers and other nationalities into "global cities," see Nicole Constable, *Maid to Order in Hong Kong*.

28. Hondagneu-Sotelo, *Doméstica*, 17–18.

29. Evelyn Nakano Glenn, *Issei, Nisei, War Bride*, 168.

30. While the term "bachelor society" common in older works of Asian American history is rightfully criticized for its connotation of privilege affixed to Asian American males as historical agents while bracketing the crucial importance of Asian American women, it is used advisedly in this study because during this time, as dictated by U.S. policy, the presence of women in the military was not found aboard the strictly homosocial spaces of U.S. Navy and Coast Guard vessels. Certainly, I am not implying that Filipina women who were wives, daughters, and family members in this migratory flow were of marginal importance.

31. Richard Miller, *Messman Chronicles*. For another incisive analysis of African American labor exploitation and racial unrest in the U.S. Navy, see John Darrell Sherwood, *Black Sailor, White Navy*.

32. Although the notion of objectivity is elusive (if not unlikely) in certain areas of the humanistic disciplines, this becomes even more pronounced within contexts of intimate personal familiarity to the scholar, especially with regard to family. For a discussion of the insider/outsider dilemma for oral histories involving family members, see Janet Wilton, "Imaging Family Memories: My Mum, Her Photographs, Our Memories," in Robert Perks and Alistair Thomson, eds., *Oral History Reader*, 268–269.

33. For a discussion regarding the tension between authorial intentionality and the interpretive biases of researchers (especially those shaped by academic interpretive frameworks), see Katherine Borland, "'That's Not What I Said': Interpretive Conflict in Oral Narrative Research," in Perks and Thomson, *Oral History Reader*, 418–420.

34. As defined by Michael Omi and Howard Winant, racial formation refers to "the *sociohistorical* process by which racial categories are created, inhabited, transformed, and destroyed" (55). Omi and Winant argue against essentialized definitions of race based on biology; rather, race is a profoundly sociohistorical process, a result of con-

stant negotiation and contestation among social forces. See Omi and Winant, *Racial Formation in the United States: From the 1960s to the 1990s* (New York: Routledge, 1994).

35. With chapter 1's emphasis on the effects of colonialism among Filipino subjects, scholars may notice that the historiography in this chapter includes both older and up-to-date works on this topic. Some older works are economistic in approach, an orientation that is criticized by many contemporary scholars as overly reductionist. Nonetheless, I have decided to appropriate certain elements in these older histories that are useful in demonstrating the economic effects of U.S. neocolonialism, especially as it relates to out-migration as a remedy to escape poverty.

36. The proclivity of exploited Filipino laborers to organize and protest—a predilection at odds with stereotypes of "Filipino passivity"—is demonstrated in Ronald Takaki, *Stranger from a Different Shore*, 152–155; further testimony is found in Craig Scharlin and Lillian Villanueva, *Philip Vera Cruz*.

37. Lloyd Prewitt qtd. in Miller, *Messman Chronicles*, 17.

38. In other instances, however, naval bureaucracy tended to frame the controversial use of Filipino stewards as an "administrative problem," rather than frontally address its racial dimension. Some naval documents reveal an effort to disguise the use of Filipino servants altogether, in full knowledge of its controversial image; hence the navy's analysis of the servant problem as a "personnel problem," rather than a racial one. This is extensively discussed in chapter 5.

Chapter 1. Colonial Past, Neocolonial Present

1. A term coined by William Taft, appointed colonial governor of Philippines, "little brown brothers" referred to America's new colonial subjects after pacification—Filipino natives. Although Filipinos were earlier referred to as "savages" before the Philippine-American War, it appears the American administrators now allowed them a degree in ascendancy in its racial hierarchy as indicated by the familial relation of "brothers."

2. A fundamental shift occurred in American foreign policy attitudes by the last decades of the nineteenth century as the nation moved from general insularity and isolationism toward internationalism. Historians point to a constellation of causal factors explaining this transition: the close of the frontier by 1890, the economic condition of overproduction, domestic social and economic crises, newfound competition with European empires, and cultural and/or racial factors related to the U.S. "civilizing mission" to spread American values abroad.

3. John O'Sullivan, "Annexation," *United States Magazine and Democratic Review* 17 (1845): 5–6, 9–10, *HathiTrust Digital Library*, 2021.

4. The historical school known as New Western History challenges the Turnerian thesis, which enjoyed currency for decades; important historical works in New West History include Patricia Limerick, *Legacy of Conquest*, and Richard White, *It's Your Misfortune and None of My Own*.

5. The period between Reconstruction and the Spanish-American War was America's industrial revolution; yet it was accompanied by social discord and problems in the forms of labor uprisings, agrarian revolt, wide social inequality, urban crowding, immigration and nativism, and economic downturn by the early 1890s. One can interpret such upheavals as the growth pains of intensive industrialization during the Gilded Age.

6. Gail Bederman, *Manliness and Civilization*, ch. 1.

7. Ibid.

8. Kristin Hoganson, *Fighting for American Manhood*, 137.

9. The term "gender frontier" is borrowed from Kathleen Brown, *Good Wives, Nasty Wenches, and Anxious Patriarchs*.

10. Hoganson, *Fighting for American Manhood*, 137. Such misinterpretations made within the "gender frontier" of the new colony not only provided evidence of a putative lack of civilization among Filipinos but also dialectically served to constitute and reinforce American constructions of manhood itself.

11. Hoganson, *Fighting for American Manhood*, 134–137.

12. "Senator Albert Beveridge Champions Philippine Colonization, 1900," in Lon Kurashige and Alice Yang Murray, eds., *Major Problems in Asian American History*, 139–142.

13. Rudyard Kipling, *White Man's Burden*. Coincidentally, Kipling's poem was published the very same day that combat first erupted in the Philippine-American War.

14. Some anti-imperialists at this time based their arguments upon a xenophobic reaction to the possibility of incorporating seven million Filipinos into the American nation. Indeed, the prevailing views of race at this time posited a cavernous gap between white Anglo-Saxons and "Orientals," and—to borrow a phrase from the English poet of Western imperialism, Rudyard Kipling—"never the 'twain shall meet."

15. Senator Beveridge's speech specifically mentioned the geostrategic importance of the "illimitable markets of China." The same year of Beveridge's speech marked the forcible opening of China's markets to the major world powers, which now included Japan and the United States.

16. Luzviminda Francisco, "Philippine-American War." The atrocities committed by U.S. troops during the Philippine-American War is further explored by Paul E. Kramer, *Blood of Government*.

17. Francisco, "Philippine-American War," 9.

18. Christopher Capozolla, *Bound by War*, 64.

19. Bruce Cumings, *Dominion from Sea to Sea*, 135.

20. Kramer, *Blood of Government*, 161.

21. Other instances of race making occurring elsewhere among America's newly acquired territories demonstrate the contingency behind racial designations of colonial subjects. Allan Punzalan Isaac shows that Puerto Ricans, by virtue of a supposed Spanish descent with only a "slight commingling of Indian blood," were thus determined by U.S. administrators as white, paving the way toward their citizenship

eligibility by 1917. This stands in contradistinction to Filipinos, who, due to their "tropical" origins and "Malay" racial stock, would remain outside of national membership. See Allan Punzalan Isaac, *American Tropic*, 28.

22. I owe the term "differential inclusion" to Espiritu, who employs it to describe the contradictory relation of Filipinos to the United States, at once excluded from the nation due to their "racial uniform" while forcibly included owing to reasons largely economic in nature—namely, the need for cheap labor. The term "differential inclusion" is appropriated throughout this work. See Espiritu, *Home Bound*, 47.

23. Daniel Immerwahr, *How to Hide an Empire*, 86.

24. Isaac, *American Tropic*, 24.

25. Lisa Lowe, *Immigrant Acts*, 13.

26. The term "second wave of occupiers" in reference to American educators brought to the islands with the war's conclusion is borrowed from Renato Constantino, "Miseducation of the Filipino," 45–47.

27. Despite the effectivity of such colonial "disciplinary mechanisms," colonial populations often sought ways—whether subtly or overtly—to subvert such knowledge or power regimes through strategies of localization and indigenization, as demonstrated in the works of scholars such as Julian Go, Vicente Rafael, and Rey Ileto. To quote Go, "This alternative scholarship on colonialism's impact . . . shows that the signs and tools of cultural power indeed permeated local societies; it is just that they were domesticated, appropriated, or indigenized in ways that tamed their otherwise powerful impact." Go, *American Empire*, 9.

28. Patricio N. Abinales and Donna J. Amoroso, *State and Society in the Philippines*, 92.

29. Teodoro Agoncillo and Milagros C. Guerrero, *History of the Filipino People*, 144.

30. Kramer, *Blood of Government*, 169.

31. Pomeroy, *American Neo-colonialism*, 43.

32. The work of Filipino nationalist and historian Renato Constantino is hardly theoretical in approach; rather, it serves as a thinly veiled polemic against the conformist-producing effects of American culture and knowledge production. It is not suggested here that Constantino's essay prefigures Foucault's reconceptualization of power. See Constantino, "Miseducation of the Filipino."

33. Constantino, *Miseducation*, 45.

34. Ibid., 47.

35. Warwick Anderson, *Colonial Pathologies*, 2.

36. Perhaps, the best example of ethnographic studies conducted as official imperial knowledge was seen in the works of the anthropologist and administrator Dean Worcester, a self-proclaimed expert on Filipino native populations both Christian and non-Christian during the early years of occupation. An examination of Worcester's photographs of Filipino non-Christian subjects especially demonstrated his treatment of Filipinos as "specimens in the colonial laboratory." Mark Rice, *Dean Worcester's Fantasy Islands*.

37. Vicente Rafael, *White Love*, 23.

38. Schirmer, "Conception and Gestation of a Neocolony," 42.

39. Ibid., 36.

40. Ibid., 36–37. For an astute analysis of how the Philippine elite landowners were able to maintain a semi-feudal political system of rulership while in collaboration with American administrators imposing American-styled democracy, see Benedict Anderson's essay, "Cacique Democracy in the Philippines: Origins and Dreams."

41. Of course, this claim should not be construed as totalizing: several prominent politicians, journalists, and businessmen opposed American imperial domination. In terms of effectivity, what is emphasized is the outcome of Philippine policy favorable to U.S. business and geopolitical interests.

42. Go, "Introduction: Global Perspectives," 6–7. Unlike Euroamerican settlement of the contiguous lands in the U.S. Western frontier, which led to the displacement of indigenous populations and the eventual territorial integration into nation (as premised on the Northwest Ordinance), the colonization of the Philippines was more administrative rather than involving settlement; it did not entail the appropriation of land nor the expulsion of the native population.

43. As opposed to Washington's experiment of direct colonialism in the Philippines, the "neocolonial experiment" was promptly launched within other territories ceded to the United States following Spain's defeat. The most conspicuous example was found with Cuba, granted independence soon after annexation, yet remaining within the tentacles of U.S. control via the passage of the Platt Amendment protecting U.S. capital while authorizing continuing American military occupation on the nominally independent country. See Stephen Shalom, *United States and the Philippines*, xv.

44. Ibid., 5–7.

45. Ibid., xiii.

46. Schirmer and Shalom, *Philippines Reader*, 87.

47. Shalom, *United States and the Philippines*, 145–146.

48. Ibid., 146. Shalom suggests that the figures of income distribution gathered at this time by the Philippine Bureau of the Census were likely understated due to the tendency of the rich to hide their income from public disclosure.

49. The term "anti-development state" is borrowed from Walden Bello, Herbert Docena, Marissa de Guzman, and Mary Lou Malig, *The Anti-Development State: The Political Economy of Permanent Crisis in the Philippines* (New York: Zed, 2004), 3–5.

50. Antonio Pido, *Pilipinos in America*, 7.

51. The interlocking relation between the military-industrial complex and U.S. full-spectrum global dominance during the post–Cold War era is uncovered by such scholars as Chalmers Johnson, *Sorrows of Empire*, and Andrew Bacevich, *American Empire*. To quote the journalist Thomas Friedman in his discussion of globalization during the 1990s: "McDonalds cannot flourish without McDonnell Douglass." Thomas Friedman, "A Manifesto for a Fast World," *New York Times Magazine*, March 28, 1999, 96.

52. Nick Cullather, *Illusions of Influence*, 2.

Chapter 2. The Navy's Search for Postcolonial Servants

1. Bureau of Naval Personnel, "Filipinos in the United States Navy."

2. Pido, *Pilipinos in America*, 60.

3. Miller, *Messman Chronicles*, 7–8.

4. In his examination of officers' preferences of messmen as related to race, Richard Miller exposes the explicit racism of high-ranking naval officers who fashioned naval policy, many of whom believed that African Americans were not as industrious, efficient, and hygienic vis-à-vis Filipinos and that, furthermore, African Americans lacked the docile quality that Filipino recruits supposedly possessed, an essentialized racial characteristic that navy officials deemed highly attractive.

5. Leonard F. Guttridge, *Mutiny*, ch. 15.

6. Jesse O. Dedmon, Secretary of Veteran Affairs, to Vice-Admiral Lewis E. Denfield, 24 January 1947, box 192, General Correspondence 1942–60. Entry A1 1022, Record Group 24, National Archives and Records Administration II (NARA II), College Park, Maryland, hereafter referred to as General Correspondence. This and all other official correspondence cited in this work are contained in the NARA II, College Park, Maryland. The particular correspondence between Dedmon and Denfield expresses concern over inquiries made by the National Association for the Advancement of Colored People (NAACP) over the navy's use of "colored personnel" within its occupational rating system.

7. Antonio N. Artuz to the Department of the Navy, 23 March 1950, file 3, box 47, Case Files Relating to Navy Rating, 1945–1978, Entry A1 1022, Record Group 24, National Archives and Records Administration II (NARA II), College Park, Maryland, hereafter referred to as Case Files.

8. Chief of Naval Personnel to Commander of U.S. Naval Forces Philippines, "Enlistment or Reenlistment in Steward Group Ratings in the Regular Navy of Male Citizens of the Republic of the Philippines," 26 August 1955, memorandum, file 3, box 47, Case Files, italics added.

9. Bureau of Naval Personnel, "Filipinos in the United States Navy."

10. Chief of Naval Personnel to Commander of U.S. Naval Forces Philippines, "Enlistment or Reenlistment."

11. Ibid.

12. Felix P. Mamaril to Charles S. Thomas, Secretary of the Navy, 15 November 1956, box 904, General Correspondence.

13. Abelardo Angeles to Senator Herbert Lehman, 19 January 1955, box 904, General Correspondence.

14. Tony Javier, in-person interview by author, 2003.

15. Sergio Norombaba, in-person interview by author, 2003.

16. Jesus Reyes, in-person interview by author, 2019.

17. Rudolfo M. San Juan to Lt. Commander C. J. Barry, written on September 17, 1947; received September 29, 1947, box 194, General Correspondence.

18. Federico Bona, in-person interview by author, 2018.

19. Paulino Maestre, in-person interview by author, 2003.

20. Vicente Bianes, in-person interview by author, 2007.

21. Norberto Amano, in-person interview by author, 2003.

22. Reynaldo Pellos, in-person interview by author, 2007.

23. Javier interview.

24. Schirmer and Shalom, *Philippines Reader*, 35.

25. Paligutan interview.

26. Ibid.

27. Franz Fanon, *Wretched of the Earth*, 51.

28. Bona interview.

29. Lucio Pontanares, in-person interview by author, 2003.

30. Ibid.

31. Teodulo James Coquilla, in-person interview by author, 2012.

32. Julian Ortiz, in-person interview by author, 2003.

33. The concern over Filipino migrants as carriers of exotic diseases was sometimes spawned by the belief in biological racism at that time: that dark-skinned inhabitants of the tropics were *biologically* predisposed to such diseases compared to whites. The earliest waves of Filipino labor to American territory aroused the xenophobic anxiety of many whites who perceived them not only as diseased agents but also as threats to American jobs. See JoAnna Poblete, "S.S. *Mongolia* Incident."

34. Bona interview.

35. Gerardo Silva, interview by author, 2019.

36. Ernie Cabanes, interview by author, 2007.

37. The view that General Douglas MacArthur's retreat from the Philippines in 1942 was an abandonment of his American and Filipino troops is explored in Richard Connaughton's book *MacArthur and the Defeat of the Philippines.*

38. The reality behind of the passage of the Tydings-McDuffie Act was the realization by American officials that the Philippines was no longer an asset but, rather, a liability to American empire. Perhaps more pertinent was the increased pressure from American labor to curb the immigration of Filipino workers, whose lower wages threatened the availability of jobs for whites during the Great Depression. Although the issue of American bases was raised in the negotiations, U.S. officials relented to resistance from Philippine nationalists; only small military installations were granted in the negotiations.

39. The Washington Naval Arms Conference of 1921, resulting in the scaling down of the U.S. Navy in the Pacific, is often cited as a demonstration of the United States' intent to demilitarize. Indeed, the Washington Conference is often postulated as an enabling possibility for the military dominance of the Japanese navy in the Pacific during the interwar years.

40. Paul Boyer, *Oxford Companion to United States History*, 87–88.

41. Harry Magdoff, "Militarism and Imperialism," 240.

42. The historiography of the Cold War in the Pacific based upon world-systems analysis is not without its critics. In his book *Illusions of Influence*, for instance, Nick

Cullather argues that analysis of U.S.-Philippine postwar relations based upon neo-colonial dependency theory and world-systems analysis are fundamentally flawed, insofar as they overstate the degree of influence the United States exerted upon its former colony purportedly engendering postcolonial economic and political dependency.

43. The term "open-door imperialism" is appropriated from the historian William Appleman Williams, who advanced an iconoclastic economic explanation of U.S. imperialism during the 1950s, an era characterized by conformist drift away from critical perspectives even by most academics. Williams employs the trope of "open door" to underscore the priority among U.S. imperialists in opening and securing overseas markets for American capital. Interestingly, it has recently been revivified by some scholars, most notably, Andrew Bacevich, in his book *American Empire*.

44. Christine Wing, "The United States in the Pacific," in Gerson and Birchard, *Sun Never Sets*, 127.

45. https://digitalcommons.usnwc.edu/cgi/viewcontent.cgi?article=2158&context=ils.

46. Schirmer and Shalom, *Philippines Reader*, 87.

47. For feminist perspectives on militarism, military bases, and prostitution, see Cynthia Enloe, *Does Khaki Become You?* and Sandra Pollack Sturdevant and Brenda Stoltzfus, *Let The Good Times Roll*.

Chapter 3. Adrift from the American Dream

1. The use of Filipino "houseboys" was pervasive during the early American colonial period, constituting 75 percent of the domestic-worker labor force, servicing American administrators and schoolteachers. See Julia Martinez, Claire Lowrie, Frances Steel, and Victoria Haskins, *Colonialism and Male Domestic Service*, 12.

2. European colonizers, justified by darker-skinned peoples' supposed inherent inferiority, often subjected them to harsh labor conditions within colonial territories, as seen with the early examples of the *encomienda* system in New Spain *(indigenous slave labor)* and African slavery in Virginia, among others. When tied to the notion of modernity, Western civilization saw itself as the harbinger of modern development, whether economic, political, or cultural; non-Westerners, on the other hand, were fated to fall behind the West, further justifying their social and economic marginalization.

3. Frederick S. Harrod, *Manning the New Navy*, 5.

4. Rick Baldoz, *Third Asiatic Invasion*, 38–41.

5. Harrod, *Manning the New Navy*, 5–7.

6. Christopher Capozzola, *Bound by War*, 75.

7. Ibid.

8. Harrod, *Manning the New Navy*, 8.

9. Ibid., 10. To quote Harrod regarding recruitment of persons of color into the Old Navy: "Once aboard navy ships, [non-white sailors] served as seamen, firemen,

jacks-of-dust (storekeepers), carpenters, water tenders, oilers, and in other specialized billets" (10). In spite of the Old Navy's more liberal policy toward nonwhites, Harrod notes that they, nonetheless, comprised most of the lower positions in the navy's hierarchical rating system.

10. Miller, *Messman Chronicles*, 18.

11. Captain Robert Emmet qtd. in Miller, *Messman Chronicles*, 8.

12. In the American racial field, Asian socioeconomic success has been occasionally used as a springboard in the criticism of comparatively lower achievement rates among other minorities, especially African Americans. This weaponization of race is particularly attached to Asians as a supposed "model minority." For discussions and analyses of racial triangulation between African Americans and Asian Americans, see Claire Jean Kim, *Bitter Fruit*, and Nadia Y. Kim, *Imperial Citizens*, 15–19.

13. Timothy Ingram, "The Floating Plantation," *Washington Monthly*, October 1970, 18. See also H. G. Reza, "Navy to Stop Recruiting Filipino Nationals: Defense: The End of the Military Base Agreement with the Philippines Will Terminate the Nearly Century-Old Program," *Los Angeles Times*, February 27, 1992, latimes.com.

14. Norombaba interview.

15. Reyes interview.

16. Norberto Amano interview.

17. "Summary of Pertinent Facts Related to Changing the Title of the 'Steward' Rating and Making It a Service Rating of the Commissaryman Rating," file 4, box 48, Case Files, 10, italics added.

18. Javier interview.

19. Paligutan interview.

20. Ortiz interview.

21. Cabanes interview.

22. Silva interview

23. K. B. Smith, assistant director, recruiting division, to director, recruiting division, 2 June 1953, memorandum, file 3, box 47, Case Files, italics added.

24. Reyes interview.

25. Norombaba interview.

26. "Recommendation: Keep Filipino Input at Minimum," file 1, box 47, Case Files.

27. Paligutan interview.

28. The steward rating had three designations: TR (steward recruit) for new recruits; TA (steward apprentice) for stewards in training; TN (full stewardsman).

29. Javier interview, 2003.

30. *Stewardsman*, Bureau of Naval Personnel, 1951, Naval Historical Center Library, Washington, DC, 1. Stewardsman is a training manual.

31. Ibid.

32. "Memorandum for Chairman, Permanent Board for Control of Enlisted Rating Structure (PBCERS), Subject: Review of Steward Rating," 19 June 1968, file 1, box 47, Case Files, 4–5,.

33. Michael Hardt and Antonio Negri, *Empire*, 292–293.

34. Norombaba interview.

35. Norberto Amano, interview.

36. Paligutan interview.

37. Norombaba interview.

38. Pontanares interview.

39. Ortiz interview.

40. Ibid.

41. Paligutan interview.

42. Yen Le Espiritu, *Filipino America Lives*, 15.

43. Pontanares interview.

44. Norombaba interview.

45. Ingram, "Floating Plantation."

46. *Administration of Officer's Messes*, 7, italics added.

47. Reyes interview.

48. Pellos interview.

49. Javier interview.

50. Silva interview.

51. Reyes interview.

52. Bona interview.

53. Teodulo James Coquilla, interview with author, 2012.

54. Javier interview.

55. Pontanares interview.

56. Coquilla interview.

57. Pontanares interview.

58. Reyes interview.

59. Jaime Ebalo, interview by author, 2012.

60. Coquilla interview.

61. Javier interview.

62. Reyes interview.

63. Javier interview.

64. Glenn, *Issei, Nisei, War Bride*, 168.

65. Martinez et al., *Colonialism and Male Domestic Service*, 14. To quote the authors regarding the connection between male domestic service and colonial mastery: "Colonial discourse sought to underline European dominance by describing male domestic workers, regardless of age, as 'houseboys' or, more generally, 'boys'" (14).

66. Silva interview.

67. Javier interview.

68. Pontanares interview.

69. Javier interview.

70. Pellos interview.

71. See Fajardo, *Filipino Crosscurrents*, and Rodriguez, *Migrants for Export*. Both authors centralize the role of the Philippine state in elevating in their boosterism the

status of overseas foreign workers (OFWs) as *bayanis* (heroes). Fajardo's exclusive focus on male seamen allows for a gendered analysis whereby their economic power constructs Filipino seafarers as key masculine figures in the face of the "feminization" of the Philippine state during the age of neoliberalism.

72. Pellos interview.

73. Norberto Amano interview.

74. Pontanares interview.

Chapter 4. Tales of Resistance

1. During the congressional debate surrounding the passing of the Reconstruction amendments, prominent radical Republicans, such as Thaddeus Stevens, proposed that naturalization be extended to Chinese immigrants, as well. This was met with vehement opposition due to Orientalist depictions of Asians as perpetual foreigners unassimilable to American civilization.

2. Serafin Cabral, in-person interview by author, 2008.

3. Coquilla interview.

4. John Darrell Sherwood, *Black Sailor, White Navy*, 9.

5. Ibid., 12. To be sure, a principal reason for this sharp decline in black recruitment stems from the navy's increased emphasis upon qualitative recruitment, and Sherwood notes that many prospective blacks received low test scores due to culturally biased exams. The fact remained that the African American community overwhelmingly regarded the U.S. Navy with contempt due to its discriminatory policies. This is evinced in sharp relief with black enlistment in the U.S. Army, which had four times as many black enlistees compared to the navy. Although black troops were utilized in more of a support capacity, African Americans evidently held ground forces in higher regard than the U.S. Navy and Coast Guard.

6. Ray L. Burdeos, *Filipinos in the U.S. Navy*, 6.

7. Harry S. Truman, "Executive Order 9981," July 26, 1946, Harry S. Truman Library and Museum, *National Archives*, www.trumanlibrary.gov/.

8. Burdeos, *Filipinos in the U.S. Navy*, 6.

9. Poblete, *Islanders in the Empire*, 6–9.

10. Ortiz interview. The term "weapons of the weak" is borrowed from James C. Scott's extraordinary book about peasant resistance, *Weapons of the Weak*.

11. Takaki, *Strangers from a Different Shore*, 333.

12. Bona interview.

13. Ortiz interview.

14. "Summary of Pertinent Facts Related to Changing the Title if the 'Steward' Rating."

15. Paligutan interview.

16. Ortiz interview.

17. Javier interview.

18. Silva interview.

19. Salvador Floriano, in-person interview by author, 2012.

20. Ibid.

21. Ebalo interview.

22. Ibid.

23. Pellos interview.

24. Coquilla interview.

25. Javier interview.

26. Ortiz interview.

27. Javier interview.

28. Ireneo "Rene" Amano, in-person interview by author, 2007.

29. Reyes interview.

30. Rene Amano interview.

31. Ibid.

32. Ibid.

33. Ibid.

34. Ibid.

35. Ibid. The term "Ilocanos" refers to persons from the Ilocos provinces in the Philippines.

36. Ibid.

37. Ibid.

38. The phrase "the subaltern speaks" is borrowed from a famous essay by Gayatri Spivak, "Does the Subaltern Speak?" The term "subaltern," in general terms, describes a person of subordinate position, especially in reference to the colonized. In her essay Spivak addresses whether the postcolonial scholar is unwittingly implicit in the project of colonialism via the use of Western-derived theoretical lenses as they aspire to be the voice of the "voiceless subaltern." Gayatri Spivak, "Can the Subaltern Speak," 271.

Chapter 5. The Navy's "Filipino Servant Problem"

1. George M. Fredrickson, *Short History of Racism*.

2. This thesis is argued by Frank Furedi in *The Silent War*.

3. See Steven Hahn's brilliant work, *A Nation under Our Feet*. Recent works on the political agency of African Americans during the nineteenth century underscore the centrality of slave agency in changing the complexion of the American Civil War from one initially fought to prevent disunion to that of slave emancipation. Such a transition was due to the slaves' emphatic insistence upon the moral imperative of emancipation as eclipsing political issues related to sectionalism, a sentiment that eventually percolated upward to the highest ranks of the military and the government itself. Interestingly, some of the strategies of resistance that Southern slaves employed during the Civil War that served to undermine the South's plantation economy were similar to those practiced by Filipino stewards during the period of the current study.

4. Timothy H. Ingram, "A 'Colonial Remnant': How the US Navy Solves the 'Servant Problem,'" *Washington Monthly*, October 1970.

5. Ibid.

6. Donald F. Duff and Ransom J. Arthur, "Between Two Worlds: Filipinos in the U.S. Navy," *American Journal of Psychiatry* 123 (January 1967): 837.

7. Ibid.

8. Ibid., 840, 841.

9. Ibid.

10. Ibid., 842–843.

11. Ibid., 842.

12. Ibid.

13. This particular interpretation of Fanon's critique of Freudianism's universality is owed to Ania Loomba, *Colonialism/Postcolonialism*, 143.

14. Ibid.

15. Frantz Fanon, *Black Skin, White Masks*, 95.

16. Official documents do not explicitly use the phrase "Filipino servant problem" but, rather, refer to the issue generically as a "steward rating problem." Moreover, earlier documents relating to this issue typically frame it as an attempt to merely restructure the rating itself—that is, the issue is posited as a bureaucratic matter rather than a racial one. Later documents (late 1960s, early 1970s), however, acknowledge criticism of the servility behind stewardship from within and without, that is, from Filipino protest as well as outside criticism. I also feel justified in using the phrase "Filipino servant problem" due to the predominance of Filipinos within the rating branch during the time of this study—according to the naval document Steward Rating Review, Filipinos made up 83.7 percent of the steward branch by the late 1960s. "Steward (SD) Rating Review," file 4, box 48, Case Files.

17. Bureau of Naval Personnel, "Recommendation: Keep Filipino Input at Minimum," circular letter, 17 March 1962, file 1, box 47, Case Files.

18. Ibid.

19. Ibid.

20. Ibid.

21. "Memorandum for the Chief of Naval Personnel, Subject: Recommendations for Improvement on Steward Rating," July 7, 1961, file 2, box 47, Case Files, italics added.

22. *SD/CS Merger*, file 3. box 47, Case Files, italics added.

23. Memo to K. B. Smith, assistant director, Recruiting Division to Director Recruiting Division, June 2, 1953, file 3, box 47, Record Group 24, Entry A1 1022, Case Files.

24. "Memorandum from Assistant Chief of Plans to Chief of Naval Personnel," March 17, 1962, file 1, box 47, Case Files.

25. Memorandum to Chairman, Permanent Board for Control of Enlisted Rating Structure, Subject: Review of Steward Rating," 19 June 1968, file 1, box 47, Case Files, 4–5.

26. "Summary of Pertinent Facts Related to Changing the Title of the 'Steward' Rating," 1.

27. Ibid., 1, 9, 10.

28. Ibid., 10, 11.

29. Ibid., 12, italics added.

30. Memorandum to Chairman, Permanent Board.

31. In fundamental respects, the issues surrounding labor within the military institutions of the U.S. Armed Forces are not exactly parallel with those found within corporate capitalism and its strictly economic institutions. The historical divide and strife between capital and labor, for instance, obviously does not apply within the military, wherein strict prohibitions against collective strikes are in place. The duties associated with Filipino naval stewardship have closer parallels to the colonial relation of master/subject rather than the capitalist employer/employee. However, the theme of "racialized labor," it is argued, traverses both institutions, especially in light of the important position the U.S. Navy has occupied within the U.S. imperial cosmology and economic hegemony. Indeed, the navy was responsible for carving out an economic sphere of interest in the Pacific—an enabling condition for the global expansion of U.S. capitalism. I owe Regina Akers at the Naval Historical Center for this important insight regarding this structural and historical distinction.

32. U.S. Naval Personnel Research Activity, "Proposed Revision of Steward Qualifications for Advancement in Rating," Annex E, Extended Discussion, E-1, 3 December 1962, file 4, box 48, Case Files, italics added.

33. T. E. White, "Change of Steward Rating to Keep This a Non-Caucasian Rating," memorandum to PERS—G12, 24 April 1968, file 4, box 48, Case Files.

34. Memorandum for Chairman, Permanent Board for Control of Enlisted Rating Structure Subject: Review of Steward Rating, 19 June 1968, file 1, box 47, Case Files, 4–5.

35. Ibid., 4–5, 3.

36. "Steward Rating Review Briefing," Case Files.

37. "Memorandum for Assistant Chief for Plans and Programs," 13 October 1972, file 1, box 47, Case Files.

38. "Filipino Stewards Still Used by Navy but Number Drops." *New York Times,* October 25, 1970, https://www.nytimes.com.

39. Rosemary Purcell, "Civilian Messmen Due by June 1972," *Navy Times,* March 10, 1971, 1.

Chapter 6. Achieving the American Dream

1. Sherwood, *Black Sailor, White Navy,* 43.

2. However, despite the new allowance of rating advancement granted to Filipino nationals, the fact remained that a disproportionate amount of Filipinos were still to be found in the mess halls and galleys well after 1973.

3. Elmo Zumwalt Jr., *On Watch,* 198.

4. Sherwood, *Black Sailor, White Navy*, 34.

5. Zumwalt, *On Watch*, 197–198.

6. Ibid., 35.

7. Ibid., 46.

8. Sherwood, *Black Sailor, White Navy*, 34.

9. Zumwalt, *On Watch*, 40, 167, 169.

10. Ibid., 174, 185, 178.

11. Ibid., 198.

12. To quote from Z-66: "I sincerely believed that I was philosophically prepared to understand the problems of our black Navymen and their families, and until [Norman and I] discussed them at length, I did not realize the extent and deep significance of many of these matters." Ibid., 202.

13. Sherwood, *Black Sailor, White Navy*, 43.

14. As evinced by oral testimonies revealed in this study, feelings of "adoration" between admirals and Filipino stewards were not always reciprocal. Indeed, interviewees who served for admirals quite often held ambivalent feelings about the appointment: while considered a prestigious appointment within the stewardship rating, it also entailed the broadening of servile duties and expectations, as Filipino stewards were often expected to serve the admiral's family and perform household duties onshore.

15. A precursor to Admiral Zumwalt's policies of racial equality within the navy is found with the issuance of the "Manual on Equal Opportunity and Treatment of Military Personnel" (SECNAVINST 5350.6), authored by the secretary of the navy in 1965. The goals delineated in this manual include equal opportunity for minorities while including educational and training programs in human relations for all levels of military personnel. This manual did not yet result in the establishment of equal opportunity as official naval policy. It is plausible to view Zumwalt's Z-66 as the culmination of such earlier precursors set in motion since Truman's declaration of desegregation of the U.S. military. See Sherwood, *Black Sailor, White Navy*, 45.

16. Sherwood, *Black Sailor, White Navy*, 47.

17. Zumwalt, *On Watch*, 204.

Epilogue

1. "Memorandum for the Vice Chief of Naval Operations, Subject: Review of Steward Rating," file 3, box 47, Case Files.

2. Espiritu, *Filipinos in America*, 16.

3. Capozzola, *Bound by War*, 272.

4. Ibid., 273.

5. Paligutan interview.

6. Javier interview.

7. Pontanares interview.

Bibliography

Abinales, Patricio N., and Donna J. Amoroso. *State and Society in the Philippines.* Lanham, MD: Rowman and Littlefield, 2005.

Administration of Officer's Messes. Bureau of Naval Personnel. Naval Historical Center Library, Washington, DC.

Agoncillo, Teodoro A., and Milagros C. Guerrero. *The History of the Filipino People.* Quezon City, Philippines: Garcia, 1972.

Anderson, Benedict. "Cacique Democracy in the Philippines: Origins and Dreams." In Vicente L. Rafael, editor, *Discrepant Histories: Translocal Essays on Philippine Culture.* Philadelphia: Temple University Press, 1995.

Anderson, Warwick. *Colonial Pathologies: American Tropical Medicine, Race, and Hygiene in the Philippines.* Durham, NC: Duke University Press, 2006.

Bacevich, Andrew. *American Empire: Realities and Consequences of U.S. Diplomacy.* Cambridge, MA: Harvard University Press, 2002.

Baldoz, Rick. *The Third Asiatic Invasion: Empire and Migration in Filipino-America, 1898–1946.* New York: New York University Press, 2011.

Bederman, Gail. *Manliness and Civilization: A Cultural History of Gender and Race in the United States, 1880–1917.* Chicago: University of Chicago Press, 1995.

Bello, Walden, Marissa de Guzman, Mary Lou Malig, and Herbert Docena. *The Anti-Development State: The Political Economy of Permanent Crisis in the Philippines.* New York: Zed, 2004.

Bonus, Rick. *Locating Filipino Americans: Ethnicity and the Cultural Politics of Space.* Philadelphia: Temple University Press, 2000.

Borland, Katherine. "'That's Not What I Said': Interpretive Conflict in Oral Narrative Research." In Perks and Thomson, *Oral History Reader,* 412–423.

Boyer, Paul, ed. in chief. *The Oxford Companion to United States History.* Oxford: Oxford University Press, 2004.

Brown, Kathleen. *Good Wives, Nasty Wenches, and Anxious Patriarchs: Gender, Race, and Power in Colonial Virginia*. Chapel Hill: University of North Carolina Press, 1996.

Bulosan, Carlos. *America Is in the Heart: A Personal History*. Seattle: University of Washington Press, 1973.

Burdeos, Ray L. *Filipinos in the U.S. Navy and Coast Guard During the Vietnam War*. Edited by Judith Farrell. Bloomington, IN: AuthorHouse, self-published, 2008.

Bureau of Naval Personnel. "Filipinos in the United States Navy." October 1976. *Naval History and Heritage Command, U.S. Navy*, 2020. https://www.history.navy.mil/.

Capozzola, Christopher. *Bound by War: How the United States and the Philippines Built America's First Pacific Century*. New York: Basic Books, 2020.

Case Files Relating to Navy Rating, 1945–1978. Entry A1 1022, Record Group 24. National Archives and Records Administration II (NARA II), College Park, Maryland,

Choy, Catherine Ceniza. *Empire of Care: Nursing and Migration in Filipino American History*. Durham, NC: Duke University Press, 2003.

Connaughton, Richard. *MacArthur and the Defeat of the Philippines*. Woodstock, NY: Overlook, 2001.

Constable, Nicole. *Maid to Order in Hong Kong: Stories of Migrant Workers*. 2nd ed. Ithaca, NY: Cornell University Press, 2007.

Constantino, Renato, "The Miseducation of the Filipino." In Shirmer and Shalom, *Philippines Reader*, 45–49.

Cullather, Nick. *Illusions of Influence: The Political Economy of the United States–Philippines Relations, 1942–1960*. Stanford, CA: Stanford University Press, 1994.

Cumings, Bruce. *Dominion from Sea to Sea: Pacific Ascendancy and American Power*. New Haven, CT: Yale University Press, 2009.

Duff, Donald F., and Ransom J. Arthur. "Between Two Worlds: Filipinos in the U.S. Navy." *American Journal of Psychiatry* 123 (January 1967): 836–843. https://doi.org/10.1176/ajp.123.7.836.

Enloe, Cynthia. *Does Khaki Become You? The Militarization of Women's Lives*. Boston: South End, 1983.

Espina, Marina. *Filipinos in Louisiana*. New Orleans, LA: Laborde, 2005.

Espiritu, Yen Le. *Filipino American Lives*. Philadelphia: Temple University Press, 1995.

———. *Home Bound: Filipino American Lives across Cultures, Communities, and Countries*. Berkeley: University of California Press, 2003.

Fajardo, Kale. *Filipino Crosscurrents: Oceanographies of Seafaring, Masculinities, and Globalization*. Minneapolis: University of Minnesota Press, 2011.

Fanon, Franz. *Black Skin, White Masks*, Revised edition. 1952; New York: Grove, 2008. Citations are to the 2008 edition.

———. *The Wretched of the Earth*. New York: Grove, 1963.

Francisco, Luzviminda. "The Philippine-American War." In Shirmer and Shalom, eds., *Philippines Reader*, 8–19.

Francisco-Menchavez, Valerie. *The Labor of Care: Filipina Migrants and Transnational Families in the Digital Age*. Urbana: University of Illinois Press, 2018.

Frederickson, George M. Racism: *A Short History.* Princeton, NJ: Princeton University Press, 2002.

Friedman, Thomas. "A Manifesto for a Fast World." *New York Times Magazine,* March 28, 1999, 96.

Fujita-Rony, Dorothy. *American Workers, Colonial Power: Philippine Seattle and the Transpacific West, 1919–1941.* Berkeley: University of California Press, 2003.

Furedi, Frank. *The Silent War: Imperialism and the Changing Perception of Race.* New Brunswick, NJ: Rutgers University Press, 1998.

Gerson, Joseph, and Bruce Birchard, eds. *The Sun Never Sets: Confronting the Network of Foreign U.S. Military Bases.* Boston: South End, 1991.

Gilroy, Paul. *The Black Atlantic: Modernity and Double Consciousness.* London: Verso, 2003.

Glenn, Evelyn Nakano. *Issei, Nisei, War Bride: Three Generations of Japanese American Women in Domestic Service.* Philadelphia: Temple University Press, 1986.

Go, Julian. *American Empire and the Politics of Meaning.* Durham, NC: Duke University Press, 2008.

———. "Introduction: Global Perspectives on the U.S. Colonial State in the Philippines." In *The American Colonial State in the Philippines: Global Perspectives,* edited by Julian Go and Anne L. Foster. Durham, NC: Duke University Press, 2003, 1–42

Gonzalez, Gilbert G. *Guest Workers or Colonized Labor? Mexican Labor Migration to the United States.* Boulder, CO: Paradigm, 2006.

Guttridge, Leonard F. *Mutiny: A History of Naval Insurrection.* Annapolis, MD: Naval Institute Press, 1992.

Hahn, Steven. *A Nation under Our Feet: Black Political Struggle in the Rural South, from Slavery to the Great Migration.* Cambridge, MA: Harvard University Press, 2003.

Hardt, Michael, and Antonio Negri. *Empire.* Cambridge, MA: Harvard University Press, 2000.

Harrod, Frederick S. *Manning the New Navy: The Development of a Modern Naval Enlisted Force, 1899–1940.* Westport, CT: Greenwood, 1978.

Hoganson, Kristin. *Fighting for American Manhood: How Gender Politics Provoked the Spanish-American and Philippine-American Wars.* New Haven, CT: Yale University Press, 1998.

Hondagneu-Sotelo, Pierrette. *Doméstica: Immigrant Women Cleaning and Caring in the Shadows of Affluence.* Berkeley: University of California Press, 2001.

———. *Gendered Transitions: Mexican Experiences of Immigration.* Berkeley: University of California Press, 1994.

Immerwahr, Daniel. *How to Hide an Empire: A History of the Greater United States.* New York: Farrar, Straus, and Giroux, 2019.

Ingram, Timothy H. "A 'Colonial Remnant': How the US Navy Solves the 'Servant Problem.'" *Washington Monthly,* October 1970.

———. "The Floating Plantation." *Washington Monthly,* October 1970, 18–19.

Isaac, Allan Punzalan. *American Tropic: Articulating Filipino America.* Minneapolis: University of Minnesota Press, 2006.

Johnson, Chalmers. *The Sorrows of Empire: Militarism, Secrecy, and the End of the Republic* New York: Owl Books, 2004.

Kang, Laura Hyun Yi. *Compositional Subjects: Enfiguring Asian American Women.* Durham, NC: Duke University Press, 2002.

Kaplan, Amy, and Donald E. Pease, eds. *Cultures of United States Imperialism.* Durham, NC: Duke University Press, 1993.

Kim, Claire Jean. *Bitter Fruit: The Politics of Black-Korean Conflict in New York City.* New Haven, CT: Yale University Press, 2000.

Kim, Nadia Y. *Imperial Citizens: Koreans and Race in Seoul to LA.* Stanford, CA: Stanford University Press, 2008.

Kipling, Rudyard. "White Man's Burden, 1899." Internet History Sourcebooks Project. *Fordham University*, 2021. https://sourcebooks.fordham.edu/mod/Kipling.asp.

Kramer, Paul E. *The Blood of Government: Race, Empire, the United States, and the Philippines.* Chapel Hill: University of North Carolina Press, 2006.

Kurashige, Lon, and Alice Yang Murray, eds. *Major Problems in Asian American History.* Boston: Houghton Mifflin, 2003.

Limerick, Patricia. *Legacy of Conquest: The Unbroken Past of the American West.* New York: Norton, 1987.

Loomba, Ania. *Colonialism/Postcolonialism.* ebook. London: Routledge, 1998.

Lowe, Lisa. *Immigrant Acts: On Asian American Cultural Politics.* Durham, NC: Duke University Press, 1996.

Mabalon, Dawn. *Little Manila Is in the Heart.* Durham, NC: Duke University Press, 2013.

Magdoff, Harry. "Militarism and Imperialism." *American Economic Review* 60, no. 2 (1970): 237–242.

Martinez, Julia, Claire Lowrie, Frances Steel, and Victoria Haskins. *Colonialism and Male Domestic Service across the Asia Pacific.* London: Bloomsbury Academic, 2019.

Miller, Richard. *The Messman Chronicles: African-Americans in the U.S. Navy, 1932–1943.* Annapolis, MD: Naval Institute Press, 2004.

Okihiro, Gary. *The Columbia Guide to Asian American History.* New York: Columbia University Press, 2001.

Parreñas, Rhacel Salazar, and Lok C. D. Siu, eds. *Asian Diasporas: New Formations, New Conceptions.* Stanford, CA; Stanford University Press, 2007.

———. *Servants of Globalization: Women, Migration, and Domestic Work.* Stanford, CA: Stanford University Press, 2001.

Perks, Robert, and Alistair Thomson. *The Oral History Reader.* 3rd ed. London: Routledge, 2016.

Pido, Antonio. *The Pilipinos in America: Macro/Micro Dimensions of Immigration and Integration.* New York: Center for Migration Studies, 1986.

Poblete, JoAnna. *Islanders in the Empire: Filipino and Puerto Rican Laborers in Hawai'i.* Urbana: University of Illinois Press, 2017.

———. "The S.S. *Mongolia* Incident: Medical Politics and Filipino Colonial Migration In Hawai'i." *Pacific Historical Review* 82, no. 2 (2013): 248–278.

Pomeroy, William. *American Neo-colonialism: Its Emergence in the Philippines and Asia.* New York: International, 1970.

Radford, Jynnah, and Abby Budiman. "2016, Foreign-Born Population in the United States Statistical Portrait: Statistical Portrait of the Foreign-Born Population in the United States." *Pew Research Center*, 2021. www.pewresearch.org.

Rafael, Vicente L. *White Love and Other Events in Filipino History.* Durham, NC: Duke University Press, 2000.

Rice, Mark. *Dean Worcester's Fantasy Islands: Photography, Film, and the Colonial Philippines.* Ann Arbor: University of Michigan Press, 2014.

Rodriguez, Robyn Magalit. *Migrants for Export: How the Philippine State Brokers Labor to the World.* Minneapolis: University of Minnesota Press, 2010.

San Juan, E., Jr. *The Philippine Temptation: Dialectics of Philippines-U.S. Literary Relations.* Philadelphia: Temple University Press, 1996.

Scharlin, Craig, and Lillian Villanueva. *Philip Vera Cruz: A Personal History of Filipino Immigrants and the Farmworkers Movement.* 3rd ed. Seattle: University of Washington Press, 2000.

Schirmer, Daniel B. "The Conception and Gestation of a Neocolony." In Schirmer and Shalom, *Philippines Reader*, 38–44.

Schirmer, Daniel B., and Stephen Rosskamm Shalom, eds. *The Philippines Reader: A History of Colonialism, Neo-colonialism, Dictatorship, and Resistance.* Boston: South End, 1987.

Scott, James C. *Weapons of the Weak: Everyday Forms of Peasant Resistance.* New Haven, CT: Yale University Press, 1985.

Shalom, Stephen Rosskamm. *The United States and the Philippines: A Study of Neo-colonialism.* Philadelphia: Institute for the Study of Human Issues, 1981.

Sherwood, John Darrell. *Black Sailor, White Navy.* New York: New York University Press, 2007.

Spivak, Gayatri. "Can the Subaltern Speak?" In *Marxism and the Interpretation of Culture*, edited by Cary Nelson and Lawrence Grossberg, 271 313. Urbana: University of Illinois Press, 1988.

Stewardsman Training Manual. Bureau of Naval Personnel, 1951. Naval Historical Center Library, Washington, DC.

Sturdevant, Saundra Pollack, and Brenda Stoltzfus. *Let the Good Times Roll: Prostitution and the US Military in Asia.* New York: New Press, 1993.

Takaki, Ronald. *Strangers from a Different Shore: A History of Asian Americans.* Boston: Little, Brown, 1998.

U.S./Philippines Military Bases Agreement of 1947. https://www.loc.gov/law/help/us-treaties/bevans/b-ph-ust000011-0055.pdf.

White, Richard. *It's Your Misfortune and None of My Own.* Norman: University of Oklahoma Press, 1991.

Williams, William Appleman. *The Tragedy of American Diplomacy*. New York: Dell, 1962.

Wilton, Janet. "Imaging Family Memories: My Mum, Her Photographs, Our Memories." In Perks and Thomson, *Oral History Reader*, 268–280.

Wing, Christine. "The United States in the Pacific." In Gerson and Birchard, *Sun Never Sets*, 123–148.

Zumwalt, Elmo, Jr. *On Watch: A Memoir*. New York: Quadrangle, 1976.

Index

affective labor, 80–81, 85, 101
African American: chattel slavery, 120, 121; comparisons and relations with Filipinos in the navy, 20, 88, 158n4; protest in the navy, 52, 100; stewards and messmen, 2, 12–13, 14, 20, 51, 73–74, 146; struggle against racism, 98–99, 120, 121
Agent Orange, 140
Aguinaldo, Emilio, 28
American exceptionalism, 8, 25–28
American Revolution, 79
Anderson, Benedict, 157n40, 163n4. *See also* imagined communities
Anderson, Warwick, 34, 38
Anti-Imperialist League, 29
Asian Americans, 3–4, 99, 158n4, 161n12

bahala na (Filipino cultural belief in fate), 118
Bederman, Gail, 27–28
Bell Trade Act, 43
benevolent assimilation, policy of, 24, 25, 28, 66
Beveridge, Albert Senator, 29
Bonifacio, Andres, 35
Bonus, Rick, 7
bracero program, 5–6, 121
Bretton Woods Conference 1944, 62
Bulosan, Carlos, 10, 38
Bureau of Naval Personnel (BuPers), 17, 79, 84, 128, 133, 143

capitalism, 3, 5–6, 45
Choy, Catherine Ceniza, 7, 9
civil rights movement, 2, 98–99, 103, 120–121
Cold War, 8, 61–65, 134
colonialism: centrality to Filipino American immigration, 6, 18; connection to race, 6; economic imperatives of, 5; and immigration, 4–5; linked to cheap labor, 5–6
Columbian Exposition of 1893, 71
Constantino, Renato, 37–38, 56
contact zones (navy ships as), 6
Cuba, 42n43

Depression of 1893, 28
Dewey, Commodore George, 28
domestic labor: Filipino houseboys for American colonials, 69, 162; Filipino stewards compared to racialized women domestics, 13–14; gendered as "women's work," 79, 89; Japanese women as domestic workers, 89; and masculine identity, 90

Espiritu, Yen Le, 5, 6, 33n22
ethnopsychiatry, 127

Fanon, Franz, 57, 121, 127–128
Filipino culture: alleged connection to passivity, 122, 124–125; *bahala na* (fate),

118; *compadrazgo*, 68; filial obedience, 141; *hiya* (shame), 105, 125; *utang na loob* (internalized debt), 124

Filipino immigration: Acapulco trade, 1; agribusiness labor, 7, 9, 51; in the context of neoliberalism, 11; to Hawai'i, 51; as an international pool of labor, 24, 44–45; nurses, 7, overseas foreign workers (OFWs), 11, 45, 91, 163n71; seamen and cargo ship workers, 10–11; transnational diaspora, 11–12

Foucault, Michel, 34, 35, 36, 40, 153

Francisco-Menchavez, Valerie, 11

Freudianism, 125

Fujita-Rony, Dorothy, 7

gender: and colonial bodies, 39; masculinity tied to naval rank and rating, 89–91; performativity, 11, 90; Philippines as a "gender frontier," 29, 155n8; and race and the Philippine American war, 29–31; tied to domestic work, 13–14; and United States overseas imperialism, 27–28

General Classification Test (GCT), 77–78

globalization, 6, 8–9

Grand Area, the Pacific as strategic, 65

Great White Fleet, 71

hiya (Tagalog word for "shame"), 105, 125

Hoganson, Kristin, 28

Ilustrados, 35

imagined communities, 99, 151n3

immaterial labor. *See* affective labor

imperialism: benevolent imperialism, 40, 42; European imperialism, 25; linked to American exceptionalism, 25–28; open door imperialism, 64, 160; in the Pacific region, 18; progressive imperialism, 34; tied to gender, 27–28

Ingram, Timothy H., 84, 97, 121–122

Insular Cases of 1901, 33

Itliong, Larry, 19

Jacinto, Emilio, 35

Jefferson, Thomas, 26

Jim Crow segregation, 51, 89, 98, 120

Kipling, Rudyard, 30. *See also* "The White Man's Burden" (poem)

"knowledge/power," 34–35. *See also* Foucault, Michel

"little brown brothers," Filipino colonials as, 24, 32, 154

Lodge, Henry Cabot, 101

Lowe, Lisa, 33

Mabalon, Dawn, 7

Mahan, Captain Alfred Thayer, 101

manifest destiny, 26

McArthur, General Douglass, 43, 61

McKinley, President William, 25, 50

mental illness: Filipino stewards and, 118, 122–128

"metaphysics of absence," 3–4, 119–120, 151n4

Military Bases Agreement of 1947, 43–44, 51, 52, 65, 74

Miller, Richard, 14, 51, 73

mutiny, 52, 100

National Security Council paper 68 (NSC-68), 64

Native Americans, 26, 27, 28, 31

neocolonialism: and Filipina nurses to the United States, 7, 43–44; and Mexico, 5–6; naval ship as neocolonial space, 2, 10, 81–82; navy base as neocolonial space, 57; U.S. Navy as a neocolonial institution, 12, 69

neoliberalism, 11

New Navy, 72–74

New People's Army (Huks), 64

Norman, Lt. Commander William, 146–147

Old Navy, 71–72

oral history, 15, 16

Organic Act 1902, 34

Orientalism: defining Filipinos as outside modernity, 73–74; and Filipino sailor's mental illness, 123–124, 126; as ideology, 19, 151n3; tied to Asians as "perpetual foreigners," 3; tied to black/white racial dichotomy, 99

Parreñas, Rhacel, 13

passive resistance (non-confrontational resistance), 97–98, 104–105, 127

Payne-Aldrich tariff law, 41

Philippine American War, 30–33, 37

Philippine colonization by the United States: as "benevolent assimilation," 24, 25; colonial Census, 39–40; colonial ethnography, 39, 156n36; Commonwealth Era, 42; education, 35–37, 56–57; as formal and direct colonialism, 42; moral justification for Philippine colonialism, 24, 29; patron-clientelism, 40–41, 42; perceived as a positive, 23, 45; the "Philippine question," 33; Philippines as a colonial racial state, 32–33; policy of Filipinization, 41

Philippine economics, 11, 44

Philippine independence, 6, 43–45, 51, 61, 74

Philippine oligarchical elite, 44

Poblete, JoAnna, 8

Proxmire, Senator William, 149

Puerto Ricans (as U.S. colonial subjects), 155–156n21

Puritans, 26

race: black/white dichotomy, 98, 112; and colonialism, 6; linked to conceptions of nation, 3–4; linked to U.S. expansionism, 24, 27; pseudoscience of, 28; "racial formation," 18, 32, 153–154; racialized labor, 69–70, 119–120, 133; racial reconstruction of Filipinos, 32

remittances, 91

Repatriation Act of 1935, 103

Rizal, Jose, 35

Rodriguez, Robin Magalit, 11

Roosevelt, Theodore, 27–28, 101

Roxas, Manuel, 43

San Diego, California, 12, 16, 68, 77, 135

Sangley Point recruitment, 47, 53, 58, 110

San Juan, Jr., Epifanio, 10

1790 Naturalization Act, 33

Spanish American War, 28, 71

Spivak, Gayatri, 57

stewards in the U.S. Navy and U.S. Coast Guard: Caucasians stewards, 130–131; college-educated Filipino stewards, 54, 58–59, 83–84, 103, 129–130; Filipinos as "perpetual stewards," 17, 23, 78, 83; Filipino steward marriage prohibition, 53, 131–132; Filipino stewards and counterhegemonic resistance, 96, 97; Filipino stewards as agents of historical change, 2, 17–18, 20, 119; Filipino stewards as transnational, 9–12; Filipino steward's

liminality, 8, 9–10, 12, 102; Filipino stewards perceived as passive, 2, 19, 20, 73, 98, 100, 104, 119, 121–122, 138; fluidity of Filipino steward identity, 70, 89–91, 102; incidents of Filipino steward labor-stoppage, 109–110, 113–114; official duties of, 78–79; paternalistic relations with officers, 84, 86; qualifying mental and physical exams for Filipinos, 59–60; as servant labor, 1–2, 80, 82–83, 130–131, 132, 149; steward contracts for Filipino nationals, 76–77; steward rating as racialized, 51–52, 69, 82; termination of steward rating, 13, 149; training of, 79–81

St. Louis Fair 1903, 71

subaltern agency, 121

Taft, Howard, 32, 40, 41, 154

Thomasites (American teachers in colonial Philippines), 36

Toqueville, Alexis de, 26

transnationalism and immigration, 8–12

Truman Executive Order 9981 (desegregation of the U.S. military), 101, 147

Turner's frontier thesis, 26–27

Tydings-McDuffie Act 1934, 51, 61

"unincorporated territory," 33, 42

United Farm Workers, 19

U.S. Coast Guard Academy, 77, 109

U.S. Naval Academy, 77, 110, 113

utang na loob (Filipino belief of internalized debt), 124

Vera Cruz, Philip, 19

Victorianism, 27

Vietnam War, 134, 139–140

westward expansion, 27–28, 157n42

"The White Man Burden" (poem), 30. See also Kipling, Rudyard

Worcester, Dean, 156n36

world-systems theory, 64, 160n42

Zumwalt, Chief of Naval Operations Admiral Elmo: early years in the navy, 144; liberal reforms, 144–145; race reforms, 20, 142, 147–148; role of Filipino stewards in Zumwalt's reforms, 87, 143; "Z-grams," 144

P. JAMES PALIGUTAN is a lecturer in
Asian American studies at California
State University, Fullerton.

The Asian American Experience

The Hood River Issei: An Oral History of Japanese Settlers in Oregon's Hood
    River Valley   *Linda Tamura*
Americanization, Acculturation, and Ethnic Identity: The Nisei Generation
    in Hawaii   *Eileen H. Tamura*
Sui Sin Far/Edith Maude Eaton: A Literary Biography   *Annette White-Parks*
Mrs. Spring Fragrance and Other Writings   *Sui Sin Far; edited by Amy Ling and
    Annette White-Parks*
The Golden Mountain: The Autobiography of a Korean Immigrant, 1895–1960
    Easurk Emsen Charr; edited and with an introduction by Wayne Patterson
Race and Politics: Asian Americans, Latinos, and Whites in a
    Los Angeles Suburb   *Leland T. Saito*
Achieving the Impossible Dream: How Japanese Americans Obtained Redress
    Mitchell T. Maki, Harry H. L. Kitano, and S. Megan Berthold
If They Don't Bring Their Women Here: Chinese Female Immigration
    before Exclusion   *George Anthony Peffer*
Growing Up Nisei: Race, Generation, and Culture among Japanese Americans of
    California, 1924–49   *David K. Yoo*
Chinese American Literature since the 1850s   *Xiao-huang Yin*
Pacific Pioneers: Japanese Journeys to America and Hawaii, 1850–80
    John E. Van Sant
Holding Up More Than Half the Sky: Chinese Women Garment Workers in
    New York City, 1948–92   *Xiaolan Bao*
Onoto Watanna: The Story of Winnifred Eaton   *Diana Birchall*
Edith and Winnifred Eaton: Chinatown Missions and Japanese Romances
    Dominika Ferens
Being Chinese, Becoming Chinese American   *Shehong Chen*
"A Half Caste" and Other Writings   *Onoto Watanna; edited by Linda Trinh Moser
    and Elizabeth Rooney*
Chinese Immigrants, African Americans, and Racial Anxiety in the United States,
    1848–82   *Najia Aarim-Heriot*
Not Just Victims: Conversations with Cambodian Community Leaders in the
    United States   *Edited and with an introduction by Sucheng Chan;
    interviews conducted by Audrey U. Kim*
The Japanese in Latin America   *Daniel M. Masterson with Sayaka Funada-Classen*
Survivors: Cambodian Refugees in the United States   *Sucheng Chan*
From Concentration Camp to Campus: Japanese American Students and
    World War II   *Allan W. Austin*
Japanese American Midwives: Culture, Community, and Health Politics
    Susan L. Smith
In Defense of Asian American Studies: The Politics of Teaching and
    Program Building   *Sucheng Chan*

Lost and Found: Reclaiming the Japanese American Incarceration
  Karen L. Ishizuka
Religion and Spirituality in Korean America   *Edited by David K. Yoo and
  Ruth H. Chung*
Moving Images: Photography and the Japanese American Incarceration
  Jasmine Alinder
Camp Harmony: Seattle's Japanese Americans and the Puyallup Assembly Center
  Louis Fiset
Chinese American Transnational Politics   *Him Mark Lai; edited and with an
  introduction by Madeline Y. Hsu*
Issei Buddhism in the Americas   *Edited by Duncan Ryûken Williams and
  Tomoe Moriya*
Hmong America: Reconstructing Community in Diaspora   *Chia Youyee Vang*
In Pursuit of Gold: Chinese American Miners and Merchants in the
  American West   *Sue Fawn Chung*
Pacific Citizens: Larry and Guyo Tajiri and Japanese American Journalism in the
  World War II Era   *Edited by Greg Robinson*
Indian Accents: Brown Voice and Racial Performance in American Television
  and Film   *Shilpa S. Davé*
Yellow Power, Yellow Soul: The Radical Art of Fred Ho   *Edited by Roger N. Buckley
  and Tamara Roberts*
Fighting from a Distance: How Filipino Exiles Helped Topple a Dictator
  Jose V. Fuentecilla
In Defense of Justice: Joseph Kurihara and the Japanese American Struggle
  for Equality   *Eileen H. Tamura*
Asian Americans in Dixie: Race and Migration in the South
  Edited by Jigna Desai and Khyati Y. Joshi
Undercover Asian: Multiracial Asian Americans in Visual Culture
  Leilani Nishime
Islanders in the Empire: Filipino and Puerto Rican Laborers in Hawai'i
  JoAnna Poblete
Virtual Homelands: Indian Immigrants and Online Cultures in the United States
  Madhavi Mallapragada
Building Filipino Hawai'i   *Roderick N. Labrador*
Legitimizing Empire: Filipino American and U.S. Puerto Rican Cultural Critique
  Faye Caronan
Chinese in the Woods: Logging and Lumbering in the American West
  Sue Fawn Chung
The Minor Intimacies of Race: Asian Publics in North America   *Christine Kim*
Reading Together, Reading Apart: Identity, Belonging, and South Asian
  American Community   *Tamara Bhalla*
Chino: Anti-Chinese Racism in Mexico, 1880–1940   *Jason Oliver Chang*
Asianfail: Narratives of Disenchantment and the Model Minority   *Eleanor Ty*

Becoming Refugee American: The Politics of Rescue in Little Saigon
  Phuong Tran Nguyen
The Work of Mothering: Globalization and the Filipino Diaspora
  Harrod J. Suarez
Discriminating Sex: White Leisure and the Making of the American "Oriental"
  Amy Sueyoshi
Muncie, India(na): Middletown and Asian America   *Himanee Gupta-Carlson*
The Labor of Care: Filipina Migrants and Transnational Families in the
  Digital Age   *Valerie Francisco-Menchavez*
Disrupting Kinship: Transnational Politics of Korean Adoption in the
  United States   *Kimberly D. McKee*
Raced to Death in 1920s Hawai'i: Injustice and Revenge in the Fukunaga Case
  Jonathan Y. Okamura
Queering the Global Filipina Body: Contested Nationalisms in the
  Filipina/o Diaspora   *Gina K. Velasco*
Manifest Technique: Hip Hop, Empire, and Visionary Filipino American Culture
  Mark R. Villegas
Shadow Traces: Seeing Japanese/American and Ainu Women in
  Photographic Archives   *Elena Tajima Creef*
Lured by the American Dream: Filipino Servants in the U.S. Navy and Coast Guard,
  1952–1970   *James Paligutan*

The University of Illinois Press
is a founding member of the
Association of University Presses.

_____

University of Illinois Press
1325 South Oak Street
Champaign, IL 61820-6903
www.press.uillinois.edu